Competing
Gospels

ROBERT G. SIMONS

Competing Gospels:

PUBLIC THEOLOGY AND ECONOMIC THEORY

E J DWYER

First published in 1995 by
E. J. Dwyer (Australia) Pty Ltd
Unit 13, Perry Park
33 Maddox Street
Alexandria NSW 2015
Australia
Phone: (02) 550 2355
Fax: (02) 519 3218

National Library of Australia
Cataloguing-in-Publication data

Simons, Robert G., 1947–
    Competing gospels : public theology and economic theory.

    Bibliography.
    Includes index.
    ISBN 0 85574 142 2.
    1. Economics — Religious aspects — Christianity. 2. Social ethics. 3. Theology.
    4. Community life. I. Title.

    261.85

Cover design by DVO Design
Text design by NB Design
Typeset in 12/14pt Bembo by Sun Photoset Pty Ltd, Brisbane
Printed in Australia by Alken Press, Smithfield, NSW

10 9 8 7 6 5 4 3 2 1
99 98 97 96 95

Distributed in the United States by:
    Morehouse Publishing
    871 Ethan Allen Highway
    RIDGEFIELD CT 06877
    Ph: (203) 431 3927
    Fax: (203) 431 3964

Distributed in Canada by:
    Meakin and Associates
    Unit 17
    81 Auriga Drive
    NEPEAN, ONT K2E 7Y5
    Ph: (613) 226 4381
    Fax: (613) 226 1687

Distributed in Ireland and the U.K. by:
    Columba Book Service
    93 The Rise
    Mount Merrion
    BLACKROCK CO. DUBLIN
    Ph: (01) 283 2954
    Fax: (01) 288 3770

Distributed in New Zealand:
    Catholic Supplies (NZ) Ltd
    80 Adelaide Road
    WELLINGTON
    Ph: (04) 384 3665
    Fax: (04) 384 3663

Acknowledgments

The author gratefully acknowledges permission for the use of material from the following works. Every effort has been made to note the sources of quoted material and to obtain authority for its use.

From *God the Economist: The Doctrine of God and Political Economy* by M. Douglas Meeks. Copyright © 1989 Augsburg Fortress.

From *The Battle for Human Nature* by Barry Schwartz. Copyright © 1986 W.W. Norton & Co.

From *Sustainability: Economics, Ecology & Justice* by John B. Cobb Jr. Copyright © 1992 Orbis.

From *Karl Marx's Philosophy of Man* by John Plamenatz. Copyright © 1975 Oxford University Press, UK.

From *Fullness of Faith: The Public Significance of Theology* by Michael J. Himes and Kenneth R. Himes. Copyright © 1993 Paulist Press.

From "The Economics of Mutual Support: A Feminist Approach," by Eva Cox in *Beyond the Market: Alternatives to Economic Rationalism*. Edited by Rees, Rodley, and Stilwell. Copyright © 1993 Pluto Press.

From *Centesimus Annus* by John Paul II. Copyright © 1991 St. Paul Publications.

Contents

Preface

Why this Book?

Competing Gospels: Public Theology and Economic Theory—is an exercise in placing Christian doctrine in dialogue with economic theory and history in the public realm. It does this from the bridging perspective of anthropology. The anthropological focus is used to gather in and consolidate a number of perspectives from Christian doctrine, as well as to highlight assumptions on the human person and community which are found in both capitalist and socialist economic theories. Throughout the book "Gospel" is used only in an analogous sense to the four Gospels of the Christian Scriptures, and refers to *a way of proclaiming a life which holds out a promise of well-being and is supposedly "good news"*.

The subtitle might also have been: "The Struggle for a Minority Opinion"—the "struggle" being specifically for that "minority opinion" which is seeking to break free from some of the hurtful consequences of global markets and to situate the operation of economic systems—of any persuasion—in a respectful way in the context and fabric of smaller interdependent human communities in the world. As such the "minority opinion" is championed both by a Catholic Christian communitarian vision of the common good, and economists who advocate a contemporary expression of local economic management.

There is yet another reason why the word "struggle" is apt. We are living in the midst of times, described as post-modern by some, when many of the cherished interpretations of Christian orthodoxy, and of economics—both capitalist and socialist—have been, and are being, seriously called into question. In the wake of such challenges the disorientation can be great. The temptation to rush to premature and simplistic alternatives can also be great. The "struggle," therefore, is also felt in the need for a commitment to, and patience with, a process—one which will have to be kept in motion for many subsequent generations—that can be threatening, and uncomfortable to all engaged in it.

There are a number of reasons for such a project. The first is *the radical need to move from viewing social relationships as embedded in an existing economy, to holding economic systems accountable to already existing sets of human relationships and communities.* Following the lead of Karl Polanyi,[1] it is necessary to think and act differently about the relationship between the economy and the human community which we have inherited. At present, the economy has become an all-pervasive and controlling system, assuming disproportionate influence on all forms of social and political interaction. Unfortunately, neither Marx's focus on the human person as alienated from the processes of production, nor Adam Smith's grasp of the human person, in a way that later came to be described as "economic man," adequately address the breadth of the connections and relations that are part of being a human person in community in the world. Is it any wonder, then, that diverse expressions of both socialist and capitalist economies have, at times, been almost devastatingly insensitive to the prior realities of individual freedom and community justice?

A second reason, suggested by the theoretical failure to integrate economic theory into a more adequately developed vision of the human person and community, is *an opportunity to place the anthropologies assumed by economists from both capitalist and socialist backgrounds in critical dialogue with a more sensitively communitarian vision of the human person derived from key Christian doctrinal perspectives.* The doctrines of the Trinity, Creation, Original Sin, and the Communion of Saints are especially rich in suggesting more adequate understandings of the human person in community, along with human responsibility for creation. In addition, and coming at the problem from a corresponding economic perspective, a growing number of economists and economic historians criticize expressions of capitalism and socialism which disregard the breadth of human concerns which are inevitably affected by economic processes.[2] The contributions from both sides of the dialogue are all preparatory to appreciating human persons as active participants in community, and justice as inclusive participation in community processes. Such understandings of persons and justice have to be part of theories of the economy which are not only sensitive to, but nurturing of, human persons-in-community contributing toward and participating in the common good.

A third main reason for this book is *the need for the voice of Christian churches on economic issues to become even more public and credible.* Both Protestant and Roman Catholic churches have attempted to bring their moral and ethical teachings to bear on a more just operation of the economy. This approach has done much to help raise consciousness and awareness of human issues which otherwise might have been lost in the midst of formal economic considerations. In Roman Catholic settings, however, the approach has largely been perceived and understood—prior to the method of composition used for the 1986 US Bishops' letter *Economic Justice for All*—as a one-way process. Indeed, within the broader tradition of Catholic Social Teaching many of the Church's pronouncements on economic policies and strategies have been heard by economists as expressions of a critique of economic systems, perhaps appropriate for Church members, but not adequately reflecting an awareness either of broader economic realities or theories. This book attempts to make a strong plea for the Church's voice and wisdom on human persons and communities, in a way which reflects a correspondingly strong and serious attentiveness to the realities and traditions of economic organization of society.

A further and final reason for the book, is *to suggest strategies to the Church for alternative ways of communicating and witnessing the relevance of its wisdom in the realm of economic organization.* The strategies point to the need for local churches, whether at the parish or diocesan or regional level, to develop an economic praxis which not only gives expression to its teachings and provides further critical insights for its refinements, but which provides a healthy and competitive alternative on how more community- and world-sensitive economies might operate.

Throughout the book, and mainly because of the broad interdisciplinary scope of the topic, my mode of proceeding is *heuristic.* That is, it is my intention *to suggest possibilities for the future for organizing societies and cultures economically.* While this suggestive process will be both critical of many aspects of present forms of economic organization, hopefully it will also be generative—especially for those better equipped and positioned than myself to respond—of both realistic and holistic future economic possibilities. Also, as a consequence of opting for a *heuristic* method it is *not* my intention to provide an exhaustive set of arguments—such is beyond my competence—which some might consider indispensable before proceeding to alternative forms of economic organization. In my opinion, however, the *heuristic* approach is very well suited for the book's overall purpose: to invite people from a variety of personal backgrounds and professional competencies to engage in further conversation about a matter that touches upon literally all aspects of our lives together—the way they are organized economically.

---

[1] *The Great Transformation: The Political and Economic Origins of Our Time* (Boston: Beacon Press [1944] 1957). For a more recent and journalistic presentation of a similar position see Chuck Matthei, "Economics as if Values Mattered: Redefining Land, Labor, and Capital," *Sojourners*: November 1993, December 1993, and January 1994.

[2] A collection of twelve such authors can be found in Mark A. Lutz (ed), *Social Economics: Retrospect and Prospect* (Boston: Kluwer Academic Publishers, 1990). See also the very helpful work coauthored by Mark A. Lutz and Kenneth Lux, *Humanistic Economics: The New Challenge* (NY: The Bootstrap Press, 1988).

Introduction

Public Theology and Economic Theory

Over twelve years ago Martin Marty wrote:

> The public church is a family of apostolic churches with Jesus
> Christ at the center, churches which are especially sensitive to
> the *res publica*, the public order that surrounds and includes
> people of faith. The public church is a communion of
> communions, each of which lives its life partly in response to
> its separate tradition and partly to the calls for a common
> Christian vocation.[1]

The public church includes believers from many different Christian
traditions. They form a movement more than a formal institution,
and are united by a desire to rescue religious belief from an
exclusive concern with the private realm, and to engage its meaning
in the wider public and social realm.

When Marty's expression "public church" is used in the present
context it refers to a community whose social mission respects the
legitimate autonomy of other social institutions, accepts some
responsibility for the well-being of the wider society, and commits
itself to work with other social institutions in shaping the common
good of society.[2] Advocates of the public church are very
uncomfortable with the idea of a faith without social meaning. For
them, the restriction of religious faith to the private and individual
realms makes it impossible for religion to serve as an integrating

element in a person's worldview and identity. Instead, life becomes fragmented into various components with religion as one area alongside others with little interaction among the fragments. Advocates of the public church, however, recognize that the restriction of religion to the private realm cannot be overcome by a return to an outmoded and discredited model of church whereby the Church tried to exert its influence in areas of society in an overextended and inappropriate way. In a post-modern and secular context the Church must be *engaged with* but not seek to *control* society.

The Church is still searching for appropriate strategies in order to become engaged in this new historical context. In that search movement beyond the private realm will probably be overcome only indirectly through the demonstrated value of religious communities to public life. For this reason, the public church is interested in working with others, not standing alone. If the aim is to contribute to the well-being of society, then other groups and individuals in the society will gradually welcome the endeavors of the public church. At the very least, they will come to judge the Church on the merits of its performance rather than assume outright that any role for the Church in public life is a threat to the common good or a veiled ploy for religious domination of the public sector.

When believers reflect upon and analyze the experiences of the Church as engaged in the public life of society, a theology emerges which strives to communicate the meaning of the Church's public involvement. Such "public theology" strives to "discover and communicate the socially significant meanings of the main Christian symbols, doctrines, and broader tradition."[3] It is a type of theological reflection which examines the resources latent within the Christian tradition for understanding the Church's public role. In this capacity, the primary task of public theology is to interpret basic Christian symbols in such a way that believers can perceive the full and broad meanings of those symbols. As Michael and Kenneth Himes have noted:

> Religious symbols not only resonate within the sanctuaries of the souls; they also give shape and insight into persons acting

publicly with others in the real world.... Public theology wants
to bring the wisdom of the Christian tradition into public
conversation to contribute to the well-being of society....
Public theology also aims at rendering an account of Christian
belief that articulates what it means to be a member of the
church.[4]

Membership in the church, for the practitioner of public theology,
however, always incorporates the social and public dimension of
human existence.

When theology is described as public the meaning of "public" is
that such theology is accessible to intelligent, reasonable and
responsible members of a society, despite otherwise crucial
differences in their beliefs and practices. David Tracy has pointed
out that public realms must include the possibility for "discussion
(argument, conversation), among various participants."[5]
Furthermore, Tracy has distinguished three "publics"—*society*,
which embraces the realms of economic structures, polity, and
culture; the *academy*, which embraces the realms of professional
intellectual discourse in all branches of knowledge; and the *Church*,
which embraces the full scope of Christianity's inherited traditions
and present experiences.[6] Failure to address any one of the publics
reduces religion to irrelevance. On this latter point, Michael and
Kenneth Himes observe that Christianity cannot presume to make
claims about ultimate values and, at the same time, say nothing
about the contexts and situations in which men and women have to
make both short-term and long-term life decisions.[7]

The public theologian searches for a way to make truth claims
which can be tested by the public without the public having to
assent to everything that the theologian believes. In general, the
criteria for public theology will be as accessible outside of, as within,
church communities: intelligibility, a critical method to assess
truthfulness, moral integrity, and fairness. Properly understood,
public theology is an issue of religion and society, not Church and
state. Religion can be understood as "the whole complexus of
attitudes, convictions, emotions, gestures, rituals, symbols, beliefs,
and institutions by which persons come to terms with, and express,

their personal and/or communal relationships with ultimate Reality (God and everything that pertains to God)."[8] Religion operates in society. The latter can be seen as a gathering of various communities that are ordered for cooperation and communication so as to enhance human well-being. Societies "... are composed of ... families, voluntary associations, colleges and universities, small businesses, corporations, labour unions, religious organisations and communities, and even governmental agencies."[9] Public theology provides one of the ways that religious institutions can contribute to the welfare of societies by providing alternative visions of what is desirable and possible for the enhancement of societal well-being.[10]

At the Second Vatican Council, in its Pastoral Constitution *The Church in the Modern World*, the Roman Catholic Church officially called upon all of the baptized to become a saving presence in the world in ways that resonate strongly with what Marty, more than fifteen years later, called the "public church." For the Council challenged Christians to become a saving presence in the world in ways that were, especially from the perspective of Roman Catholic church history, both different and innovative. Different because of the manner in which the Church was called to be present: not simply as a teacher and witness but also as a dialogue partner with all women and men of goodwill in taking responsibility for those tasks which are shared by all. Innovative because of the skills that the Church would have to learn and develop in order to engage in dialogue constructively and to be able to assume appropriate levels of responsibility for tasks which would take it beyond its usually acknowledged realms of competence.

One such realm, not usually regarded as part of the Church's ordinary competence, is economics. How does the Church, on the level of broad general assumptions, decide from a spectrum of views about the proper scope of economic activity? At one end of the spectrum of economic paradigms, economics is understood as a science for allocating scarce resources in order to satisfy a variety of competing ends. With this understanding economics is simply a science of means. At the other end of the spectrum economics can be understood as one among many ways of constructing a particular kind of society. With this understanding, economics is a more complex project which proposes an end to which scientifically informed economic activity might contribute.

Throughout this work, economics will be understood as incorporating elements from both understandings: that is, it will assume as a starting point and a goal a broad understanding of the common good which goes beyond strictly economic growth, and yet also will attempt to be respectful of the scientific and technical complexities of contemporary market theories of the economy. This understanding reflects the conviction that the shape and operation of the economy affects all levels of life and all persons in community. Unfortunately, because societies have, in many instances, been forced to conform to the operation of an almost exclusively scientific understanding of economic institutions, and such economic institutions have not adapted either readily or easily to already existing societies, the economy has often been experienced as overpowering and oppressive in its pervasive impact.

All men and women, and not simply members of the Christian churches, who choose to participate responsibly in society, cannot avoid the need to make decisions about the way economies throughout the world affect communities. Their attempts to do so, however, can leave them feeling overwhelmed. Nonetheless, responsibility for economies cannot be left simply to professional economists anymore than responsibility for good health can be left totally to professionals who administer health services. In both instances there is a need for intelligent, adult, public conversation, interaction, and cooperation for human health and welfare.

Competing Gospels hopes to stimulate a broadly based conversation on the need to take human persons in community as the prior context in which all market economy exercises have to be situated. It offers an anthropological, theological and economic rationale for making decisive moves toward locally managed economies more readily accountable to already existing sets of human relationships and communities. Repeatedly posing the question "What is an economy for?", the book's aim is to engage people of goodwill to think more seriously and deeply about the negative impact which market economies have had upon the possibility for community-based economic organization. The book invites economists to be attentive to the voices of Christian theology on the nature of human persons and community. The book also invites theologians to be attentive to market realities and strategies as they attempt to respond to some of the most recurring challenges of organizing human societies. Overall, it intends to provide a meeting place whereby conversation can occur between Christian traditions and economic theories for further and more effective contributions toward the greater welfare of individuals, communities, and the environment.

The book, however, is by no means limited to professional theologians or economists. Indeed, it is written primarily for Christians who are confronted and troubled by some of the most persistent societal problems in need of being addressed more compassionately and effectively, respectively by market economists and Christian social justice teachings: unemployment, poverty, homelessness, and despoliation of the environment. It is also hoped that the book can assist all who, whether for religious, economic or humanitarian reasons, wonder why market systems which have an impressive track record on many counts, also consistently result in "booms and slumps" which create great disparities of wealth and welfare, as well as threaten the environment and its limited resources. To that end lecturers and university students of Christian doctrine, political economy and economics in general, Christian social ethics, systems of justice, and philosophical anthropology will also find the book touching on a number of their concerns.

The work's distinctive contribution is twofold. In its first part, it offers a developed reflection on understandings of human persons in community, as the common ground on which theologians and economists can meet. The differing anthropologies reflected in economic theory and Christian doctrine are interfaced critically with a view toward mutual learning. In its second part, and building upon the interdisciplinary dialogue in the first part, it proposes ways that the Catholic Church, along with other Christian churches, might enhance the effectiveness of its official teachings on economic matters, as well as ways to model alternative, credible forms of community-based economic management.

In Part One, *Responding to the Great Transformation*, the focus will be upon an understanding of the human person and community which can contribute to a more humane operation of the economy. Chapter One will survey some of the main factors which brought about the transformation from a pre-industrial to a capitalist market economy. Critical to this history is the development of an economic realm which exerts more influence than the broader social fabric and community relations in which it operates. The chapter will then look at the contemporary economic and social character of market economies, and in a concluding section will suggest a method for bringing the operation of the market and a Christian vision of the human person and community into dialogue.

Next, Chapters Two and Three will attempt to show respectively how the capitalist and socialist theories and systems which emerged during and after the Industrial Revolution were significantly flawed in their respective understandings of the human person and community. Both systems have experienced and continue to experience serious difficulties in accepting how economic doctrines and strategies might actually have to be adapted and adjusted to existing societies, and become more responsive to individual and community needs as they arise. Economic criticisms of such systems provide some helpful suggestions for moving beyond the hurtful aspects of their legacies.

Then, in Chapter Four, a Christian vision will be proposed for moving toward communities which are more inclusive of all persons and which strive to overcome some of the exclusions and excommunications brought on by economic rationalism and economic imperialism. The anthropological vision, in response to the problems and challenge, will be derived largely from the doctrines of the Trinity and Creation. Chapter Five, the last in Part One, will address the shadow side of any anthropology and community by drawing on the wisdom conveyed in the doctrine of Original Sin. Then it will address the challenge of working for communities in which a greater number of persons can participate in the common good, especially by appealing to the wisdom in the doctrine of the Communion of Saints. Wherever economic and theological criticism and contribution converge it will be brought together to suggest how such combined understandings might provide an alternative way for thinking about an exercise of the economy which more sensitively respects human freedom and more adequately fosters justice in the community. At the same time, such insights might also alert us to the realistic limits inherent in any vision of the person and community, as well as to the ever-present need for therapeutic and reconciliatory adjustments in economic practice.

Part Two, *Reconstructing the Context,* focuses on how the Church, both in its universal teaching, but even more so in its local witness to a more humane economic praxis, might continue to make significant contributions in the public realm. Chapter Six will evaluate the strengths and weaknesses of the Church's more recent teachings on economic issues. In doing this it will survey some of the most notable contributions made by the Roman Catholic hierarchy to the public conversation on the economy.[11] Chapter Seven will then take up Paul Lakeland's contention that, while such teaching has done much to communicate the Church's seriousness about speaking out on issues which affect everyone's economic welfare, there is a need for a more coherent critical theory to undergird future exercises of the Church's papal and episcopal teaching on social and economic issues.[12]

It will be suggested how an appeal to, and adaptation of, Jurgen Habermas' theory of communicative action might provide greater coherence in official church teaching.[13] Chapter Eight will project a scenario in which local churches might arrange the economic organization of their households, and model ways to situate the operation of the economy within a set of already existing community relationships. Such an economic praxis aims at empowering individuals to greater freedom, providing greater opportunities for participation in community, and equipping the community to witness to a more just world order. Then Chapter Nine will address the limits on natural and human resources which have to be respected by any emerging form of economic organization. It will also consider the need to rethink the limits of growth-based economics and the desirability of moving toward steady-state economies. The latter give priority to more whole understandings and measures of growth and development.

Finally, Chapter Ten will consolidate some of the main themes throughout the book. It will do so in order to make the final argument for the book's "minority opinion" in favor of a new economic order in which local economies can become more self-reliant. For only then will they be able to exist in global interdependence freed of some of the most hurtful aspects upon human communities, brought about by the most recent and powerful stage in the development of conventional economic wisdom: world markets.

---

[1] Martin Marty, *The Public Church* (New York: Crossroad Publishing, 1981), 1.

[2] See Michael J. Himes and Kenneth R. Himes, *Fullness of Faith: The Public Significance of Theology* (NY: Paulist Press, 1993), 2.

[3] See David Hollenbach, "Editor's Conclusion" in Hollenbach, Lovin, Coleman, Hehir, "Theology and Philosophy in Public: A Symposium on John Courtney Murray's Unfinished Agenda," *Theological Studies 40* (1979): 700–15 at 714. See also Ronald F. Thiemann's *Constructing a Public Theology: The Church in a Pluralistic Culture* (Louisville, Kentucky: Westminster/John Knox Press, 1991); and Himes and Himes, *Fullness of Faith*, 1–27.

[4] Himes and Himes, *Fullness of Faith*, 5.

[5] David Tracy, "Particular Classics, Public Religion, and the American Tradition," in *Religion and American Public Life*, 115–31 at 115, cited in Himes and Himes, *Fullness of Faith*, 16.

[6] David Tracy, *The Analogical Imagination* (NY: Crossroad Publishing, 1981), 6–28. In general, Tracy's contribution has been acknowledged and developed largely in the North American context. See Don S. Browning and Francis Schussler Fiorenza (eds), *Habermas, Modernity, and Public Theology* (NY: Crossroad Publishing, 1992), 5; also Max L. Stackhouse, *Public Theology and Political Economy: Christian Stewardship in Modern Society* (Grand Rapids, MI: Wm. B. Eerdmans Pub. Co., 1987), 94.

[7] See Himes and Himes, *Fullness of Faith,* 17.

[8] Richard P. McBrien, *Caesar's Coin: Religion and Politics in America* (New York: MacMillan Publishing, 1987), 11.

[9] McBrien, *Caesar's Coin*, 25.

[10] See Robert Reich, "Introduction," 4 in Robert Reich, (ed), *The Power of Public Ideas* (Cambridge: Ballinger Publishing, 1988).

[11] Two recent examples from episcopal conferences include *Economic Justice for All: Pastoral Letter on Catholic Social Teaching and the U.S. Economy*, National Conference of Catholic Bishops, Washington, D.C., 1986; and *Common Wealth for the Common Good*, Australian Catholic Bishops' Conference (Melbourne: Collins Dove, 1992). Furthermore, both bishops' conferences operated in the context of an impressive output of recent papal teaching on issues pertinent, either directly or indirectly, to the operation of the world economy: *Redemptor Hominis* (1979), *Laborem Exercens* (1981), *Sollicitudo Rei Socialis* (1988), and *Centesimus Annus* (1991).

[12] See Paul Lakeland, *Theology and Critical Theory: The Discourse of the Church* (Nashville: Abingdon Press, 1990), c.3 "The Value of Critical Theory for Catholic Theology," 70–102.

[13] I originally proposed the initial stages of such a project in "Towards Accountability Criteria Within a Theologically Informed Paradigm For Economics," *The Australasian Catholic Record* 71(1994), 298–313.

PART ONE

Responding to the Great Transformation

Markets and the Societies in Which They Operate

ECONOMIES SIMULTANEOUSLY AFFECT AND ARE AFFECTED BY the societies in which they operate. As it will soon be seen, however, their respective impacts upon each other are neither mutual nor even. The first part of this chapter will look at the ways societies were organized economically prior to the emergence of a market economy. Then it will briefly describe how the change from a market pattern to a market system exercised an immense impact upon the structures of society and the expression of its priorities. The particular economic character of the market eventually changed the manner in which goods and services were made available to the members of society. The corresponding impact which societies have been able to exert upon the operation of the market, however, has not been nearly as great.

Despite some influence upon the distribution and allocation of the market's goods, and a limited degree of regulation of the production processes, many dynamics of the market have continued to develop independently, and in a way which escapes significant accountability to the commonly agreed upon social goals of the peoples and governments which depend so heavily upon them. It is precisely this imbalance in the interrelationship between markets and societies that calls for a number of adjustments from a variety of sectors of life. The concluding section of the chapter, then, makes some initial suggestions about a method for Christians to begin to enter a public conversation about redressing that imbalance.

The suggested ways of proceeding will then be further developed throughout the remaining chapters of the book.

The Principles of Economic Organization Prior to a Market Economy[1]

Prior to our time no economy has ever existed that, even in principle, was controlled by markets. Gain and profit made on exchange never before played such a critical role in the organization of human societies. Although the institution of the market has been fairly common since the later Stone Age, its role was no more than incidental to the broader economic life of a community.[2] Up to the end of the Middle Ages, markets were neither central to, nor defining of, the economic system. Other institutional patterns prevailed. From the sixteenth century onwards markets were both numerous and important. Under the mercantile system[3] they became a main concern of government. Yet, there was still no sign of the coming control of markets over human society. On the contrary, the markets themselves were regulated strictly.

The outstanding discovery of recent historical and anthropological research is that human economy, as a rule, is submerged in a broader context of social relationships. Every single step in the processes of production and distribution is geared to a number of social interests. In fact, order in production and distribution is ensured by a number of principles of behavior which are not, in the first instance, economic: *reciprocity* in regard to patterns of mutuality in the pairing off of individual relations in the give-and-take of goods and services; *redistribution* in regard to the collection, storage and subsequent dispersal of goods and services; and *householding* in regard to "production for one's own use." The Greeks called the latter *oeconomia*, the etymon of the word "economy." The practice of catering for the needs of one's household is very different either from the motive of gain or from the institution of markets. Its pattern is the closed group, and its principle is that of producing and storing for the satisfaction of the needs of members of the group. Aristotle insists on "production for use" as against "production for gain" as the essence of householding proper.

Broadly, we can say that all economic systems known to us prior to the end of feudalism in Western Europe were organized either on the principles of reciprocity or redistribution, or householding, or some combination of the three. These principles were institutionalized with the help of a given form of social organization. The orderly production and distribution of goods was brought about through a great variety of individual motives. Among these motives, however, gain was not prominent. Custom and law, magic and religion cooperated in inducing individuals to comply with rules of behavior which, eventually, ensured their functioning in the economic system. The very idea of a self-regulating market was absent. To comprehend the sudden change-over to an utterly new type of economy, the "great transformation" in the nineteenth century, a brief survey of the history of the market will be instructive.

The Emergence of the Market Pattern and the Self-Regulating Market[4]

The economic system of feudalism could not be incorporated into the market economy because the latter, even in its origins, systemically ignored the social realities of the human person[5]. The emerging market system, in its tendency to relate to persons almost exclusively as individual workers for the production process, was heedless of the basic human need for a cohesive society.[6] The major tragedy of the Industrial Revolution was the social devastation of an uncontrolled and unregulated market economy. While the economic changes were taking place people failed to realize what the cohesion of society meant. The tremendous problem of the social control of a revolutionary change was unappreciated. In the face of the Industrial Revolution's remarkable advances in the tools and methods of production, those who were profiting from the advances did not stop to notice the disruption and the dislocation in the lives of so many people.[7] The good news of increased productivity was so intoxicating in its tangible results, that its accompanying dislocation of families and whole communities was virtually ignored in the process. A further element of tragedy in the process is that many of its worst abuses might have been avoided if the changes it wrought had been regulated. Such regulation might have done much to safeguard the welfare of the community. Some of the worst consequences of rapid uncontrolled change might also have been averted if, in the eighteenth century, there had been a keener memory of the consequences of rapid, uncontrolled economic change brought on by the enclosure movement just a few centuries before during the Tudor period in England.[8]

Unfortunately, the two-century break from the beginning of the enclosure movement until the start of the Industrial Revolution obliterated from the memory of the nation the horrors of the enclosure period and the achievements of government in overcoming the perils of depopulation. An avalanche of social dislocation far surpassing that of the enclosure period came down upon England with the Industrial Revolution. No single factor deserves to be lifted out of the chain of events which comprised the Industrial Revolution as does the establishment and institutionalization of the market economy. The institutionalization of the market implies a change in the motive of action, from community subsistence to individual gain, on the part of the members of society. All transactions are turned into money transactions. These, in turn, require that a medium of exchange be introduced into every aspect of industrial life, and that all incomes must derive from the sale of something or other. The most startling peculiarity of the market system, however, is that prices must be allowed to regulate themselves. Self-regulating markets are at the heart of a market economy.

For a long time historians of economic liberalism have assumed that the market's self-regulating practices and methods were the natural outgrowth of a general law of progress. To make those practices fit the pattern of evolutionary progress, the principles underlying a self-regulating market were projected backward into the whole history of human civilization. As a result the true nature and origin of trade, markets and money, of town life and national states were distorted almost beyond recognition.

Barter and exchange, as principles of economic behavior, are dependent for their effectiveness upon the societal *pattern* of the market, with the latter understood as a *meeting place for the purpose of barter or buying and selling.* Unless such a *pattern* is present, barter cannot produce prices. The market *pattern,* with the peculiar motive of buying and selling as its own, is capable of creating the market *system,* a specific *institution.* Ultimately, that is why the control of the economic system by the market is of overwhelming consequence to the whole organization of society. It means no less than the running of society as an adjunct to the market system. The economy is no longer situated respectfully in the context of existing social relations. Indeed, the latter are compelled to change and fit into a powerful economic system.[9] For once the economic system is organized in separate institutions, based on specific motives and conferring a special status, society must be shaped so as to allow that system to function according to its own laws. This is the meaning of the assertion that *a market economy can function only in a market society.*

The Economic Character of the Market

According to Allen Buchanan the market economy raises moral, social, and political issues of the utmost importance both in our time and in the foreseeable future.[10] It is critical, then, to understand some of the basic economic factors with which a market economy, as well as any system of economics, has to deal.[11] One such factor is *scarcity,* the most basic economic assumption, problem and challenge. In the notion of scarcity economists acknowledge that our infinite wants can be met by only a finite amount of resources.[12] They include land, the natural elements of soil and minerals; capital, the man-made elements of factories, machines and the infrastructure; and labor, the human effort put into the production process. These three constitute what economists call the *factors of production* or the *factors market,* the means by which our wants are satisfied. With the concept of scarcity economists also acknowledge that finite resources can be brought together in different combinations to produce different goods and services. The question is which to produce and which not to produce. For example, the full cost of using land for a tennis court also includes the cost of not using it for growing vegetables; that is, the "opportunity cost." Finally, scarcity also arises out of the problem of the timescale: of having to choose between meeting present needs or investing to meet future needs.[13]

With scarcity as an indispensable consideration, the basic economic task of all systems concerns the allocation of scarce resources to meet people's needs. Economic tasks center on *what* to produce, *how* to produce, and *for whom*.[14] The basic tasks are distributed among four functions: the *demand function* determines what to produce—that is, which wants should be met; the *production function* determines how to produce, that is, how to combine the resources of land, labor, and capital to produce the goods and services. Then two further sets of functions determine *for whom* production is carried out. The *exchange and distribution functions* determine how to share out the product to those who produce and those who cannot; and the *savings and investment functions* determine how to divide the product for present and future use.[15]

The influence of scarcity on the economic task developed into modern economics through the Industrial Revolution. Industrialization provided both structure and motivation for the transformation of basic economic problems and tasks into modern economics and market economies. Most economists argue that the fulcrum of that transformation was the emergence of the price system or mechanism.[16] The task of the price mechanism was to coordinate the demand and supply of many thousands of different goods and services produced by thousands of firms for millions of households. Such developments were required by the rise of specialization and the subdivision of labor. Thus, individuals no longer made goods for their own use, but for sale in the market. As a result, the price obtained for the goods produced and the price to be paid for what the individual wanted became of vital importance. Barter between individuals ceased to be the manner of exchange.

The problem, however, was the coordination of the demand of consumers and the supply of producers so that both were satisfied. The provision of the required goods and services in terms of quantity, quality and price was needed at prices that enabled the producers to make sufficient profit to stay in business. It was these realities and problems that the price mechanism or system of modern economics and the market economy rose to meet. Indeed, it was so dominant that some economists have referred to the market as "the price economy."[17]

Relying on private ownership of the factors of production, and on money as the medium of exchange and not barter, the price mechanism had two main functions: as an incentive and as signals of information. Regarding the former, a rising price signalled to a producer the value of obtaining more resources to produce more of a desired product. Regarding the latter, prices signalled two kinds of information to be harmonized or coordinated: the intensity of the consumer's demand for a product; and the costs incurred and the resources or factors needed to produce that product. Consumers were seen to buy more as prices were lower, and producers to produce more, and therefore achieve greater profit, as prices moved higher.

The two, the prices indicating consumer demand and producer costs, were seen to meet at the point where the demand of the consumer matched what the producer would supply. It is this *equilibrium price* that reflects the satisfaction of consumer demand and the producer's sale of the goods.[18] If the price goes above the equilibrium level, the goods are not all sold because the consumers buy fewer. As a consequence, the reduced demand results in the reduction of the price until it returns to the equilibrium point. If the price falls below the point, demand increases, the goods are all sold, and so the price rises because the demand is no longer satisfied. Again, the price moves until it reaches the equilibrium point. The interests of consumers and producers are therefore reconciled by the way both respond to the price signals. This in turn then determines the output of products. It is where consumers and producers encounter one another that the market comes into being.[19]

The concept of the market is an aggregate term for a variety of markets. The *factors market*, which we have already looked at, is for the resources of land, capital and labor. It provides producers with the essential means for the production of commodities. As a market for buyers and sellers, the interaction of demand and supply determines the price of the resources of land and capital. The price of labor, however, is not determined by higher prices generating more supply. Other influences also play a major part, including training, geography and social class, and the value of specific forms of work as the primary determinant of labor costs.[20] The *commodities market* refers to the final goods and services purchased by consumers from companies. The decisions regarding the output of such goods are determined principally by the interaction of demand and supply.

Lastly, in the *monies market*, financial intermediaries such as banks, allocate the savings deposited with them, including passing them on to borrowers for investment purposes. The advantage of such a market is that there is no need to match savers and borrowers, and the risk of lending for investment is spread. Again, as with the other markets, prices, like interest rates, provide essential information and incentives. So, despite the variety of markets each with their special features, they basically operate according to the same principles which are derived from a unified economic theory and practice.[21] The latter emerge as the coherent center of the market economy. The latter also provide the reason why market economy places a strong faith in the impersonal working of the price mechanism to bring consumers into contact with resources.[22]

There are a number of key actors in this market of markets. Apart from the state, they consist principally of consumers and producers. Producers include firms who purchase factors in the *factors market*, organize production to meet the particular demands registered through the price mechanism, and then sell to other firms or consumers. The prices suggest how best to allocate or deploy the resources in order to anticipate the demands of the market. Consumers consist of individuals and households with sufficient income to purchase final goods and services in the *commodities market*. They also act as suppliers in the *factors market* of labor and capital. Indeed, there is a circular flow of the income received for labor being used to purchase goods or invest. For consumers, the prices of goods and services enable them to assess their relative value and so prioritize their needs.

Businesspersons, as mediators between consumers and producers, perform two important functions in the market economy: they initiate production by forecasting demand and so take the risk of assembling the resources necessary to meet it. They also seek to coordinate production in order to meet the price messages from consumers by bringing together the requisite sources to produce what is demanded at the lowest cost. The probability of profit acts as an incentive to entrepreneurs, who consistently act on the basis of the profit motive when making such decisions.[23]

Despite some of the obvious advantages of the market economy, any attempt to inflate its achievements by losing sight of or overlooking some of the persistent problems which plague it, such as cyclical unemployment, concentrations of wealth and power, and threats to the environment, has to be rejected. The market economy must be distinguished from its ideal type as developed in economic theory. The latter assumes that consumers bid rationally and freely for goods in the market, that prices reflect costs, that competition is unrestrained and therefore removes excess profit, and that resources go to the most efficient firms.

Although such theorizing is essential for the development of any academic discipline, a realistic understanding of the market economy must take account of the actual characteristics of market economies as they have developed, particularly in the West. This means that the significant contributions of the market economy to standards of living in more advanced societies have to be qualified by its equally significant defects in those same societies. For example, firms are often not in full competition, so prices do not fully reflect costs and firms do not simply respond to consumer demand. The market is an essentially human construct which attempts to bring order out of potential chaos but does not always succeed.[24]

The Social Character of the Market

In the eighteenth century the concept of "political economy" in economics reflected the conviction that the market economy could be realistically and sympathetically located within the wider framework of society. "In its most comprehensive sense, political economy involves the social relationships of power that exist in the human attempt to gain livelihood for the community and its members . . . . There are at least four basic components of every political economy: power, property, work [as production], and needs [as consumption]."[25]

Before the end of the nineteenth century, however, "political economy" was replaced by "economics" as the specialist-operating concept for understanding wealth creation in society. In recent years there has been a renewed interest in the older concept, among theologians as well as others. John Atherton, however, is doubtful whether the rediscovery of "political economy" reflects sufficiently the complexity of the contemporary context.[26] His doubt, in my opinion, issues out of an insufficiently critical analysis of the ways in which political contexts and cultural values contextualize an otherwise self-regulating market adequately. A more realistic and critical presentation of the complexity of the contemporary context can be found in Robert J. Holton's *Economy and Society*.[27] Holton argues for the perspective of economic sociology, a view which not only situates the operation of the market in the context of the power relations of political economy, but also within the broader and diverse cultural contexts in which markets operate.

Within the Western market tradition, according to Atherton, specific *institutions* and *politics* have exercised a limited socializing influence upon the market. Both have prevented market economies from falling prey to the most crude forms of *laissez-faire* capitalism. Although Atherton does not deal with the further problem of how these restraining factors still enable the market in many instances to operate without sufficient attention to social goals,[28] he has rightly noted how the major institutions of property and values have made limited contributions respectively to the sustaining and restraining of the market. With the dismantling of feudalism and mercantilism and the rise of *laissez-faire* capitalism, private property began to play a central role in the development and sustaining of market economies.[29]

Some economists even argue that private property is a basic determinant of a market system.[30] Within this broad acceptance of the role of private property, market economies also acknowledge that all property does not need to be in private ownership. Public services like education, roads and parks provide salient examples of the point. While performing the key function of defending property rights and contracts, both indispensable to the market economy, the state has also been the principal agency for restraining the undue use of these rights in contravention of the public good or as a means of oppressing others.

Values comprise the second major contextualizing *institutional* form for the market economy. Adam Smith contended that the effective operating of the market depended on the support of values both as a resource for market behavior and a restraint of its tendency to imbalance. The former included truth, honesty, obligation and trust, which the market system did not provide, and yet without which it could not survive: "Market relations are so pervasive in a capitalist economy, that it would be impossible to regulate every transaction by a legal contract. An element of general social assent to standards of honesty and truth is also needed."[31] Many of these values are historically part of Christianity initiating and sustaining virtues in the private and public realms. The restraining function of values in the market relates particularly to the use of self-interest as the principal motivating force in economic life.[32]

Modern economics has given a primary role to the individual as consumer and producer acting in a rational, calculating and self-interested mode.[33] As expressed in personal responsibility, initiative, rational and calculating choice, self-interest provides an essential complement to the need for community. Indeed, the liberation of the individual from the corporatism of feudalism and mercantilism was achieved partly at the continuing cost of traditional human solidarities. Unfortunately, self-interest has a tendency to develop sometimes into what Preston and MacPherson have described as "possessive individualism."[34] Once again, there emerges the need to balance the excesses of individualism in the market with communitarian habits promulgated by families and a wide variety of mediating structures or intermediate associations. It is here that the Church as institution has an essential role to play in nourishing those values that both resource and restrain the performances of market economies.

In addition to the institutions of private property and values, politics and political life provide the second major characteristic for socializing market economy. The modern state in Western market economies, which has emerged only in the last 100 years, both supports and restrains the market economy. It supports it by legitimizing and protecting private property and contracts. Since the Second World War, through the development of macro-economics,[35] the state also seeks to oversee economic activity by using, for example, fiscal and monetary policies to control aggregate demand and supply.[36] The maintenance of high employment, economic growth and low inflation are valued objectives shared with economic actors, but no longer left to them alone.

Indeed, recently emerged East Asian market economies, along with France and Germany, now foster the closest collaboration between government and industry in carrying out industrial policies and activities. Japan's Ministry of International Trade and Industry (MITI) is the prime example of this development. Similarly, supporting the population through the collective provision of key services like education and health is regarded as an essential contribution, as well as a counterbalance to economic activities. On the other hand, the state also acts as a corrective to known defects in the market economy, and pursues a whole host of regulatory interventions in the market, including the labor market as proposed in the European Community's Social Charter.[37]

The claim has often been made that the market economy, on a variety of levels, is highly compatible with liberal or political democracy.[38] Proponents of the claim assert that intrinsic to both projects is the decisive separation of the political and economic arenas. Without this degree of autonomy it is highly unlikely that the market-price economy would be able to operate effectively. There is a serious reason for challenging this claim, mainly on the basis that an insufficiently regulated market will result in the breakdown of a shared political vision of the common good.[39]

From its very inception, the survival and growth of the market system has been tangentially constrained by a number of powerful social forces, and to that extent, socialized in a very limited fashion. The socialization, however, has not been sufficient to restore a priority to social goals on most levels of operation of the market. A major portion of the task ahead will involve finding a way to restore that priority by integrating a professionally credible understanding of market theory with the values with which Christianity has criticized market economy. The present is a time of significant opportunity to take up such a task. For as Thomas S. Johnson, a former president of Manufacturers Hanover Corporation and former president of Chemical Bank, has noted, the collapse of communism in Eastern Europe presents an important opportunity to move the discussion of the relationship of market economies and moral-religious values to a deeper level.[40]

A significant and important part of moving to a deeper level will involve engaging a view of the human person and community which moves considerably beyond the limitations of the anthropology assumed in both classical and neoclassical economics. Such an anthropology will also have to be more developed than that found in Marxist writings, especially since the latter were offered as a critique of all that was either wrong or deficient in a market economy. It is to the task of developing such an anthropology by placing capitalist and socialist writings in critical dialogue with a Christian vision of the human person and community that the next four chapters especially are directed. Before moving on to them, however, it will be helpful to address some prior methodological concerns involved in a constructive Christian response to and interaction with market economies and the communities in which they operate.

A Christian Response to Markets in Our Present Context

Economies, both in their day-to-day operations and especially when significant changes occur, have a major impact on the societies, cultures and communities in which they operate. It has already been pointed out how both the enclosure movement and the Industrial Revolution, as significant economic changes in their times, had profound consequences on the broader fabric and structure of the societies in which they took place. While some Christian responses to market economies have been made directly to market theory and the operation of the market economy,[41] others have concentrated on the consequences and impact of those economies on the general welfare of persons and the communities in which they reside.

In either case, however, there is a recognition of a need for the market to be made more broadly accountable to the societies and communities in which it operates. The focus of accountability, if it is to be adequate, can be neither exclusively economic, nor social, nor theological. Ultimately, it will have to involve a more commonly agreed upon and articulated vision of the human person and community, and specifically a vision of them as economic agents. It is especially important for the Christian churches in First World countries to contribute to such a vision, because they have exerted the greatest degree of influence in the same Western societies in which the market has had the longest history and the most dominating position.

John Kenneth Galbraith has noted that economic ideas are not only influenced powerfully by their situations, but that as contexts change so must economic ideas if they are to retain their relevance.[42] How, then, might Christians view the functioning of market economies in the contemporary context of change— especially in view of the introduction of market systems into so many formerly socialist countries, and the potential impact of that development on global markets and the societies in which they operate? What does it mean for Christians, operating out of the values and perspectives in their doctrinal and moral traditions, to discern and read the significance of market economies upon the fabric of the societies in which they attempt to provide a Gospel witness? Somewhere along the line a Christian has to ask: "What, from a Christian perspective, are economies for?" Ultimately, a Christian reading of the contemporary context involves, at least, a serious dialogue between the economic understandings of the human person and community and a religious understanding of the same realities.

John Atherton has described the economic understanding as part of a "secular identification of disclosure movements." Such an identification has two moments.[43] The first emerges out of the empirical recognition by a significant proportion of people, disciplines and experiences, of market economies, as a major trend in our times. Secondly, it reflects the judgment that we are generally right in what we affirm and wrong in what we deny.[44] By these two tests, according to Atherton, and with the support of *most* practicing economists, market economies are more confirmed than rejected as the most effective ways of managing economies in modern societies.[45]

However, there are very serious differences with, and problems about, the economic assumptions upon which Atherton bases the main lines of his "secular identification." Indeed, a growing number of market economists are taking greater and greater distance from some of the previously unchallenged major assumptions upon which the whole economic enterprise has rested.[46] When that critical distance is both supported and strengthened by a dialogue with Christian understandings of God's purposes for human living, then the depth and seriousness of the challenge becomes even more probing.

If such a combined challenge is to be heard outside, as well as within, the Christian churches, however, the latter will have to learn how to communicate their potential contributions to the economic debate more credibly in the public realm. At the very least, this will mean avoiding an identification of God's will directly with specific events, or in a fundamentalist or immediate sense. Instead, the churches' economically and theologically informed understandings in a secular context will have to be offered as purposeful though provisional, related to a particular place and time, without presuming validity for all times and all places. Also, if economics can be criticized for not sufficiently acknowledging the breadth of the social responsibilities inherent in its operations for persons and communities, then Christianity in addressing the economy might be criticized for not making a more economically informed and detailed clarification of its vision of a moral and/or ethical economic organization of society.

Even when these criticisms are acknowledged, however, Christians in market societies will still have to examine their own presuppositions about capitalism: that is, whether they place more emphasis on the financial gains which it brings about, or whether they stress a variety of negative social consequences which it simply does not address.[47] Neither emphasis alone provides an adequate picture and avoids the complexities involved in a truly helpful analysis.

Peter Berger has recently argued that an adequate study of contemporary capitalism presupposes locating it in its social, political, economic and cultural contexts.[48] Berger rightfully points out that market economies involve an aggregate of perspectives. One very important perspective involves their international nature. The international dimension emerged partly as a result of the recognition by particular market economies that economic policies pursued in one country directly affected, and were in turn influenced by, policies pursued in others.[49] The extension of the market capitalist system from a single economy to a group of interacting economies has become a central feature of both market economies and their contexts.[50] That feature is a "force of cataclysmic transformation" in one country after another, beginning in Western Europe and North America and spreading as far as East Asia.[51]

Market economies are now essentially a global phenomenon, particularly through their dramatic advance in East Asia. That growth has been powerfully expressed in the achievements of Japan, South Korea, Taiwan, Hong Kong and Singapore. All five have been characterized by the interlocking of business and government in the promotion of national economic policy.[52]

Market economies, however, have been seriously and rightly challenged on the negative impact which they have had on the international stage. The most obvious manifestation has been seen in the growing gulf between First World economically "developed" countries and the Third World "underdeveloped" or "developing" countries in terms of income per head, social welfare and mortality rates. It is the precise nature of the relationship between the achievements of these "two worlds" that has become the major source of division between them. Critics of market economies contend that, far from contributing to the overall economic welfare of Third World countries, they have actually contributed to making them dependent upon those of the more powerful and influential First World. Emerging in the late 1950s, the dependency theory confronted the claims of the market's development theory.[53] The former stressed that the increasing immiseration of the Third World resulted from international capitalism's search for new markets.

While Third World poverty can be explained predominantly as the result of First World economic exploitation, it is important to acknowledge that, whatever theory is used to explain the relationship between the First and Third World economies, greater attention must also be paid to the broader societal and cultural differences which distinguish the communities in such geographically distant and distinct settings, differences which the international economy often overlooks. In many situations the introduction of a market system into an already established local economy has been fraught with experiences of culture shock and disorientation.[54] No matter how an opinion is formed about the relationship between advanced market economies and the Third World, economists and theologians agree that the relationship is of the greatest importance for national and world economies. The increasingly international character of the market economy has ensured that this will be one of the great foundational questions at the end of the twentieth century.

Another important perspective for understanding market economies in a contemporary setting is the perduring significance of command economies. State socialist centrally planned economies still dominate much of China and some Third World societies. Historically, socialism[55] and socialist economies emerged as the countermovement to capitalism or market economies. Command economies are largely a major component of a political system. That system tries to ensure that the central planning authority makes the basic economic decisions with regard to what to produce, in what quantities and qualities, and how it is distributed as commodities and incomes—including deciding between present consumption and investment for future production. The decision-making of consumers registering their wants through the price system, and producers deploying equipment and labor in response to consumer wants registered again through the price system, is replaced by a centralized bureaucracy. When an economy becomes more complex and consumer needs more sophisticated, the command system responds and adapts neither readily nor flexibly.[56]

The discernment leading to appropriate Christian responses to market economies, then, has to deal with a variety of complex and interrelated factors. Most basically, there is the challenge to develop a contemporary Christian vision of human persons and communities as socially responsible economic agents. In order to do this, the Christian tradition must engage in a truly interactive dialogue with the visions of the human person and community that have been assumed by both market and socialist economists. Secondly, there is the further challenge of becoming more literate in the details and operations of the market economies, especially in view of the implications of the recent collapse of so many command economies for market economies throughout the world. Thirdly, Christians will have to acknowledge that for the most part, the common good has not been adequately served by the market's limited socialization by the institutions of property and values, as well as by the politics of setting very limited social goals.

Finally, in coming to terms with the international and global nature of market economies, a Christian response will have to involve further study of the impact of multinational corporations on the communities and cultures in which they operate. Within the same international perspective, an adequate Christian response will also have to pay attention to the significance of the perdurance of command economies, and especially to which elements of market economy they either incorporate or reject. It is to the most basic task, however, of developing a contemporary Christian vision of human persons and communities as socially responsible economic agents that we must now turn. The first part of our task will involve becoming acquainted with the assumptions about the human person and community reflected in classical capitalist and socialist writings.

---

[1] Throughout this first section I am especially indebted to Karl Polanyi, *The Great Transformation: The Political and Economic Origins of Our Time* [1944] (Boston: Beacon Press, 1957), Chapter 4 "Societies and Economic Systems," 43–55. Following Polanyi, market economy implies a self-regulating system of markets. It is an economy directed by market prices.

[2] See Marshall Sahlins, *Stone Age Economics* (Chicago & New York: Aldine. Atherton, Inc., 1972).

[3] A system of political and economic policy, evolving with the modern national state and seeking to secure a nation's political and economic supremacy in its trading rivalry with other states.

[4] See Polanyi, *The Great Transformation*, Chapter 5 "Evolution of the Market Pattern" 56–67, for a more detailed presentation of the material in this section.

[5] See Robert M. MacIver, *Foreword*, p. x in Polanyi's *The Great Transformation*.

[6] See Ronald H. Preston, *Religion and the Ambiguities of Capitalism* (London: SCM Press, 1991), 42, where as part of his presentation of a Christian socialist critique of capitalism he states that society is prior to the individual and that it has to be understood as more than a collection of individuals taking part in voluntary economic and cultural activities.

[7] See Polanyi, *The Great Transformation*, 33.

[8] Enclosure of open fields and conversion of arable land to pasture occurred when fields and commons were hedged in by lords, and whole counties were threatened by depopulation. Lords and nobles upset the social order by literally robbing the poor of their share in the commons, tearing down the houses which, by the force of custom, the poor had long regarded as theirs and their heir's.

[9] See Polanyi, *The Great Transformation*, 57.

[10] See Allen Buchanan, *Ethics, Efficiency and the Market* (Clarendon Press 1985), 1.

[11] Although I will argue for a substantially different position, throughout the remainder of the chapter I have been greatly assisted by the research compiled in Part One of John Atherton's *Christianity and the Market: Christian Social Thought for Our Times* (SPCK, 1992), 1–77.

[12] Today, the question of scarcity also has to include data about the environment that is pertinent to the question of sustainable development. See, for example, Donella H. Meadows, Dennis L. Meadows, Jorgen Randers, *Beyond the Limits: Confronting Global Collapse, Envisioning a Sustainable Future* (Post Mills, VT: Chelsea Green Pub., 1992). A fuller treatment of the question of the economy and the environment will be given in Chapter 9.

[13] John F. Sleeman, *Basic Economic Problems: A Christian Approach* (SCM Press, 1953), 22. On the assumption that scarcity will be part of the future as long as we can imagine see J. Bennet (ed), *Christian Values and Economic Life* (Harper, 1954), 186. Also, on the recognition of scarcity in premodern society see B. Gordon, *Economic Analysis Before Adam Smith: Hesiod to Lessius* (Macmillan, 1975), 4.

[14] Robert Benne, *The Ethic of Democratic Capitalism: A Moral Reassessment* (Philadelphia: Fortress Press 1981), Chapter 6 quoting Samuelson.

[15] See John F. Sleeman, *Economic Crisis: A Christian Perspective*, (SCM, 1976), Chapter 7.

[16] The price system is part of that branch of economics referred to as microeconomics. The latter frames the decisive problem of economics as determining how prices are formed and incomes distributed. It offers explanations of price formations and their relationship to the distribution of the income created as wages, profit and rent.

[17] G. Williams, *The Economics of Everyday Life* (Penguin 1951), Chapter 2. See also Denys L. Munby, *Christianity and Economic Problems* (Macmillan 1956), Chapter 9.

[18] "Equilibrium price" is part of the theory of marginal utility. Marginal utility *for the consumer* relates price to the value of the last item of a specific product consumed; *for the producer*, the value of a resource relates to the marginal contribution of the last unit of the resource used when it is equal to the cost of any alternative use. See H. Daly and J. Cobb, *For the Common Good: Redirecting the Economy Toward Community, the Environment, and a Sustainable Future* (Boston: Beacon Press, 1989), 47–48. Also, see c.2, 28, 34; and c. 4, 66–8.

[19] See Peter Donaldson, *Economics of the Real World* (BBC and Penguin, 1973), 23–24.

[20] See Preston, *Religion and the Ambiguities of Capitalism*, 26: "Pure market theory inappropriately treats humans as it treats land, presupposing that they [both] respond to market changes automatically."

[21] See Gordon, *Economic Analysis Before Adam Smith*, 262.

[22] See Donaldson, *Economics of the Real World*, 23.

[23] See Denys L. Munby, *God and the Rich Society* (Oxford University Press, 1961), 202f.

[24] In *Christianity and the Market*, p. 62, John Atherton contends that, despite universally agreed defects, there is general recognition that no effective substitute exists, whether of a socialist command economy or a substantial "third way." Atherton's position will not only be challenged in Chapters 8–10 of this book, a case will also be made for taking on alternative economic strategies, within the present market system, in order to lead to significant alterations in it.

[25] See M. Douglas Meeks, *God the Economist: The Doctrine of God and Political Economy* (Minneapolis: Fortress, 1989), 1 and 7.

[26] See his *Christianity and the Market*, 63.

[27] (London and New York: Routledge, 1992).

[28] See G. Hodgson, *The Democratic Economy* (Penguin, 1984) on the need for incorporating a social dimension for the effective functioning of a market economy.

[29] See Buchanan, *Ethics, Efficiency, and the Market*, 2.

[30] Donald Hay, in *Economics Today: A Christian Critique* (Apollos, 1989), 147, regards the institution of private property as one of the two essential features of a "capitalist market economy." The other essential feature is that exchange is mediated through markets.

[31] See Hay, *Economics Today*, 149. V.A. Demant in *Religion and the Decline of Capitalism* (Faber, 1952) argued, with others, that capitalism was parasitic on such external values and would gradually consume them.

[32] See Milton L. Meyers, *The Soul of Modern Economic Man: Ideas of Self-Interest—Thomas Hobbes to Adam Smith* (Chicago and London: University of Chicago Press, 1983).

[33] See Mark A. Lutz and Kenneth Lux, *Humanistic Economics: The New Challenge* (New York: The Bootstrap Press, 1988), c.3 "Self-Interest and Economic Man: A History," and c. 6 "Beyond Rational Man: The Reasonable Person."

[34] See R. Preston, *Religion and the Persistence of Capitalism* (SCM Press, 1979), p. 73, and his use of C.B. MacPherson's *Theory of Possessive Individualism* (Oxford University Press, 1962). Also see Robert Bellah (ed.), *Habits of the Heart* (New York: Harper & Row, 1986).

[35] In contrast to microeconomics (see fn. 16 above), macroeconomics poses the decisive problem of economics as the determination of the level of output and employment in a given economy.

[36] See John Maynard Keynes, *The General Theory of Employment, Interest, and Money* [1936] (London: Macmillan rpt., 1973).

[37] See Lutz and Lux, *Humanistic Economics*, c.10 "Government and the Market: The Vital Link," 202–22.

[38] See Peter Berger, *The Capitalist Revolution: Fifty Propositions About Prosperity, Equality and Liberty* (Wildwood House, 1987), 74: By "democracy" is meant a political system in which governments are constituted by majority votes in regular and uncoerced elections. For an interpretation from the left affirming the connection between market economy and democracy see G. Therborn, "The Rule of Capital and the Rise of Democracy," in *New Left Review*, No. 103, May–June 1977, 3–42.

[39] See c. 4, 82–83, on the detrimental effects of economic imperialism on democratic processes.

[40] "Capitalism After Communism: Now Comes the Hard Part," in *One Hundred Years of Catholic Social Thought: Celebration and Challenge*, John A. Coleman, S.J. (ed), (Maryknoll, NY: Orbis Books, 1991).

[41] Atherton in *Christianity and the Market*, Part Two, 79–201 describes and criticizes three major responses: the conservative response affirms market economies largely as the most appropriate expression of a Christian political economy; the radical response rejects market economy; and the liberal response which subordinates the operations of the market to social purposes and goals. In my opinion, a more accurate and fair description of Christian responses can be found in J. Philip Wogaman's *Christians and the Great Economic Debate* (SCM Press, 1977), 98–154. In the latter, social market capitalism is closest to Atherton's liberal response and democratic socialism corresponds to Atherton's radical response. Unfortunately, Atherton's description of a conservative response is a thinly veiled apologia for much of present market operations. Furthermore, Atherton, writing fifteen years after Wogaman, does not treat as a separate response what Wogaman calls economic conservationism or steady-state economic management. The response developed in this work, which accepts the need to be familiar with the workings of market economies, argues strongly for reforms and adaptive strategies suggested by what Wogaman calls social market capitalism.

[42] John Kenneth Galbraith, *A History of Economics: The Past as the Present* (Penguin, 1989), 1.

[43] Atherton, *Christianity and the Market*, 17.

[44] See Munby, *God and the Rich Society*, 12.

[45] Atherton, *Christianity and the Market*, 17.

[46] Some of the most serious challenges to the reigning economic orthodoxy include: Paul Ormerod, *The Death of Economics* (London/Boston: Faber & Faber, 1994); Paul Krugman, *Peddling Prosperity: Economic Sense and Nonsense in the Age of Diminished Expectations* (New York/London: W.W. Norton & Company, 1994); and *Beyond the Market: Alternatives to Economic Rationalism,* edited by Stuart Rees, Gordon Rodley and Frank Stilwell (Sydney: Pluto Press, 1993).

[47] Preston, in *Religion and the Ambiguities of Capitalism*, 28, points out that the free market left to itself cannot cope with "externalities"—that is, the bad effects, from a public and societal point of view—which an entrepreneur can create without any self-cost. Pollution is an obvious example.

[48] Berger, *The Capitalist Revolution*, 8.

[49] A whole series of international bodies were developed to handle such interconnections, from the meeting of the seven most advanced economies, the G7, to the European Economic Community.

[50] Hay, *Economics Today*, 248.

[51] Berger, *The Capitalist Revolution*, 3.

[52] For a detailed description and analysis of the operation of a market economy in an interlocking fashion with the government in Japan see James Fallow's three-part series in *The Atlantic Monthly* "Looking at the Sun," Nov. 1993, 69–100, "How the World Works," December 1993, 61–87, and "What Is An Economy For?", January 1994, 76–92.

[53] By the 1970s dependency theory came to dominate much Third World thinking, particularly through the efforts of Fernando Cardoso. He linked it to the role of multinational corporations which rapidly became the major source of the inequities brought on by financial exploitation.

[54] Both Berger, in *The Capitalist Revolution*, 124–5, and Atherton, in *Christianity and the Market*, 32–3, in an effort to distribute responsibility for the market's hurtful effects in the Third World, assign more weight to political and cultural shortcomings in Third World settings than I find either credible or culturally sensitive.

[55] See Ronald H. Preston, *Church and Society in the Late Twentieth Century* (SCM Press, 1983), 13, where he refers to thirty-nine definitions of socialism.

[56] See A. Nove, *The Economics of Feasible Socialism* (Allen & Unwin, 1983), 33.

CHAPTER TWO

Self-Interest and the Behavior of "Economic Man"

The Reduction of Needs to Wants

AN ECONOMICS WHICH DOES JUSTICE TO AND RESPECTS THE human condition has to acknowledge the operation of complex needs and motives in human persons and communities. Only then can an economics that is in accord with human wholeness be derived. While mainstream *neoclassical economics*[1] has rightly observed that people often seek their own personal advantage, it too often takes this part of human behavior to be the whole picture as far as the science of economics is concerned. Such an economics does not take account of the complexity and persistence of human needs and reduces the human person to the construct sometimes called "economic man."[2] In such a construct the human person can be understood completely by self-interest motives.

Unfortunately, conventional neoclassical economic theory has inherited from eighteenth- and nineteenth-century British philosophy an image of the person which has effectively eliminated the reality of human needs, as well as narrowed the breadth of human motivation. One example of the British philosophical heritage, from which neoclassical economics operates, utilitarianism, provides the basis for "economic utility theory." It was first formulated by the Englishman Jeremy Bentham (1748–1832). The philosophy assumes that people do the things they do, not because of need, but because actions are useful to them; that is, they "have utility" in the sense of bringing people happiness or pleasure.

Bentham maintained that pleasure and pain alone point out what we ought to do, as well as determine what we should do.[3]

Also, according to Bentham, pleasures do not differ between themselves in type or kind, but only in their strength or intensity. Therefore, the difference between the pleasure of eating a piece of chocolate and the satisfaction of a job well done is not that they are different kinds of pleasures, but that they differ in their impact. The importance of Bentham's view for the study of the person is that, in substituting pleasures for needs, it also sidesteps the classic human issues of ethics and justice, or values. It treats these problems as if they were only a matter of quantity. The need to discriminate between the good and the pleasurable, between what is true and the personally expedient, is increasingly seen as only the difference between two amounts of pleasure.

Utilitarianism's quantitative approach to the human person, as well as to the person's intensity of pleasure, led to a physicalist focus on the body and bodily sensations. The physicalist and quantitative emphases of utilitarianism also laid the foundation for a major theoretical direction in early psychology, behaviorism. From Pavlov's work with laboratory dogs, conditioned reflexes were assumed to be the simple unit upon which the whole edifice of human personality and culture was built. Later on, the psychologist B.F. Skinner refined and broadened these behavioristic concepts in his formulation of what was called the "Reinforcement Theory." For Skinner, as for Pavlov, these principles were the actual foundations upon which all other complex and sophisticated human behavior was built.

The quantitative concept of utility, the physicalist pleasure principle, and the behaviorist reinforcement theory came together to shift the focus, in the emerging conventional view of economics, from human needs and motivations to human behavior. In this view, an understanding of human behavior was thought to be able to be charted by describing the wants and desires which characterized human choices. A good illustration of the influence can be seen in the way that certain behavioral economists have come to use the Skinnerian reinforcement model in their study of economic behavior.[4]

The shift away from human needs and motivations to human behavior was given further impetus by William Stanley Jevons (1835–1882). He began to redefine the phrase "hierarchy of needs" in a way which gradually disassociated it from human needs and moved it closer to wants and desires: for Jevons it was far more appropriate to speak about a "hierarchy of feeling" which correlated more easily with the pleasures and pains with which the economy deals.[5] Jevons decided that an economic "hierarchy of feeling" occupied a place within the broader hierarchy of human needs. His decision soon led to the rejection of the idea of a hierarchy of needs and along with it the elimination of the concept of needs itself within economic theory. Economics, following Jevons and others of his time, did away with the concept of needs and instead substituted the concept of "wants," or more specifically what is called "demand."

By reducing all human needs and desires to wants, economics makes no distinction between activities as different as reading a book, eating a hamburger, or going for a walk. They all provide the same thing, the fulfillment of a want; and whether this is called satisfaction, pleasure or utility, it is all seen as the same thing. Utility is contained in all useful goods, and because of this common property all goods are seen not only as comparable but also as substitutable. In the concept of "utility" economics has invented a category into which all things fit. Expressing needs as wants allows the economist to assume that persons can substitute needs in the same way that they can substitute wants.[6]

Today, mainstream neoclassical economics views the nature of the person as a collection of infinite wants. Paul Heyne in *The Economic Way of Thinking* uses the example of water to demonstrate the economist's conviction that, upon closer inspection, needs turn out to be nothing more than wants.[7] After he asks whether or not we *need* water, Heyne tells us that we do not, and further that the best way to turn a drought into a calamity is to pretend that water is a necessity. Expressing the view of standard economics, his point is that if we take a supposed need, such as water, and we increase its price, then people will use less of it, just like anything else. Therefore, the economist reasons, it is not a need. Critically, Heyne says that the economist is not comfortable with talk about needs, and that the "law of demand" is preferable to the concept of need, because demand relates the amounts that are purchased to the sacrifices that must be made to obtain these amounts.[8] The "sacrifices" that the economist refers to in the concept of demand is purchasing power. By this standard a rich person will make more "sacrifices" for water than a poor person. To the economist a poor person just does not seem to want water as much as a rich person. Also, all wants can be reduced to one general abstract want called "utility." The theory based on such a construct assumes consumers who have a relatively ample income and their economic choice is guided only by the available quantities of commodities.[9]

When economics reduced all wants and needs to the concept of utility two consequences followed. First of all, a theoretical acknowledgment of the fundamental difference between needs and wants was virtually lost. Secondly, after absorbing the concept of needs into that of wants, economics also assumed that wants are infinite and insatiable.[10] With these consequences, economics then developed a theory, that of *diminishing marginal utility*, to account for human behavior when faced with a variety of insatiable wants.

> Diminishing marginal utility is an expression of the 'variety is the spice of life' philosophy—that people prefer to have one or a few of a lot of different goods and services rather than a great many of only a few goods and services. . . . An individual will derive more satisfaction from eating a first apple than a second apple, . . . than a third apple and so on—where all the apples are eaten at one sitting.[11]

Notice that for the economist it is not a fulfilled need that leads an individual to go from one item of consumption to another, but a satisfied want, and further wants which demand variety. The doctrine of wants and utility came about largely as a product of the history of economic activity, with the key role played by England in that history and the special attention that was given there to the concept of self-interest.[12] It will be helpful to look at some of the people who contributed to that history.

Self-Interest: From Unacceptable Vice to Scientific Law

In 1705 the Dutch physician Bernard de Mandeville published a small booklet of verse that later became known as *The Fable of the Bees*. It is a satiric social commentary, which reflects on economic activity in society with the analogy of a busy beehive. In it Mandeville states that the various vices—pride, indulgence, avarice, and so forth—are actually the cause of social and economic development.[13] In the story the moralists in the beehive complain about all the sinfulness, and finally Jove, moved by indignation, turns "all the knaves honest" and brings the supposed "benefits" of virtue upon them. The "benefits," however, turn out to be dubious since the presence of virtue removes the motivation, the means by which all their luxuries and comforts came to be. As a consequence, the whole economy of the hive runs down, and the hive's honey stock diminishes. In his conclusion, Mandeville tells the moralists to stop complaining, because to have a society of wealth and yet be without great vices is a contradiction.

One of Mandeville's critics, Francis Hutchenson, occupied a chair of Moral Philosophy at the University of Glasgow in Scotland. Hutcheson's student, and in turn the occupant of that same chair of Moral Philosophy in 1752, was Adam Smith, the venerable father of economics. Smith's first book, which originally brought him to public recognition, was *The Theory of Moral Sentiments*, published in 1759. In the opening lines Smith states the nature of his inquiry: "How selfish soever man may be supposed, there are evidently some principles in his nature, which interest him in the fortune of others, and render their happiness necessary to him, though he derives nothing from it, except the pleasure of seeing it."[14]

In general, Smith's theory of the basis of moral sentiments is a person's ability to take the position of a third party, an impartial observer, and in this way to form a sympathetic idea of the moral, as opposed to the selfish, merits of the situation. Near the end of the book, under the category of "Licentious Systems," Smith deals with Mandeville. All traditional systems of morality rest, as Smith says, on the belief that there is a real and essential distinction between vice and virtue. A licentious system, such as that of Dr. Mandeville, says that such a distinction is false, so that one need not attempt restraint and control of the so-called lower passions because they are not really lower after all. In that way Mandeville's system gives "license."

The so-called virtues are really disguised or masqueraded forms of what we ordinarily call vices, such as pride and vanity. In other words, so many of the seemingly virtuous are really hypocrites. Smith regards Mandeville's ideas as "pernicious," and "in *almost* [emphasis added] every respect erroneous." Nonetheless, Smith concedes that "how destructive soever this system may appear, it could never have imposed upon so great a number of persons nor have occasioned so general an alarm among those who are the friends of better principles had it not in some respect bordered on the truth." This truth for Smith, at least in his first book, is just a bit of sophistry by which Mandeville establishes his favorite conclusion that "private vices are public benefits."[15]

Seventeen years later, in 1776, Smith comes out with *The Wealth of Nations* and the book goes down in history as the origin of the economic theory of self-interest. In one of its most famous passages, Smith says:

> It is not from the benevolence of the butcher, the brewer, or the baker, that we expect our dinner, but from their regard to their own self-interest. We address ourselves not to their humanity but to their self-love, and never talk to them of our own necessities, but of their advantages. Nobody but a beggar chooses to depend chiefly upon the benevolence of his fellow citizens.[16]

In the excerpt Smith sounds much closer to Mandeville than he was in *The Theory of Moral Sentiments*. Ironically, while he opposed the unrestrained lower passions or vices which Mandeville cited as the energy of prosperity, he came to see self-interest as a socially acceptable way of restraining the vices and of generating wealth in society.[17]

Smith's later appraisal of self-interest, however, was also based on an analogy with the impersonal force of gravity. In Smith's time, the intellectual climate in Britain was heavily influenced by Sir Isaac

Newton's *The Mathematical Principles of Natural Philosophy*, published in 1687. The Scottish universities of which Smith was a most prominent member were highly active in spreading the ideas of Newton. In one of Smith's essays he describes Newton's system as "the greatest discovery ever made by man."[18] The keynote of Newton's system was the law of universal gravitation. It stated that a universally present "force," which Newton called gravitation, caused a phenomenon to follow mechanical and mathematically regular laws. It appears that Adam Smith effectively brought together his socially acceptable understanding of self-interest with his later view of "the invisible hand" as an analogous illustration of the law of gravitation. He advanced the principle that "the invisible hand" operates in economics analogously to the way gravity operates in physics.

Smith's shift from a moral to a scientific understanding of self-interest is reflected in the differences between his *Moral Sentiments* and *Wealth of Nations*. In the former Smith uses the invisible hand concept for the first time and aligns it with God's providence:

> The rich . . . in spite of their . . . own vain and insatiable desires . . . divide with the poor the produce of all their improvements. They are led by an *invisible hand* to make nearly the same distribution of the necessaries of life which would have been made had the earth been divided into equal portions among all its inhabitants; and thus, without intending it, . . . advance the interests of . . . society . . . . When Providence divided the earth among a few lordly masters, it neither forgot nor abandoned those who seemed to have been left out in the partition.[19]

The "providential" effect of the invisible hand is a more just distribution of the necessities of life.

When Smith introduces the invisible hand concept in *The Wealth of Nations*, it no longer refers to a guiding force moderating the social effects of the "vain and insatiable desires of the rich." Now, it provides a justification for economic agents following their own self-interest. "[The economic agent] intends only his gain, and . . . in this, . . . [is] led by an invisible hand . . . . By pursuing his own interest [the economic agent] frequently promotes that of the society more effectually than when he really intends to promote it." Furthermore, Smith positively disdains those who think that economic agents should operate from any motive other than self-interest: "I have never known much good done by those who affected to trade for the public good."[20] Effectively, Smith's later interpretation of the invisible hand had as wide an influence on classical economics[21] as had Newton's understanding of gravity on modern physics. Self-interest became the universal governor of social behavior, just as gravity was understood to order all earthly and heavenly phenomena.

From a Science of Wealth to a Science of Value-Free Human Behavior

In the early formulations of the principle of self-interest by Smith and his followers, economics as the *science* of wealth production investigated the causes and the reasons that would bring about the betterment of society at large, and the adequate provision of material goods for the less well-off. After Smith a number of "classical economists" moved the emphasis upon self-interest from being an "impersonal natural force," to being an acceptable "personal motivation." One of them, David Ricardo (1772–1823), was instrumental in shifting the focus of economics from that of a science of making wealth to one which described the *human behavior* which promoted wealth production. When this happened economic theory developed an understanding of human behavior which reinforced the economic theory in possession.

The compatibility between economic theory and human behavior can be seen in Ricardo's insistence that self-interest and business motivation were perfectly compatible.[22] In fact, the entire economics of Ricardo presupposed self-interested individual motives and actions, especially as they can be instrumental in the development of income distribution in an economic system.

The shift onto the nature of the individual seeking wealth was developed further in the writings of John Stuart Mill.[23] In his view of the individual, Mill broke with his father, James's, and Jeremy

Bentham's, strict quantitative and utilitarian view of human nature.[24] He wrote several essays on how to recast economics into a science "depending on laws of human nature," but only those which did not relate to the feelings of affection, love, conscience, duty, and a sense of personal dignity. These other aspects were not relevant for economics, even though they might interfere with its applicability. Thus was born a hypothetical image of the human person that, on the one hand, acknowledged *abstractly* all human passions and motives—especially the more noble ones—but, on the other hand, chose to deal *concretely* only with the less noble ones which pertain to economics.[25] Mill's analytical abstraction of human nature establishes him firmly as the *conceptual* father of *homo economicus*, the "rational economic agent."

The focus on the self-interested nature of the individual received an immense boost in the person of Hermann Heinrich Gossen (1810–1858), an obscure and long ignored Prussian civil servant. His economics emphasized pleasure-seeking, atomistic individuals interacting with one another in market-exchange. The maximization of individual pleasure was for Gossen not only life's ultimate purpose, but God's will. Furthermore, it was his opinion that any moralistic efforts to contain the increase of pleasure were contradictory to God's purposes.[26] If they were attempted, however, they would be frustrated because the desire for maximized self-interest is so strong. Even if that desire were suppressed, it would always reappear with increased strength in an unexpected and unforeseen new manifestation.[27]

According to Gossen most humanitarian legislation to help the poor will indirectly backfire and make the poor even worse off. It is the task of economics to demonstrate the social reformers and moralists wrong. The egoism of the human race is the true force which moves the human family.[28] The Creator himself has made egoism " . . . the sole and irresistible force by which humanity may program in the arts and science for both its material and intellectual welfare."[29] With such convictions, Gossen effectively raised egoism to a divine principle and declared it the root of all that is good, not only in the economic sphere, but for the entire social domain as well. His "gospel" of self-interest emerged decades later under the guise of two fundamental assumptions about economic behavior in market societies: the God-given goodness of self-interested behavior; and suspicion of all humanitarian legislation to improve welfare, whether by minimum wage laws, social security, or relief for the poor.

Gossen's framework of divinely ordained individual self-interest was essentially ignored until capitalist economists of the late nineteenth century discovered in it an anthropological foundation on which to bring the notion of value-free economic behavior to the forefront of economic thought. One of them was William Stanley Jevons in his *Theory of Political Economy*.[30] He, along with other defenders of capitalism at the time of Marx's attacks on its legitimacy, finally found in Gossen a way to move away from the labor theory of value held by classical economists since Adam Smith.[31] That theory had been held even in the face of some fundamental problems about the nexus between labor and the value of commodities. One was how tools or machines, by reducing labor while increasing output, thereby reduced the amount of labor value imparted to commodities. A second problem was that of market value. The prices which people are willing to pay for goods are determined in markets, not simply by the amount of labor required to make them. Smith was particularly troubled by this latter problem and phrased his dilemma in what has been called the paradox of value: Why it is that something which has great use, such as water, should cost us so little, while something with very little use, such as diamonds, should be so dear in its exchange value in the marketplace? Thus Smith recognized two kinds of value, use value and exchange value.

It was Jevons, however, who proposed an ingenious theory to account for the paradox of differing types of value. The key lay in the concepts of marginal and total utility. Marginal utility represents how much a consumer is willing to spend for the last unit bought of a particular commodity. Total utility, by comparison, represents the overall number of individual units of a particular commodity which have been consumed. The paradox of value is solved because *use value is the total utility of a good*, whereas *exchange value is its marginal utility*.[32] Unfortunately, while the paradox may have been solved, there is still a very serious flaw in the explanation. The goods which are compared, in this case water and diamonds, are not substitutable. Also, the reasoning simply does not acknowledge the difference between water as a necessity of life and diamonds as a luxury consumer item.

Jevons, like Gossen before him, was a strong advocate of a more mathematically, and by implication, value-free economics. On the question of whether or not economics was a physical or a moral science, Jevons insisted that his theory of economy was an example of a physical science, as was mathematics.[33] For Jevons, economics and its calculus of utility, need to be limited to material wants and wealth. Questions of morality do not enter the picture until we have to decide what is right and wrong in the way we employ wealth earned through the skillful and scientific management of economics. So, while self-interest and calculated utility maximization are appropriate for economics, they are not appropriate for all human actions. In effect, Jevons' designation of separate spheres on the basis of methodology establishes a context in which it becomes accepted to exclude economics from the moral accountability that applies to all other areas of life. It also helped to consolidate the assumption of classical and neoclassical economics that economic behavior operated in a value-free realm. Or, at least, that it was accountable only to a set of scientific criteria that were not applicable to other realms of life.

The classical development of value-free economics culminated in the work of Alfred Marshall (1842–1924).[34] Marshall, an ex-theology student who once planned to become a Protestant minister, refined Jevons' concept of "economic man" and coined the phrase in his lectures of 1885. He found that the proper focus of economics was human conduct in the *business* part of life.[35] For Marshall, the most pervasive motive in the business part of life is the desire for material rewards. Higher motives need only to be recognized in the way income and wealth are spent. They cannot be included within the scope of economics, and were a worthwhile topic only for some distant future.[36]

In the meantime, Marshall treated the consumer as a self-interested utility maximizer who interacts with a basically profit-maximizing businessman. Interestingly, whether or not the social good increases depends, not on the highest or most noble expression of human nature, but on the strongest.[37] By this conviction Marshall was expressing the long-standing belief in Western social thought, which can be traced to Hobbes,[38] that the higher aspects of human nature were largely ineffective in curbing the much more powerful human passions. For social progress to occur, economic self-interest, not virtue, had to be set against the lower passions.

The Time and Relationships of "Economic Man"

When Marshall, in his lectures of 1885, coined the term "economic man," he gave a name to the already forty-year-old intellectual offspring of J. S. Mill. The neoclassical meaning of the concept "economic man" referred only to that behavior which was considered "economic." In that domain humans were seen to behave selfishly and motivated only with regard to their own welfare. The psychology was derived from Bentham's utilitarianism and since J. S. Mill, great care was taken to ensure that any kind of ethical or moral considerations were not allowed to determine, or even co-determine, human behavior. "Economic man" was not only the prime pillar in the economic foundation but was also responsible for making economics the science of value-free self-interested behavior.

It was with Philip Henry Wicksteed (1844–1927) that the understanding of self-interested behavior characteristic of the economic realm was extended to the organization of all human resources. He did this by suggesting that the principle of diminishing marginal utility should no longer be restricted to industrial or commercial firms. In The Common Sense of Political Economy, Wicksteed proposed that the principle be understood as a universal and vital force in the administration of all deliberate or conscious human action.[39] All human enterprises were to be seen as part and parcel of economics. Wicksteed referred to two areas of life in particular to make his point: time management, and relationships.

Wherever there is a question of choice, for example whether to study or go out with a friend, we are in a process of managing our time. Our time is limited to twenty-four hours a day and to the span of our life. Wicksteed's suggestion represented a new way of looking at life. Economists like Jevons and Marshall identified scarcity with *material* shortage. And while it is true that Gossen pioneered in taking time itself as the bedrock of scarcity in the German-speaking world, Wicksteed was the first to introduce such a notion into the English intellectual scene.[40]

The implications of Wicksteed's move were far-reaching. It allowed not only the consumer but also the human being in general to be analyzed the same way we look at a businessman—calculating, commercial, and impersonal in his dealings. Everything we do relates to the economic category. Simply because we all have to live with finite time, we are all administering that limited resource in order to squeeze out maximum gain, pleasure, or utility. The noneconomic category either does not exist or is subordinated to the economic. Gone are the reservations of Mill, Jevons and Marshall, as well as the traditional focus emphasizing applications in business and commerce. What results is much more subtle: economics becomes a new *way of thinking*, the way of extremely time-conscious beings always aware of what they are forgoing by doing what they do.

In addition to defining and conceptualizing economics as a way of life that applies to all human behavior, Wicksteed also believed that he was able to show that this way of thought had nothing to do with selfishness. "Economic man" may be constantly calculating to achieve his own ends, but these ends need not be selfish. Indeed, they could be philanthropic. The purposes, however, had nothing to do with what economics was about. Economics was merely about the most efficient *means* to achieve specific ends. For Wicksteed what defines the economic relationship is that each party enters into it with only the intent of serving his or her own purposes and not those of the other with whom one is dealing. The critical point for Wicksteed is that one's purposes in entering into the exchange need not be selfish. The only thing that matters from the standpoint of economics is that genuine altruism is not applied to the person one is dealing with and exchanging with. In this way, the self-interest principle going back to Adam Smith is still maintained, and yet the discipline need not conceive of itself as the science of selfishness.

One of the most celebrated attacks on the self-interest assumed in the underlying image of the human person in economics came from the American economist Thorstein Veblen (1857–1929). He caricatured nineteenth-century "economic man" as a hedonistic calculator of pleasure and pain, a homogenous globule of desire and happiness who has neither antecedent nor consequence.[41] It was Lionel Robbins, however, in *The Nature and Significance of Economic Science* who attempted to respond to the critics of "economic man" by showing that the concept was morally neutral.[42] In the final analysis, his "defense" failed to account for how moral neutrality could justify treating people as means rather than ends in themselves.

Summary

At the beginning of this chapter it was stated that an economics which is respectful of human wholeness has to acknowledge the presence of complex needs and motives in human persons and communities. Only then will the growth and development of the economy be able to be in a sympathetic relationship with the growth and development of persons and the communities in which it operates. Yet the history of the idea of self-interest and other closely associated ideas in mainstream neoclassical economics has largely been a history of the blocking out of many of the needs and motives that are properly part of any human enterprise. Once the foundation had been set in place with the concept of utility, whereby the distinction between needs and wants is virtually lost, self-interest could begin to be interpreted without the need for putting it in dialogue with other human motivations. Not only did it become an expression of human nature whereby the lower and more disruptive passions could be kept in tow, it took on the respectability of an impersonal force, a scientific law, which inevitably guided the growth of the economy.

J.S. Mill, while acknowledging the higher human activities of the pursuit of truth, the love of beauty, and a sense of personal dignity, nonetheless made an apologia for self-interest as the only appropriate motive for engaging *in the market*. Furthermore, he suggested that any efforts to better the plight of the needy beyond giving free rein to the laws of self-interest are useless and doomed to failure. It was then easy for other British economists like Jevons and Marshall to argue for human behavior in commerce and industry as value-free. For in the latter realms human behavior was simply guided by the laws of human nature and of the marketplace.

The prominence of self-interest was given a further boost by the German/Austrian economist Hermann Gossen, who identified it with the will of God and who also left his mark on other English economists in the persons of Wicksteed and Robbins. With the latter, the self-interest which had been the hallmark of economic activity is extended to all realms of life via the concept of time. Since time is the ultimate resource, everything we want and do is inherently limited. We are all more or less self-interested all the time, not just in the domain of what traditionally had been regarded as economics—in production, consumption, work and leisure—but also in our family and love-life. In any deliberate action there is only one purpose; we have to make the best use of our time.

The British tradition ever since J.S. Mill has been able to point out problem areas where economic laws left to themselves will produce undesirable outcomes as judged from a "higher" or holistic point of view. Gossen and other economists from the Austrian tradition, on the other hand, claim to be speaking not about laws restricted to the economic realm but about laws applicable to a broader range of human experiences. The recommendations of such an economic/human science are limited only by the limitations of nature itself. There is no social, noneconomic point of view from which to criticize "economic" outcomes. In the final analysis, however, whether we are dealing with the British or the Austrian view, self-interest is the characteristic motive of the behavior of "economic man." In both instances we are presented with a "gospel of *self-interest* of one kind or another."[43]

[1] See Stephen L. Slavin, *Economics: A Self-Teaching Guide* (NY: John Wiley & Sons, Inc., 1988), 182. Neoclassical economics, also referred to as rational expectations theory, says no to any form of government economic intervention in the operation of the market. It is based on three assumptions: (1) that individuals and business firms learn, through experience, to anticipate instantaneously the consequences of changes in monetary and fiscal policy; (2) that they act instantaneously to protect their economic interests; and (3) that all resource and product markets are purely competitive.

[2] For the general outline of the history of the idea of "economic man" throughout this chapter I am indebted to Mark A. Lutz and Kenneth Lux, *Humanistic Economics*, especially cc.1–3, 1–63. Also see Ronald H. Preston, *Church and Society in the Late Twentieth Century*, 33–55; and *Religion and the Persistence of Capitalism*, 69–82.

3 See Jeremy Bentham, *An Introduction to the Principles of Morals and Legislation* (London: T. Payne & Sons, 1789), Chapter 1, Part 1.

[4] See John Kagel et al., "Experimental Studies of Consumer Demand Behavior Using Laboratory Animals," *Economic Enquiry*, 13 (1975), 22–38.

[5] See William Stanley Jevons, *The Theory of Political Economy* [1871], (NY: Augustus M. Kelley, rpt. 1965), 26–27.

[6] See Lutz/Lux, *Humanistic Economics*, 324–5. The authors point out that "substitutability" was developed into the "equimarginal principle/rule" by Alfred Marshall in the latter's *Principles of Economics* [1890] (London: Macmillan Press, 1949). Nicholas Georgescu-Roegen demonstrated that substitutability and the equimarginal rule, assumed by all economists since Marshall to be applicable in the choice of all goods, is only valid within a certain need category, such as clothing. As soon as it is applied to basic goods representing different needs, it breaks down. Georgescu-Roegen thereby responded with the "principle of the irreducibility of needs."

[7] See Paul Heyne, *The Economic Way of Thinking*, 4th edition (Chicago: Science Research Associates, 1983), 16.

[8] Heyne, *The Economic Way of Thinking*, 32.

[9] Nicholas Georgescu-Roegen, "Utility and Values in Economic Thought," in Philip P. Wiener, ed. *Dictionary of the History of Ideas* Vol. 4 (NY: Charles Scribner & Sons, 1973), 458. Since the 1930s "utility" has been conceived as the satisfaction of an individual's subjective desires. See Paula England, "The Separative Self: Androcentric Bias in Neoclassical Assumptions," in *Beyond Economic Man: Feminist Theory and Economics* (Chicago: University of Chicago Press, 1993), 37–53, at 41.

[10] Campbell McConnell, *Economics*, 8th edition. (NY: McGraw-Hill, 1981), 23.

[11] Werner Sichel and Peter Eckstein, *Basic Economic Concepts* (Chicago: Rand McNally, 1974), 128–9. Also, see c. 1, 20, fn. 18; 34 of the present chapter; and c. 4, 66–8.

[12] Lutz and Lux, *Humanistic Economics*, 31.

[13] Bernard de Mandeville, *The Fable of the Bees* [1714] Vol. 1 (Oxford University Press, 1966), 18, 24, 36. For a detailed commentary see Louis Dumont, *From Mandeville to Marx: The Genesis and Triumph of Economic Ideology* (Chicago and London: University of Chicago Press, 1977), c. 5 "Mandeville's Fable of the Bees: Economics and Morality," 61–81.

[14] Adam Smith, *The Theory of Moral Sentiments*, edited by D.D. Raphael and A.L. Macfie (Indianapolis: Liberty Classics [1759] rpt. 1982), 9.

[15] See Smith, "Of licentious Systems," in *The Theory of Moral Sentiments*, 306–14.

[16] Adam Smith, *An Inquiry into the Nature and Causes of the Wealth of Nations* [1776], The Edwin Cannan Text of the Fifth Edition (NY: The Modern Library, 1985), 16.

[17] For an excellent and insightful treatment of the relationship between economic self-interest and the taming of socially disruptive passions see Albert O. Hirschman, *The Passions and the Interests: Political Arguments for Capitalism before Its Triumph* (Princeton, NJ: Princeton University Press, 1977).

[18] Cited by E.R. Canterbery in *The Making of Economics* (Belmont, CA: Wadsworth, 1976), Liv.

[19] Smith, *The Theory of Moral Sentiments* 184–5.

[20] Smith, *The Wealth of Nations*, 225. Despite the different meanings of the "invisible hand" in *Moral Sentiments* and *Wealth of Nations*, see "Introduction," 20–25 in Adam Smith, *The Theory of Moral Sentiments*, edited by D.D. Raphael and A.L. Macfie for the view that Smith's respective views were substantially the same in the two works.

[21] See Slavin, *Economics*, 171: "The classical school of economics dominated mainstream economics from roughly 1775 to 1930. . . . The classical economists believed that [the] economy was self-regulating [and thereby pleaded for no government interference]: Recessions would cure themselves, and a built-in mechanism would always push the economy toward full employment."

[22] See Israel Kirzner, *The Economic Point of View* (Kansas City: Sheed & Ward, 1960), 53.

[23] Mill's textbook *The Principles of Political Economy*, first published in 1848, held sway in the field through numerous editions until it was finally replaced as the premier text in the field by Alfred Marshall's *Principles of Economics* in the 1890s.

[24] See John Stuart Mill, *Utilitarianism, On Liberty, Essay on Bentham and John Austin* [1838] M. Warnock, ed. (Cleveland: World Publishing, 1962), 88, 99–101.

[25] J.S. Mill, *Essays on Some Unsettled Questions of Political Economy* [1844], Reprinted in David Hausman, ed. *The Philosophy of Economics*, (NY: Cambridge University Press, 1984), 57.

[26] H.H. Gossen, *The Laws of Human Relations*, [1854] (Cambridge, MA: MIT Press, 1938), 4.

[27] See Gossen, *The Laws of Human Relations*, 6.

[28] Gossen, *The Laws of Human Relations*, 218.

[29] Gossen, *The Laws of Human Relations*, 299.

[30] Recall the earlier discussion of Jevons' role in reducing human needs to wants on p. 27, as well as the full reference to his *Theory of Political Economy* in fn.5.

[31] See Smith, *Wealth of Nations*, 34: "Labor alone, therefore, never varying in its own value, is alone the ultimate and real standard by which the value of all commodities can at all times and places be estimated and compared. It is their real price; money is their nominal price only." See Lutz/Lux, *Humanistic Economics*, 43–4, where they point out the irony of Marx having derived his labor theory of value from Adam Smith.

[32] For a further explanation see W. Sichel and P. Eckstein, *Basic Economic Concepts* (Chicago: Rand McNally, 1974). Also see p. 28 for related comments on diminishing marginal utility.

[33] See Jevons, *The Theory of Political Economy*, 3.

[34] See Alfred Marshall, *Principles of Economics* [1890] (London: Macmillan Press, 1949).

[35] Alfred Marshall, *Principles of Economics*, 12.

[36] See Marshall, *Principles of Economics*, 72, 76–7.

[37] See Dennis Robertson, *Economic Commentaries* (London: Staple Press, 1956), 148.

[38] See Thomas Hobbes, *Leviathan*, [1651]. Reprint (Indianapolis: Bobbs-Merrill, 1958).

[39] See Philip Wicksteed, *The Common Sense of Political Economy* (London: George Routledge & Sons, 1933), 3.

[40] Lutz and Lux, *Humanistic Economics*, 55.

[41] See Thorstein Veblen, *The Place of Science in Modern Civilization and Other Essays* [1915], Reprint (NY: Caprice Books, 1969), 73–4.

[42] See Lionel Robbins, *The Nature and Significance of Economic Science* [1932]. (London: Macmillan, 1984), 95, 97.

[43] Lutz and Lux, *Humanistic Economics*, 60.

CHAPTER THREE

Human Needs and Freedom from Alienation

The Anthropological Basis of Marx's Critique of Capitalism

WOLFHART PANNENBERG HAS SUGGESTED THAT MARX'S thought draws its power from its anthropological roots.[1] The purpose of this chapter is to push that assessment further, namely, to uncover and highlight Marx's anthropological insights in his writings on economics. For Marx's critique of capitalism's effects on human persons and their relationships to each other and to their communities highlights major traits of the modern world that orthodox economics consistently ignores.[2] Indeed, it is Marx's anthropological insights and criticisms, albeit insufficiently developed, and not his better known economic alternatives to capitalism, which challenge neoclassical economics to rethink its anthropology and to integrate a more adequately developed view of persons in community into its overall theory.

A great part of the challenge, however, is to know where to turn in Marx's vast writings on economics to gather his anthropological insights. One problem is that the primary and significant works on anthropology were not published until 1932.[3] The twentieth century has witnessed a growing interest in these earlier writings. There has been a gradual realization among scholars that a more full picture of Marx's intellectual development was necessary in order to see how the young Marx wrestled with the problem of human individuals in relationship to society and nature.[4]

To those who had become disenchanted with the scientific, impersonal, "mature" Marx, the concern of the "early" Marx for the individual provided a new impetus to the study of his philosophy.[5] The early Marx's philosophy was first and foremost concerned with humanity in its predicament of alienation under the capitalist system. Some Marxists also saw in the early period a necessary corrective to the ideological excesses of official Marxism.[6] There is unanimity among scholars that in his early texts, Marx's preoccupation is with philosophical anthropology and a "corresponding critique of human culture."[7] There is only general agreement, however, that in his later writings Marx was more the economist, sociologist and political scientist than the philosopher.[8] Nonetheless, Marx's later pursuit of economic theory never became completely separated from his more fundamental preoccupation with human alienation. Beneath his discussions of political economy there was always the primary motivating consideration: the condition of human beings in capitalist society.[9] The explicit philosophy in Marx's early writings continues to provide the basic framework for his later economic analysis of capitalism.

The continuity in Marx's thought between his earlier and later years depends upon the fundamental influence of Hegel. It is most clearly seen in Marx's discussion of the theme of alienation in both the early and the later works. Viewed as a whole, Marx's writings are primarily concerned with humanity as the creator of its own history. The philosophical anthropology of the early Marx is present in the social and economic analysis of the mature Marx. Indeed, it is the theme of the human person as capable of achieving eventual control of the world by technological mastery that provides the foundation upon which Marx's later thought is methodically developed.[10] Human beings create themselves and history is the account of human creative activity. Even salvation, understood as the transcendence of alienation, will be ushered in by human beings. In order to grasp and evaluate Marx's vision of the human person and community, however, it is necessary first to look at his understanding of alienation. Then, it will become clearer *how* and *why* Marx's ideas on human nature have handicapped contemporary perceptions and critiques about what is possible or impossible in proposals of economic reform.

Marx on Alienation

Steeped in Hegelian philosophy and confronted by the exploitative character of modern industrial capitalism, Marx could not avoid the question of alienation.[11] It was Hegel's usage of "alienation" that had the most lasting impact upon him. Marx, however, appears either to have *misinterpreted* or *reinterpreted* Hegel's usage of the term. For Hegel, alienation had two meanings: a fundamental one which refers to a separation or a discordant relation; and another, derivative one which refers to surrendering the willfulness, which is a cause of separation, and thereby reattaining unity.[12] For Hegel, the fundamental sense of alienation is transcended precisely *through* the derived sense of alienation as a surrender of willfulness. Marx's interpretation, however, combines Hegel's two meanings in a single general sense of "separation through surrender." For Marx, separation is the *consequence* of surrender; surrender is no longer the way of overcoming separation.[13] In Marx's later writings "surrender" became the relinquishing of one's control over one's product and labor.

Marx argues further that in relation to production, humankind's creative work, there are essentially four categories of the workers' alienation: from their products, from the process of production, from their free, self-conscious creativity, and from other human beings. First of all, workers are alienated from the products of their labor. The capitalists, who own the means of production, usurp them and the workers' right to their value.[14] To the capitalists the workers are mere producers of commodities whose value rests in their capacity to produce. In producing commodities, the laborers create themselves as commodities as well. Thus, under the exploitative capitalist system, the workers are the architects of their own alienation. A product is not an affirmation but a denial of the human value of the workers. Consequently, Marx concludes that the externalization of the workers in their products results in their labor not only becoming an alien object outside of them, but one which also becomes an affront to their personhood.[16]

Secondly, workers are alienated from the processes of production.[17] The primary symptom is the division of labor into fragmented tasks so that no one worker is responsible for the final product. Such an organization of production is geared to maximize profits for the capitalist. The workers' welfare is secondary to the capitalists' amassing of wealth, the primary motive of production. While the workers expend physical energies, the capitalists elevate themselves to positions of authority and expend only mental energy. The separation of mental from manual labor, along with the separation of various manual tasks, constitutes the characteristics of the division of labor which gives rise to alienation.[18] Workers can no longer take pride in their work, and they lose motivation and incentive. The workplace exposes their bodies to abuse, and provides virtually no mental stimulation.[19] In this situation, workers feel at home only outside of their work and feel like strangers in the process of working. Their labor is not voluntary but forced. It cannot satisfy any of the workers' needs. Over extended periods of time the workers' activity turns into passivity, and when there is no outside compulsion, labor is avoided like the plague. For Marx, this is the epitome of the workers' alienation from the productive process.

A third type of alienation occurs when labor in its *alienated* state separates workers from their "free, self-conscious creativity." Humans have a spiritual need to create. Most basically, it is expressed when they satisfy their physical needs.[20] The satisfaction of physical needs, however, is secondary to the expression of human freedom as the primary manifestation of the spiritual need to create.[21] In addition, the spiritual need to create is reflected in humanity's capacity for culture and for the cultivation and appreciation of the aesthetic.[22] In an *unalienated* state labor connects laborers with their "free, self-conscious creativity,"[23] and thereby enables the experience of work to be life-giving. Unless this happens workers "become animal," because the separation and discordance created by the capitalist system in the labor force spills over into other important areas of a person's life.[24]

One of those areas is alienation from nature, understood as the organic objective world. Humans perceive nature in two complementary ways: as the source of resources for survival, and as an extension of their ability to be creative.[25] In the first or physical way, humans *live from* the products of nature: food, heating, clothing, habitation, etc. In the second or creative way, humans *relate* to nature as the material object and tool of their vital creative activity. Unalienated human beings will live in creative harmony with nature. Even in an alienated way, however, they fashion things according to the laws of beauty. Advanced technology and human ways of using such technology are integral to this complex process.

The sad commentary on the condition of human beings in capitalist society, according to Marx, is that alienation tears human beings from their creativity and from nature. Furthermore, in an alienated state, their creativity and nature progressively heighten their sense of separation. In the type of world they have created, alienated human beings do not see that they have duplicated their own personal experiences of separateness in their products and in their relationship to nature.[26]

A fourth and final type of alienation is that which entails a person's separation from other humans. Marx declares that every self-alienation of persons from themselves and nature appears in their relationships to others.[27] In their alienated state, human beings continue to create further alienation. Their perception of reality is distorted, and their actions are selfish and hostile. This experience of alienation throws light on Marx's understanding of the human being as a social being.[28]

For Marx, becoming self-conscious and aware of other selves are distinct but inseparable parts of the same process. In the pursuit of the satisfaction of their creativity and relational needs, humans act communally. They affirm themselves within community, not apart from it. In the unalienated society, unalienated human beings will experience concord and harmony with each other.[29] There will be mutual exchanges of creative activities without the dehumanization of the workers which characterizes alienated, capitalist society.

The extent to which Marx attempted to grapple with the experience of alienation in the wake of the Industrial Revolution is impressive. In my opinion, however, it is also disappointing to see how Marx short-circuited the possible outcome of his analysis by making the condition for free creativity so dependent upon overthrowing the capitalist processes of production. In doing that, he and the capitalists whom he criticized apparently could not begin to imagine how significant adjustments to those processes, as opposed to their radical overthrow, might have resulted in a situation in which workers and their communities were not as exploited, and the relations in which communities could grow and be strengthened would be situated in a more healthy context. Neither could easily imagine such adjustments, in my opinion, because neither had paid enough attention to the full range of human needs—material and nonmaterial—and the types of communities in which they might be met. Neither moved sufficiently beyond a scientific understanding of the operation of the economy to a more holistic understanding of an economic organization of society.

Unfortunately, Marx's restriction of the human spirit's activities to the processes of production reflected one of the main ways in which his later economic analysis began to overpower some of the more important anthropological insights from his earlier period. The increasing attention he gave to the oppressive impact of capitalist processes of production inhibited the breadth of his understanding of the economic welfare which economic organization should serve and foster.

Other than describing human nature as an "ensemble of social relations," Marx does not define in precise terms what he means by humanity.[30] Rather, he simply insists that human nature is self-created precisely as workers participate in the processes of production. Humanity considered in isolation from a specific socioeconomic class, for Marx, is little more than a philosophical fantasy.[31] Human nature is socioeconomically determined. As such, human nature is relative to, and a function of, the economic mode of production.[32] Marx virtually ascribes a metaphysical status to production and productivity. They exercise a constitutive power over the shape of people's lives.[33] By assigning such importance to production, Marx places humanity in a relationship that has the potential to become as alienating as the very dynamics of the capitalist system which he rejects. Effectively, he reduces human nature to the freedom to cooperate in the processes of production, and thereby greatly limits the possibility for an ever-developing human nature to transcend the limits of that process.

Also, Marx's emphasis upon self-alienation in the processes of production appears to have prevented him from developing more positive reasons for the formation of human community. Instead of proclaiming the importance of community among workers on the basis of the need for collaborative relationships among them and management, community is portrayed as the result of the workers' opposition to capitalist production processes. Such a negative basis for communal identity reflects yet another way in which economic categories progressively exerted more influence upon Marx than philosophical reflections on the nature of human person and community.

Marx's Scientific and "Ethical" Perspectives on Economics[34]

In his treatment of human nature, Marx also leaves unanswered some other very important questions: "What are the specific *criteria* for delineating what human nature is?" Also, "Where might such criteria originate?" Marx believes that they are immanently present in humanity's socioeconomic base. As such, they are also a cultural construct. Unfortunately, he did not bother to develop this contention further.[35] Instead, his primary concern in this area was to reject the criteria offered by religion and other forms of what he considered false consciousness.

The lack of development is illustrated further in Marx's discussion of morality and law. In anticipation of the unalienated society, Marx gives the impression that there will be harmony in the nature of unalienated beings. He suggests that the laws of the future society will reflect the inner core of human nature—freedom. State law will have to compel a person to be free only when a person's behavior shows that he or she has ceased to obey the natural law of freedom. Again, Marx's discussion of freedom is weak. He assumes that once persons are free *from* the exploitative processes of production, then they will be freed *for* the harmonious satisfaction of all of their needs. He does not appear to grasp how the selfish dynamics of freedom expressed in the exploitative processes of capitalist production, and the false consciousness which they both reflect and reinforce, might resurface, albeit in alternative forms, in communist societies. As a result, he does not seem to recognize the need for a more sophisticated understanding of ethical norms.

The problem of humans exploiting one another will be corrected by radically changing the economic structures of production and bringing about the altered consciousness which such changes effect. We still have no clue, however, about ethical criteria upon which he makes his contrasting condemnation of capitalism and commendation of communism. Pushing the question further, however, suggests that Marx is moving toward replacing ethical judgments about human persons and community with presumably scientific analyses of human-beings-in-society.

Marx is convinced that, when he criticizes philosophy and religion as ideological, his premise is historical and scientific rather than moral or ethical.[36] The workers must overthrow the existing mode of production, because the very forces of history make the revolution possible. For Marx, there is a vast gulf between his philosophy of revolutionary praxis and a philosophy of ethics on how to behave in this world under the present order of things. Where the former advocates a radical transformation of the economic base of society, the latter merely attempts to preserve the status quo. The latter is the product of alienated, false consciousness. It is ideology. Nonetheless, the question still remains how Marx can appeal to a historical scientific analysis of communism in a way that is not vulnerable to self-interest, distortion, and a false consciousness, which while different from that of capitalism might be equally as oppressive.

Marx simply keeps going back to the claim that the root of alienation lies in the alienated productive process which has been alienating since the very beginning of humankind's interaction with nature. The arrival of the capitalist mode of production brought with it total and complete alienation. There is a cruel injustice inherent in the system. It forces the exploiter to enslave the exploited, and it robs both of their freedom. One of Marx's strongest reasons for condemning the capitalist system was because in it wealth meant political power in the sense of power over others. For when labor power is a commodity, as it is in capitalism, all workers must sell themselves on the market. The system, in Marx's judgment, therefore, resembled slavery.[37]

The moral tone in Marx's critique of capitalism cannot easily be traced either to a moral principle or to some vision of what capitalism ought to be and how it is falling short. Rather, the judgment is based on "feelings of antipathy."[38] Feelings of antipathy and sympathy are natural to human beings. This is consistent with Marx's assumption that human beings are the measure of what is human. Yet it is not self-evident that the capitalist and the proletariat cannot and do not share the same feelings about many significant things. It is also not self-evident that they have different and conflicting reactions to other significant phenomena. Why should the feelings that appeal to the revolutionary workers be any more true, any more free of illusion than the feelings of capitalists and those not sympathetic to revolutionary praxis? This is a question that Marx does not answer. He is merely dogmatic and resorts to persuasive rhetoric.[39]

Marx, however, is not content to rest his position on natural feelings of antipathy and sympathy. For he and Engels are convinced that they have discovered the laws of history which show that history itself is moving toward the proletarian revolution. History is inevitably working toward freedom, toward the communist society where workers' production will no longer enslave them, but will become part of them.[40] Marx's determinist understanding of history does not leave much room for a moral dimension in analyzing humanity's role in the making and shaping of history. When the process is inevitable, the responsibility is simply to discover, and preferably with a scientific analysis, what has to be, rather than to judge what ought to be. And in Marx's view, having discovered the laws of history, he was providing a scientific and empirical basis upon which human morality could be based, and placed at the service of the proletariat.[41]

The premise upon which Marx bases his argument for the historical transcendence of alienation is revolutionary praxis—that is, effective transforming action.[42] The world cannot be changed by merely changing our notions of it, by theoretically criticizing what exists. Change requires revolutionary praxis. Such praxis is not restricted to a given culture or geographical area. It is universal in its scope. Over the years, through successive epochs, the base has been broadened until the whole of humanity is divided into two camps or classes: the exploited and the exploiters.[43] After that has happened the struggle continues with a growing intensity.[44] At the heart of this class conflict is the basic socioeconomic conflict out of which all other conflicts in history arise. It leads to change when changes in the mode of production result in disharmony between the forces of production and the relations of production.

Marx's optimism for a resolution of alienation rests upon the new possibilities contained in ever-advancing technology. Every succeeding generation finds itself in possession of the productive forces won by the previous generation which serve it as the raw material for new production. In his survey of nineteenth-century capitalist society, however, Marx concluded that as long as private property persists, developments in technology can only bring about a partial satisfaction of human needs. With the abolition of private property, technology will permit humanity to regain its human, social existence in the satisfaction of its needs in a more adequately human way.[45] Then workers, in universal solidarity with one another, will engage in a revolutionary transformation of the productive processes.

Some of Marx's rhetoric supports the argument that he was a-ethical in his philosophy: in *The German Ideology* he states that communists cannot preach morality at all. For, in specific situations, egoism can be as necessary a form of self-affirmation as self-sacrifice. Indeed, communists recognize that in many instances law, morality, and religion, are little more than vehicles for conveying bourgeois prejudices and interests.[46] Other sections of Marx's writings support the view of those who see ethical content present in his thinking, for example when he insists that the proletariat must overthrow all circumstances in which humanity is humiliated, enslaved, abandoned and despised.[47] The human qualities which are needed for such a project, however, are not those which are fostered by Christianity. The revolution calls for the characteristics of authentic, unalienated humanity: courage, pride and a sense of independence. The social principles of Christianity, according to Marx, preach cowardice, self-contempt, abasement, submission, and humility.[48] In Marx's ethics of revolutionary freedom, the former characteristics are even more important than the meeting of basic physical needs.[49]

One way to get beyond the ambiguity in Marx's thought is to remember that Marx did not construe the terms "scientific" and "moral" respectively to mean "value-less" and "value-laden." Scientific refers to the material conditions of life, while moral refers to whatever is abstracted from the real situation. The distinction enables us to affirm that, in some senses, Marx's outlook is both ethical and scientific. In Marx's thought, that which is and that which ought to be form a unity in creative tension.[50]

Marx is convinced that the socioeconomic dissolution of the capitalist mode and relations of production would lead to a moral revolution. Moreover, complete and total human emancipation cannot and will not occur if appeal is made only to morality without attempts to understand and change the mode of production. Coming to terms with the practical and historical dimensions of ethics and morality in Marx's thought is crucial for a more accurate appraisal of his emphasis upon human creativity and responsibility for the abolition and transcendence of all forms of alienation. It is critically important, however, that the centrality of human activity is in no way obscured. For when this happens the human struggle is left to the caprice of unexpected and uncontrollable accidents in the historical process.[51] When the indispensable importance of human activity is in any way overlooked, a dynamic unity and interaction between human creativity and the material forces of production is no longer possible.[52]

Marx's emphasis on human agency is seen most strongly in his preoccupation with human beings as subjects of history, subjects who will be self-determined when freed from alienation. Such an emphasis leads him to reject utilitarian concepts of humanity for utilitarianism lacks the ethics of human freedom to create the new. Utilitarianism merely seeks to live in harmony with its environment by adapting to and being accommodated by a given situation. For Marx, utilitarianism takes human desires and expectations at any given moment as ultimate. Marx's "morality," in contrast, seeks to transform humanity's wants and to increase its expectations. Utilitarianism works within a given social and political system and criticizes it only where it fails to satisfy demands expressed within the system. Humanistic Marxism, however, is prepared to transcend the system, to criticize the system itself for the wants and demands it creates.[53]

It is hard to deny that, in contrast to the ethics of utilitarianism and of Christianity, as Marx conceived them, there are great possibilities for human realization and fulfillment in the "ethics" of Marxian humanism. His vision of transcending alienation in history, and humanity's pivotal role in that alienation, is both ennobling and inspiring. Unfortunately, his vision does not seem to recognize where humanity can and might go wrong. Because his anthropological reflections are not more systematically developed, the problem of alienation, for him, is largely one which comes from outside of humanity. The challenge of humanity is largely one of becoming aware of the problem and overcoming it. Marx does not seem to envision how distorted consciousness could still be a problem even after we have passed beyond the oppressive structures of capitalism.

At the end of the first subsection of this chapter the point was made that grasping Marx's understanding of alienation would help to clarify *how* and *why* his ideas of human nature were stifled in their possible further development. Basically, the threads of Marx's anthropological thinking appear to have been co-opted and gradually controlled by the assumption of scientific materialism as the controlling dynamism in the processes of production. When that happened, the potential power of his critique of capitalism to suggest more humane ways of organizing society economically was also stifled.

For Marx, the scientific laws of history appear to have become as foreordained and irrefutable as did capitalism's assumption of the "invisible hand" guiding the operation of the market. Unfortunately, both scientific perspectives allowed little or no room for the integration of values to direct and correct the operation of the economy. The failure of the Marxist critique to have integrated values more adequately becomes especially evident in Marx's attempt to pay more attention to human needs in the face of capitalism's almost total theoretical denial of them. Even in this regard, however, the possible impact of Marx's critique was seriously jeopardized by its ultimate dependence upon a view of the human person which only partially acknowledged the interdependence between the satisfaction of material and spiritual needs. A major source of the inability of Marx's critique to address the full range of human needs more adequately was his view of human creativity also through the limiting perspective of scientific materialism.

In order to be able to begin to imagine visions of economic organization that do not fall prey to the severe limitations either of neoclassical economics or central command economies, a significantly more developed view of human persons in community, and their needs, has to be drawn up as an utterly indispensable starting point for *any* future system of economic management. Only then will we be able to hope for ideas and policies of economic organization that can more adequately address a whole range of human and community needs presently overlooked by the economic systems which we have inherited.

---

[1] See his *What is Man?* translated by Duane A. Priebe (Philadelphia: Fortress Press, 1979), 116–17. Also, for many of the insights about the relationship between Marx's anthropology and economic theory in this chapter I am indebted to Winston D. Persaud's *The Theology of the Cross and Marx's Anthropology: A View From the Caribbean* (NY: Peter Lang, 1991), c.1: "Marx's Anthropology," and c.2: "Marx's Theory of History," 9–65, and 67–112.

[2] See Guy Routh, *The Origin of Economic Ideas* (2nd ed.) First Published 1975 (London: Macmillan, 1989), 217.

[3] They have a variety of titles: the *Paris Manuscripts*, the *1844 Manuscripts*, or *Economic and Philosophic Manuscripts*. See Karl Marx, *Early Texts*, translated and edited by David McLellan (Oxford: Basil Blackwell, 1971), xxvii–xxix.

[4] Adam Schaff, "Studies of the Young Marx: A Rejoinder," in *Revisionism*, edited by Leopold Labedz (London: George Allen and Unwin Ltd., 1962), 188–9.

[5] For alternative classifications of the different stages of Marx's thought see Alvin Gouldner, *The Two Marxisms: Contradictions and Anomalies in the Development of Theory* (NY: Seabury Press, 1980); and Dermot Lane, *Foundations for a Social Theology: Praxis, Process, and Salvation* (NY: Paulist, 1984), 39–40.

[6] See Raymond Geuss, *The Idea of Critical Theory: Habermas and the Frankfurt School* (NY: Cambridge University Press, 1981), 4–44. In a descriptive sense, ideology covers all the beliefs held by the members of a particular society, or those beliefs which cohere in some form of worldview, or those beliefs consciously held as a program of action for the transformation of the world. In a pejorative sense, ideology is some set of beliefs or attitudes that distorts reality, creating a false consciousness. The latter can result from an epistemological error, the legitimizing of a social illusion, or the conscious or unconscious defense of the interests of a particular subgroup in society. A positive sense of ideology is as an enabling mechanism for the satisfactory cohesion of a culture.

[7] Donald Clark Hodges, "The Young Marx—A Reappraisal," *Philosophical and Phenomenological Research*, vol. xxvii, no. 2 (December, 1966), 219.

[8] Raymond Aron, *Main Currents in Sociological Thought* (NY: Basic Books, 1965), 111. The later works include *Communist Manifesto*, *German Ideology*, and *Capital*.

[9] Daniel Bell, *The End of Ideology* (NY: Collier Books, 1961), 361–2.

[10] See Kostas Axelos, *Alienation, Praxis, and Techne in the Thought of Karl Marx*, translated by Ronald Brunzina (Austin: University of Texas Press, 1976), 49.

[11] Leszek Kolakowski, *Main Currents of Marxism Vol I: The Founders*, translated by P.S. Falla (London: Oxford University Press, 1978), 132–4.

[12] See Richard Schacht, *Alienation* (London: George Allen and Unwin, 1971), 35.

[13] Schacht, *Alienation*, 83.

[14] See Karl Marx, *Early Texts*, translated and edited by David McLellan (Oxford: Basil Blackwell, 1971), 140–3.

[15] Marx, *Early Texts*, 134. See also Kolakowski, *The Founders*, 139; and Bertell Ollman, *Alienation* (London: Cambridge University Press, 1971), 198–204.

[16] See Marx, *Early Texts*, 135.

[17] See Ollman, *Alienation*, 137–47, for a more elaborate treatment of Marx's understanding of the worker's alienation from his/her own productive activity.

[18] John Plamenatz, *Karl Marx's Philosophy of Man* (London: Oxford University Press, 1975), 149–60.

[19] See Marx, *Early Texts*, 137.

[20] See Plamenatz, *Karl Marx's Philosophy of Man*, 69–78, and Ollman, *Alienation*, 111–15, for discussions on how humans express their distinctive character.

[21] Ollman, *Alienation*, 116–20.

[22] See Axelos, *Alienation, Praxis, and Techne*, 175–94 where he notes that Marx displays an extremely ambiguous and ambivalent attitude towards art. Perhaps the ambivalence reflects Marx's desire to replace the Spirit in Hegel's philosophy with the material processes of production, while, at the same time, trying to affirm human creativity in that process. Also, see Plamenatz, *Karl Marx's Philosophy of Man*, 49, where he criticizes Marx's dichotomy between physical and spiritual needs. For Plamenatz, both types of needs are more interrelated than Marx acknowledges. Indeed, the satisfaction of material needs has a properly moral and spiritual dimension.

[23] In the *Early Texts*, 167, Marx talks about the workers' alienation from their "species-being." Since the meaning of the latter is both highly technical and complicated, I have opted for "free, self-conscious creativity" as a "user-friendly" paraphrase.

[24] See Marx, *Early Texts*, 138, 139. Also, "Economic Imperialism's Threat to the Non-Economic Sectors of Life," in c.4, 69–71.

[25] See Marx, *Early Texts*, 140, 149–54.

[26] Marx, *Early Texts*, 140.

[27] See Marx, *Early Texts*, 142.

[28] Marx, *Early Texts*, 149–51. Also see Plamenatz, *Karl Marx's Philosophy of Man*, 153–5.

[29] Marx, *Early Texts*, 193–4.

[30] See Plamenatz, *Karl Marx's Philosophy of Man*, 48. See also Axelos, *Alienation, Praxis, and Techne*, 131–42.

[31] See *The Communist Manifesto Vol. 1* (Moscow: Foreign Language Publishing House, n.d.), 55; Vol 2, 8; Vol 3, 12 quoted in Kamenka, *Ethical Foundations of Marxism* (London: Routledge and Kegan Paul, 1962), 146.

[32] Erich Fromm, *Marx's Concept of Man* (NY: Frederick Unger Publishing Co., 1961), 24.

[33] See Axelos, *Alienation, Praxis, and Techne*, 315–16, 135; also see Plamenatz, *Karl Marx's Philosophy of Man*, 34.

[34] A detailed study of Marx's ethics can be found in Eugene Kamenka, *The Ethical Foundations of Marxism*; and *Marxism and Ethics*, 2nd ed. (London: Macmillan Publishers, Ltd., 1970).

[35] See Charles Taylor, *Hegel* (Cambridge University Press, 1975), 180–1, 551–6, where he points out that the absence of criteria in Marx concerning the constitution of human nature is directly related to Marx's failure to provide a material substitute for Hegel's *Geist*, which Marx rejected.

[36] See Marx's "Fourth Thesis on Feuerbach," in Marx and Engels, *Collected Works* (London: Lawrence and Wishart, 1976) 4.

[37] See K.R. Popper, *The Open Society and Its Enemies, Vol. II* (London: George Routledge and Sons, Ltd., 1945), 199.

[38] Kamenka, *Ethical Foundations*, 145.

[39] See John Plamenatz, *Karl Marx's Philosophy of Man* (London: Oxford University Press, 1975), 177–8: "[Marx] resorts to forms or words whose persuasive power comes largely of their being echoes of Holy Scripture. The most alienated, the most dehumanised of men, in redeeming themselves will redeem mankind. What is this but another way of saying that the last will be first, that the humble will be raised up?"

[40] Kamenka, *Ethical Foundations*, 145.

[41] Svetozar Stojanovic, *Between Ideals and Reality: A Critique of Socialism and Its Future*, translated by Gerson S. Sher (NY: Oxford University Press, 1973), 173.

[42] "Preface," in Karl Marx and Frederick Engels, *Collected Works Vol. 5*, xv.

[43] See Karl Marx and Frederick Engels, *The Communist Manifesto* (NY: International Publishers Co., Inc., 1948), 9.

[44] Marx and Engels, *Collected Works*, 60.

[45] Axelos, *Alienation, Praxis, and Techne*, 222.

[46] See Marx and Engels, "The German Ideology," Part III, Vol. 3, 229; and *The Communist Manifesto*, 21. Also see Stojanovic, *Between Ideals and Reality*, 142–3.

[47] Marx, *Early Texts*, 123.

[48] See Stojanovic, *Between Ideals and Reality*, 141.

[49] Karl Marx, *Early Texts*, 139–42.

[50] Stojanovic, *Between Ideals and Reality*, 142.

51 "Marx's Letter to L. Kugelmann of April 17, 1871," in Marx and Engels, *Selected Correspondence*, 320, quoted in Stojanovic, *Between Ideals and Reality*, 145–6.

52 "The Eighteenth Brumaire of Louis Bonaparte," in Marx and Engels, *Selected Works*, 2 Vols. (Moscow: Foreign Languages Publishing House, 1951), 97.

53 Eugene Kamenka, *Marxism and Ethics*, second edition (London: Macmillan Publishers, Ltd., 1970), 22.

CHAPTER FOUR

Toward More Inclusive Communities

T HE ANTHROPOLOGIES IN BOTH CLASSICAL AND NEOCLASSICAL economic theory, as well as in Marxist revolutionary praxis, entertain scientific assumptions about human nature and activity which are shortsighted and deficient. "Economic man's" emphasis on self-interest for the creation of wealth and the satisfaction of insatiable wants lamentably ignores the existence of human motivations and values which are necessary for the cohesiveness and welfare of any society. Marx's scientific analyses of the capitalist processes of production, with their resulting alienation of laborers from the products of their labor, from nature, and from each other, fail to grasp the breadth of the human spirit's self-transcending possibilities. In doing this, and despite its insightful diagnoses of some of the most blatant excesses of an uncritical approach to capitalist theory and practice, the Marxist analysis also ignores the presence of human motivations and values which are a necessary part of any adequate and lasting attempt to organize diverse peoples and cultures into stable societies.

In my opinion, there are two great ironies emerging out of the scientific anthropological assumptions of both capitalist and Marxist theories. First of all, neither capitalists nor Marxists could easily imagine how significant adaptations to market price theory might have addressed some of the most glaring problems of market economies. Capitalists, by and large, opted to keep the free market as unregulated and unchanged as possible. Marxists, by and large, opted for a totally different system, often described as a centralized command economy. Secondly, they both inadequately grasped the scope and range of ways in which individual welfare is dependent upon a broadly based inclusion in the life and activity of communities. Both were narrow and constricted in their grasp of the range of the free activity of individuals as well as in the understanding of the range of projects that have to be harmonized for an adequate experience of community welfare.

Neither capitalism nor Marxism has yet come to terms sufficiently with the priority of general community welfare for the emergence and continued development of individuals. In failing to do this both systems have contributed to the stratification and fragmentation of societies. Each of them, in their own respective ways, have excluded and marginalized significant numbers of individuals from fair and just participation in the workings of society: Marxism by a type of political excommunication of democratic processes; and capitalism by a form of economic excommunication and marginalization. In both cases, neither have provided sufficient bases upon which to build more inclusive communities.

Increasing the breadth of inclusiveness in community is a goal for which the entire human family has to strive constantly and persistently. It must be intentionally chosen. Inclusive communities are neither automatically nor necessarily formed because of special interests such as gender, occupation, or even common oppression. None of these emphases is adequately inclusive. Rather, inclusive communities are an expression of our conscience's most basic affirmation that living and loving are coextensive. Living means living together in a loving way, one which is marked by equality and mutuality. It is a long journey, however, to inclusive communities which are marked by such traits. We often treat people as things, rather than as other persons like ourselves. We see them only as means to an end.

Inclusive communities characterized by lived communion are the central focus of religion, inasmuch as the latter concerns what binds us together, what we bind ourselves to, and what we must bind ourselves to again and again if we are to live. In a wide variety of ways, religions seek to express this consciousness of community and its connection with the hope for salvation as the fullness and oneness of life. This chapter will look at how the Christian religion's doctrines of the Trinity and of Creation can make a contribution to humanity's striving and working for more inclusive human communities. For they proclaim how community is prior to, indeed absolutely indispensable to, personal growth and identity. They also proclaim how all persons in community are also part of and in relation to all of creation.

Before moving on to that development, however, we will look first at two very serious threats to the realization of greater inclusivity in community: neoclassical economic theory's reduction of human nature to the individualistic behaviors of rational economic agency; and the incursions of economic imperialism into the noneconomic sectors of life, where values and goals are more broadly based than the instrumental rationality of most economic theory.

The Rational Economic Agent

For the most part, contemporary neoclassical economics is a utilitarian science of means. It aims at describing how economies, markets, firms and even individuals work. In some ways, it also aims at revealing the laws of *economic human nature*[1]. A successful economic science, however, is not especially concerned with contributing toward, and working for, more inclusive communities. The latter is a goal or value, and economics presumably does not aspire to tell people what their goals or values or needs should be. Rather, it is a science of means, means to satisfy whatever wants people happen to have.

In his provocative work, *The Battle for Human Nature: Science, Morality and Modern Life*, Barry Schwartz proposes that there is a "struggle" between the language of science and the language of morality for a controlling influence in describing what it means to be a person. He argues that the languages of various sciences of human nature and action—rational choice economics, sociobiology, and behaviorist psychology—provide descriptions of, and share a common vision of, human nature:

> . . . Human beings are economic beings. They . . . pursue self-interest to satisfy wants, to maximize utility, or preference, or profit . . . . The interests of society (collections of individuals) are the summed interests of its members. The wants of society are the agglomerated wants of its members.[2]

This vision leaves out any consideration of values, goals or morality.

The moral neutrality which is claimed for economics reflects some significant assumptions about human nature and human desires. In everyday discourse, people make distinctions between what they *need* and what they *want*, but economics tells us that such distinctions will not stand up under close scrutiny. For the economist, the market is the only yardstick for determining value available.

Also, the idea that individuals are the best judges of their own welfare implies that there is no way to make interpersonal comparisons of welfare, and that there is no way to say what is good for society as a whole. Largely as a result of this assumption, modern economics limits its proper object to the behaviors of "rational economic agents" aimed at increasing the sum of individual welfares. Individual welfares do not merely result from the satisfaction of unlimited wants, but from the making of choices in the market that *maximize limited preferences*.[3]

The "rational economic agent" is a theoretical construct presumed to be an accurate description of human behaviors in the market, as well as a reliable reference point from which to *predict* such behaviors.[4] The construct incorporates a number of identifiable behaviors. Acknowledging that rational economic agents always want something, the construct affirms that human desires are *individual, idiosyncratic, and not capable of being compared.* In addition, they always reflect *preferences between commodities.* When asked whether they prefer commodity A to commodity B, rational economic agents can always give an answer, either A or B or indifferent. Rational economic agents, also according to the construct, *prefer more of a desirable commodity to less, and they prefer that more at a lower price to a higher one.* But the behavior which reflects even more strongly economic theory's assumption to be able to predict accurately the choices people make is the *manifesting of relatively stable preferences over time.* The meaning of "relatively" is that no one has absolutely stable preferences. People change and acquire tastes for some things and lose tastes for others. In addition, rational economic agents also have *commodity preferences that are transitive.* Generally, transitivity of preference means that if A is preferred to B, and B is preferred to C, then A is preferred to C. Transitivity of preference as a feature of economic rationality also confers a great deal of predictive power on a theory of economic behavior.

Another behavior of rational economic agency is that the *more that rational economic agents have of a commodity, the less will further increases in that commodity contribute to their satisfaction.* This is known as the principle of *diminishing marginal utility,*[5] and reflects the most important behavior upon which market predictability is based. Diminishing marginal utility attempts to account for human behavior when faced with a variety of insatiable wants. Because of its predictive potential, the principle is the heart of microeconomics, sometimes called the price system. So, for example, a loaf of bread is worth a great deal to a starving man. The second loaf is also worth a lot, though less than the first. The third loaf is worth still less, the tenth, still less, and the hundredth, perhaps little or nothing. *The more a person has of something, the less interested he is in having more of it.* Think also for a moment about two people deciding whether to trade in the marketplace. One of them has eggs, while the other has cheese. Will they be able to strike a bargain, trading so much cheese for so many eggs? Since people are free to do whatever they want in the market, no bargain will be struck unless both parties feel that they are gaining from the exchange.

The principle of diminishing marginal utility applies to all commodities in the marketplace. It is a force that makes people willing to give up some of which they have a lot for relatively little in return. By doing this, the principle—at least theoretically—also drives toward equity in the distribution of goods and services in the marketplace. Indeed, through the market, the principle works to allocate resources where they will provide the greatest satisfaction, for the best prices. The one significant exception to this principle may be money. Since money can essentially become any commodity, its utility may not diminish, or may diminish much more slowly, than the utility of other commodities. Even with money, however, people with plenty of it seem willing to trade large quantities for goods and services that others, with less money, would not dream of purchasing.

Perhaps one of the most surprising assumptions about human behavior, according to economic theory, is that rational economic agents *act in the marketplace on the basis of "complete information."* This characteristic assumes that rational agents know everything about what is available, for what price, now, and about what will be available, for what price, in the future. This notion that people in the market have "complete" information is an abstraction, an idealization. While this abstraction is unrealistic, it is nevertheless important to economic theorizing's claim to predict how persons will act. One way economists try to make the assumption of "complete" information more realistic is to treat information itself as a commodity and to ask how much time and effort people will spend in gathering it. The economist's task, then, is to estimate the costs of information gathering and compare them with the benefits of having that information available.

When looked at critically, the "rational economic agent" that economics assumes to be reflective of human behavior, credits people with more calculation and consistency than they actually possess. It also fails to appreciate a range of noneconomic influences on economic decision-making.[6] For real people cannot express preferences among all possible commodities, do not always prefer that which is cheap to that which is expensive, do not always have transitive preferences, do not act with "complete" information, cannot always act to maximize preferences, and do not have consistently stable preferences. Furthermore, the approximation of economic rationality is heavily influenced by factors that are themselves noneconomic in nature. One's ability to seek and to manage relevant information, and to restrict the infinite number of possible choices, depends upon a network of traditional cultural practices and individual habits about which the economic framework is silent.[7]

Economic Imperialism's Threat to the Noneconomic Sectors of Life[8]

The areas in which the economic framework is silent are fraught not only with limitations, but also with a serious threat: namely, *economic imperialism*, the spillover of economic self-interest into domains of life that most people do not regard as economic.[9] Economic imperialism makes it progressively more difficult to achieve collective goods by undermining various significant social *practices*—that is, established and developing social traditions that are kept on course by their specific and peculiar purposes. Various everyday social relations, like friendship, marriage and parenting, are all *practices*, and are each complex social activities with long histories. They are each goal-directed, with noneconomic ends that continue to evolve. Economic imperialism turns the goals that direct "practices" from noneconomic into economic ones. So the activities of doctors, lawyers, teachers, scientists, professional athletes, and even husbands and wives look very different when they are guided by the pursuit of gain than when they are guided by the pursuit of health, just resolutions of conflict, enlightened children, truths about nature, excellence in physical accomplishment, and intimate emotional bonds.

For Alaisdair MacIntyre, the concept of a *practice* has a central place in a theory of what it is to be a good person.[10] Good people, who engage successfully in *practices*, possess a number of characteristics or virtues: justice, honesty, courage, wisdom, respect, constancy, determination, and so on. When economic imperialism transforms *practices* simply into means to external goods, important vehicles for realistic expressions of moral worth disappear. If that happens, then there is only one *practice*—utility maximization. Then the virtuous, "moral man" will have become indistinguish-able from "economic man." In the face of such a probability Karl Marx pondered about a time:

> When everything . . . considered inalienable became an object of exchange, . . . and could be alienated. . . . When the very things which till then had been . . . given, but never sold; acquired, but never bought—virtue, love, conviction, knowledge, conscience, . . . passed into commerce.[11]

Economic imperialism, and many of the collective bads that result from the unrestrained pursuit of individual goods, affects everyone: polluted air and water, inflation, and overcrowded jobs, neighborhoods and highways. In affecting everyone, the spread of economic imperialism also threatens all noneconomic institutions. Paradoxically, two institutions threatened by economic imperialism are the market itself and political democracy. The market cannot function in the smooth and efficient way that economists say that it should if people behave as thoroughly economic agents. For in order for the market to work, people must make moral commitments to agree on what can be bought or sold, to tell the truth, and to honor their contracts. In the absence of these commitments, the market will grind to a halt. And as the market grinds to a halt, so will our system of political democracy.

In recent years, a view of democratic politics known as the "economic theory of democracy" has become increasingly popular among political and social theorists.[12] It treats democracy as nothing but a market in which citizens "buy" social policies with their votes. Many of the problems with our democratic institutions that have surfaced in recent years can be traced directly to the idea that the voting booth is nothing but a department store. If people treat the democratic state as a market, democracy may explode under the pressure of millions of self-interested individuals making competing and often incompatible demands. Freedom and democracy in the market may undercut freedom and democracy in society as a whole. For unless people are willing to submerge their individual interests, at least some of the time, for the common good significant aspects of political life will be taken out of the hands of economic actors who have little influence in the market and left to those whose presence in the market is predominant. When this happens the inclusiveness in political processes that is presupposed by democratic governments will have been greatly jeopardized.

To determine appropriate boundaries on the sphere of market activity, people must distinguish market goods and services—that is, commodities—from nonmarket goods and services. When it becomes possible to buy things with money that are not commodities, the barriers between different spheres of social life are broken down. Then, money becomes a "dominant good" whose influence extends beyond the market to all spheres of social life. Money will buy not only cars and houses but education, political power, love, friendship, respect and prestige. Restraining the progressive tyranny of economic imperialism will require action on a number of fronts. One front involves structuring different spheres of life and justice,[13] reflected in social institutions like the family, the Church, the school, and the state, so that the practices proper to each can retain their distinctiveness.[14] Preliminary to that task, however, communities and individuals have to learn to think about the human nature to which their communities and lives give expression, in ways that challenge the incursions of economic imperialism, issuing out of an uncritical and unlimited exercise of rational economic agency. It is a foundational vision for that prior project which the next section now addresses.

Self-Giving Love: A Critical and Humanizing Response to Rational Economic Agency[15]

No belief is more central to the Christian tradition than the doctrine of the Trinity, an elaborate spelling-out of the most basic Christian proclamation that God is "love-for-us" (1 Jn 4:8, 16), pure self-gift. The classic doctrine of the Trinity is an attempt to understand the freedom of that self-gift. In traditional Christian imagery, the Father gives himself totally to the Son, the Son gives himself totally to the Father, and the Spirit, proceeding from both, is the bond of that pure self-giving love. At the heart of the doctrine and the deepest claim which Christianity makes about being, including human being, is that "to be" and "to love" are synonymous. The doctrine developed because Christians found it a most suitable description of their experience of shared life. Basic to that experience is that we know ourselves as social, as communal in the very structure of our being—that is, as essentially political. Thus the doctrine makes a political statement: it maintains that not only is human existence social but that the ground of all being is relationship.

A public theology grounded in the Trinity provides the deepest foundation possible within the Christian tradition for a radical challenge and alternative to the individualistic bias of the anthropology of "the rational economic agent," as well as of its understanding of society as an aggregate of individuals. Placing the doctrine of the Trinity in conversation in the public realm argues for two changes in the way the relationship between individuals and communities is understood. First, since being and self-giving love are identical, individual existence finds its origin in and out of a relational context. Individual existence is not the precondition for community; community is the indispensable context out of which individual identity emerges. For God is community, relationship, Trinity, self-giving love. Where Aristotle observed that the human person is intrinsically political,[16] Christianity teaches firstly that God is intrinsically relational and, by implication, political. Then, as a consequence of God's relational/political existence as the ground of all being, it also teaches that humanity, existing in God's image, is radically and fundamentally relational/political. Second, the "image of God" motif is often employed as the theological basis for claiming that the human being, like God, is capable of self-gift.

The human person is the point at which creation is able to respond by giving itself in return. With the Christian trinitarian and communitarian understanding of God, the individual and the community give life to one another. Indeed, the broader and deeper the network of relationships, the more truly human the community and the individual. The most fundamental human activity, then, is not rational economic agency motivated by self-interest, but the exercise of the power of self-giving love, the opportunity for entrance into relationship, for deeper participation in the life of the human community.[17]

A trinitarian understanding of personhood as relatedness to others in a politically inclusive community also helps us to claim a number of identifying traits of personhood.[18] The first is that persons are interpersonal and intersubjective. An isolated person is a contradiction in terms, just as an isolated God or a God incapable of relationship is irreconcilable with the revelation of God in Jesus Christ. The doctrine of the Trinity is indispensable for preserving the relational character of God, the relational nature of human existence, and the interdependent quality of the entire universe.[19]

When Augustine defended the Latin use of *persona* in speaking of the Trinity, he did so by insisting that a person does not exist "as directed to self," but "as directed to others."[20] Consistent with his position that terms predicated of God and creatures are done so properly of God and only by extension of creatures, Thomas Aquinas taught that "person" applies preeminently to God.[21] This is because, in God, relation is not something added to God's existence, but is already an expression of how God exists.[22] We, therefore, existing in God's image, become more fully relational precisely by engaging in the political processes of community existence. Communal existence is the precondition for the possibility of individuals developing their relational capacities. It is also a corollary of the Trinity that selfhood becomes possible directly in proportion to communal relatedness.

A second identifying trait of personhood is that persons are unique and unrepeatable. No two relational histories are identical. No two sets of relationships which are constitutive of personal identity could ever be the same. Nonetheless, unique personhood emerges in interdependence. Personhood requires a balance of self-love and self-gift. Each new relationship or cluster of relationships brings about a new and evolving reality. Every time we give some of our being to another and have some of our being from another, we "exist" in a new way. In addition, unique personhood is the bridge between ourselves and everything and everyone else, past, present and future. The inclusiveness of the person invites us to overcome a fear of diversity and loss of personal identity. Furthermore, the basic good of a person's life is of its very nature something which also involves the life of the whole creation. The life of individual persons is something which is part of and relative to the whole. The life of each individual is the life of the whole and vice versa. Thus, the final good of each and every individual human person must be seen as the mutual interrelationship of persons in community which includes all persons, in which each cares for the others and for the nonpersonal creatures placed in their care.

The challenge of inclusive community requires that a person's egocentric and competitive traits be tempered with attentiveness not only to his/her own needs but also to the needs, hopes and dreams of others. The achievement of such an expression of personhood requires discipline, and only develops over a period of time. It is a significant accomplishment and does not occur easily.

Finally, living as persons in communion, in right relationship, is the meaning of salvation and the ideal of Christian faith. Walter Kasper has described the doctrine of the Trinity as the "grammar and summation" of creation and salvation.[23] "Creation" and "salvation" are categories which attempt to describe what it means to find one's origin in God's self-giving love and to be sustained by that same love, precisely as they are gifted dimensions of humanity's historical existence.

The Trinity is the proclamation of the Christian community's most fundamental experience of itself in the context of such love. Human beings are created in the image of the relational God and gradually are being perfected in that image, making more and more of the real communion of all creatures with one another. Thus, in contrast to the individualistic self-interest which motivates the rational economic agent, a trinitarian view of the human person and human salvation provides a decisively more respectful alternative for affirming the importance of community welfare for individual well-being. It also has the potential, if incorporated into an anthropological starting point for economic organization, of humanizing the exercise of economic agency and of responding to the social bads which can eventuate when such agency acts independently of the communities in which it operates.

Companionship: Recovering a Broader Sense of Relatedness and Community

For Christians, one of the most useful ways in which to affirm the priority of social relationships and community for the development of persons, as we have seen, is the doctrine of the Trinity. Another way is via the doctrine of Creation—especially inasmuch as the latter heightens our sense of relatedness to, and community with, not only other humans, but all of nature.[24] The doctrine finds its origins in the two creation accounts of Genesis (1:1–2:4a; 2:4b–25). Both depict the human capacity for relationship as that which makes humanity "like God." They suggest the ways human beings "in the image of God" relate to one another and to the nonhuman world. The first of the two stories has been the basis of both the overlordship and stewardship images for the role of humanity in the natural world. Part of the human being's likeness to God is the exercise of dominion over the rest of creation. There is a contrasting theme, however, in this story of the beginning of all things. "And so God created the human being in God's image; . . . male and female did he create them" (Gen 1:27). The point is not that God is male or female, or male and female, but that God is relational.

The only God that the Hebrew tradition knows is the God who is about the business of creating; that is, bringing into existence, not simply by "making," but by inviting all of creation into a covenanted relationship of life and love. The Hebrew Scriptures contain nothing about God considered apart from the creating God, the God in continuing and developing relationship with all of creation. To be the image of this God, the human being must be relational.

God's relationality is also a central theme of the second of the Genesis creation stories (Gen 2:4b–25). It is in the context of humankind's hunger for companionship, that names are conferred on all of the animals. In the second story, companionship is the explicit ground given for the creation of the two sexes. It is, however, also the reason for the creation of "the various wild beasts and birds of the air" (2:19). The natural world is not intended merely for subjugation by human beings, but for companionship. Unfortunately, the recourse of both rational economic agency and economic imperialism to instrumental rationality—that is, to using people and nature as resources for production—militates against an awareness of the "companionship" of all persons and creation.

The theme of companionship, the relationship which exists not only between human persons but between human beings and nonhuman beings, implies mutuality. It excludes the reduction of either side of the relationship to a tool of the other's purposes.

Martin Buber explored the meaning of companionship by describing the quality of some relationships as "I-Thou."[25] The contrasting relational possibility is "I-It." When I relate to some person or thing as an "it," that to which I relate has no intrinsic value, only the instrumental value which I designate. In contrast, when I relate to some person or thing as a "thou," that to which I relate has intrinsic value and is viewed as such and not merely as a means to an end. The challenge, as an appeal is made to the doctrine of Creation to broaden our understanding of the relational scope of the human person, is how to present nonhuman creation as companion to humanity. The Catholic tradition offers two important symbols for reappropriating the biblical theme of companionship in creation: poverty and sacramentality.

The Franciscan emphasis on poverty is grounded in one insight: all creatures are united in the depths of their being by the fact of being creatures. The source and foundation of one's being is not in oneself, there is no intrinsic reason for one's being at all. This "poverty" unites all creatures. In this fundamental poverty there is equality of *intrinsic value*. The human person has intrinsic value as a person, just as a plant has intrinsic value as a plant, an animal as an animal, and a stone as a stone. Equality of intrinsic value criticizes a crudely instrumental approach to nonhuman creation. The principle, however, does not imply that nonhuman creation has *rights* comparable to human rights. For the human person plays a unique role in the divine economy: namely, to exist as that point in creation to which the fullness of the self-gift of God can be given, as well as be responded to with a gift of self. The Christian doctrine of the Incarnation affirms humanity's role as one of extraordinary dignity. That dignity, however, involves the recognition of the inherent *value* of all creation. The role of every creature is as sovereignly the gift of God as is the unique role given to humanity.

The doctrine of "creation out of nothing" simultaneously affirms the fundamental poverty of the universe, and also that the only reason for anything to exist is the free self-giving love of God. To see creation as a whole or any creature in particular as totally dependent on the gracious will of God, is to see everything as a sacrament of the goodness and creative power of God. Indeed, the themes of creation and poverty intersect in the Catholic vision of sacramentality, in which the identifying trait of a sacrament is the capacity to reveal the self-giving love of God by being what it is. A sacrament gives bodily expression to the self-giving love of God that undergirds both it and all of creation. Every creature, human and nonhuman, animate and inanimate, can be a sacrament. The discovery that every creature can be a sacrament of the love of God that causes all things to be provides the deepest foundation for reverencing creation, and for recovering the companionship motif of the Genesis narratives.

Both rational economic agency and economic imperialism militate against an awareness of the sacramentality of all persons and creation. Their recourse to an instrumental rationality is also inimical to the companionship motif and to the types of inclusive communities to which it points. If their combined threat to working for more inclusive communities is to be addressed effectively, their individualistic anthropology must be confronted critically with an anthropology which insists on the priority of communities for the development of persons, as well as with the sacramentality of all creation that is part of human dignity.[26] Both creation stories in Genesis agree in their depiction of the human capacity for relationship as that which makes humanity "like God." The companionship motif provides an orientation which can guide us in developing an anthropology for inclusion in community that is not compromised by instrumental rationality, either toward humans or the nonhuman creation.

An anthropology which fosters greater inclusiveness in community also has to be reflected, and complemented, in an expanded notion of the common good which includes nonhuman creation. Both John XXIII and John Paul II have contributed to such a notion.[27] In addition, an anthropology which nurtures the possibility of more inclusive community also suggests means whereby an expanded/universal notion of the common good can be safeguarded and promoted: namely, a transnational perspective for analyzing social questions.[28] Issues which touch upon the universal common good, such as the operation of the economy, go beyond the competence of individual nation-states to participate in a global economy. It is necessary to develop structures which protect the well-being of the global community.[29] The persistent tendency of nations to define narrowly their economic self-interest remains a major obstacle to building effective vehicles for the universal common good. We have to ask what economic mechanisms on both national and transnational levels must be devised so that the varied activities of citizens, while respectful of their own local needs, are also directed to the common good, understood as including the good of all nations and creation.

Economic strategies which attempt to incorporate an anthropology for greater inclusiveness also cannot avoid confronting the pressing question of economic development. Does such development take account of the types of communities which are needed for the overall welfare of persons? It is only when economic development begins with an anthropology for greater inclusivity, and sensitivity to creation in all significant aspects of the world community, that it can approach adequate standards of justice and fairness.[30] The Jewish and Christian traditions on creation highlight some of the deeper anthropological issues which are part of the makeup of more inclusive communities which foster the development of persons. Those traditions remind us that the development of persons within communities, and the economic development of such communities, are fundamentally interdependent.

Evaluations of economic success must be made in tandem with evaluations of the overall and comprehensive welfare of communities. The question must constantly be asked: "Are economic strategies enhancing the community's ability to be inclusive of more persons and respectful of the limits of nature in the process?" The most inclusive understanding of the common good has to be a prior point of reference for measuring economic and human development. Building a shared understanding of the common good is a crucial enterprise for any economic development strategy which respects the need to work for more inclusive human communities. Significant dimensions of engaging the participation of the greatest possible number in the formulation of the common good are taken up in the next chapter.

[1] Of those who have contributed to a description of human nature as "economic," understood analogously with the operation of scientific economic principles, probably none has done so quite as boldly as Gary S. Becker in *The Economic Approach to Human Behavior* (University of Chicago Press, 1976); esp. cc.1 and 8.

[2] Barry Schwartz, *The Battle for Human Nature: Science, Morality and Modern Life* (New York: W.W. Norton & Co., 1986), 148; also see 18. Schwartz says that the three disciplines operate similarly to Gordon Kaufman's view of the function of theology: they "create a framework of interpretation which can provide an overall orientation for human life," (Gordon D. Kaufman, *Theology for a Nuclear Age* [Westminster Press; and Manchester University Press, 1985], 26). For Kaufman, however, it is theology's, not science's, principal concern to create a framework of interpretation, namely God, which can relativize and humanize thoroughly our contemporary existence, institutions and activities. In the last two sections of this chapter, theology's relativizing and humanizing perspective will be derived primarily from a reflection on what the doctrines of the Trinity and Creation convey about human nature and personhood.

[3] While there was a time when a number of economists held that the goal was the maximization of pleasure (Stanley Jevons, *Theory of Political Economy* [NY: A.M. Kelly, 1871], 9), today virtually all modern economists concur on the "maximization of limited preferences" (Schwartz, *The Battle for Human Nature*, 74).

[4] For the remainder of the present section I am especially indebted to Schwartz's analysis of the behaviors of the rational economic agent in *The Battle for Human Nature*, 65–74. Also, for a further critique from a variety of feminist perspectives of rational economic agency, see Marianne A. Ferber and Julie A. Nelson (ed) *Beyond Economic Man: Feminist Theories and Economics* (Chicago and London: University of Chicago Press, 1993).

[5] See c. 1, 20, fn. 18; c. 2, 28 and fn. 11; and, again c. 2, 34 for the distinction between *total utility* and *marginal utility*.

[6] See, for example, Amartya K. Sen's "Rational Fools: A Critique of the Behavioral Foundations of Economic Theory," in Jane J. Mansbridge (ed.) *Beyond Self-Interest* (University of Chicago Press, 1990), 25–43. Sen shows the effect of introducing "commitment," as a noneconomic factor, on the predictive power of rational economic theory. "The characteristic of commitment . . . drives a wedge between personal choice and personal welfare, and much of traditional economic theory relies on the identity of the two" (*Ibid.*, 33).

[7] For a more thorough critique of the behaviors of the rational economic agent, see Schwartz, *The Battle for Human Nature*, c. 6 "The Limits of Economics," 152–81.

[8] The ideas discussed in this section have been distilled principally from Schwartz's discussion of economic imperialism in cc. 9 and 10 of *The Battle for Human Nature*, 247–80, and 282–309. Schwartz himself incorporates much of the analysis found in Fred Hirsch, *Social Limits to Growth* (London and Henley: Routledge & Kegan Paul, 1977).

[9] Economic self-interest's overflow into noneconomic sectors of life is discussed by A.K. Sen in *Collective Choice and Social Welfare* (San Francisco: Holder-Day, 1970), and M. Olson, *The Logic of Collective Action* (Cambridge: Harvard University Press, 1965).

[10] See his *After Virtue* (South Bend: University of Notre Dame Press, 1981).

[11] K. Marx, *The Poverty of Philosophy* (London: Lawrence and Wishart, 1955), 29, cited in Schwartz, *The Battle for Human Nature*, 280.

[12] An example of this theory can be found in Joseph Schumpeter, *Capitalism, Socialism, and Democracy* (London: Unwin University Books, 1942).

[13] See Michael Walzer, *Spheres of Justice* (New York: Basic Books, 1983).

[14] See Chapter 8: "Contributing to the Emergence of Economic Alternatives," for an example of how diocesan churches might be structured with this very purpose in mind.

[15] Throughout this section I am especially indebted to Michael J. Himes and Kenneth R. Himes, *Fullness of Faith*, 56–61.

[16] Aristotle, *Politics* 1253 a.3, cited in Himes and Himes, *Fullness of Faith*, p. 59.

[17] See *Gaudium et Spes, 24*: "Indeed, the Lord Jesus, when He prayed to the Father, 'that all may be one . . . as we are one' (John 17:21–22), . . . implied a certain likeness between the union of the divine Persons, and [that] of God's sons in truth and charity"; also, see John Paul II's *Centesimus Annus*, 41: "A man is alienated if he refuses to transcend himself and to live the experience of self-giving and of the formation of an authentic human community . . . . A society is alienated if its forms of social organization, production and consumption make it more difficult to offer this gift of self and to establish this solidarity between people."

[18] For the following characteristics of personhood I have adapted a presentation by Catherine Mowry LaCugna, *God For Us: The Trinity and Christian Life* (San Francisco: Harper , 1991), 288–92.

[19] LaCugna, *God For Us*, 289.

[20] Augustine, *De Trinitate* 7, 6, 11.

[21] Aquinas, *Summa theologiae* I, q. 13, a.2; the general principle is found in I, q. 13, a. 2.

[22] Aquinas, *Summa theologiae*, I, q. 29, a.4.

[23] Walter Kasper, *The God of Jesus Christ* translated by Matthew O'Connell (New York: Crossroad, 1984), 311.

[24] For the remainder of the present section I am indebted to Himes and Himes, *Fullness of Faith*, 105–20. See also Charles Murphy, *At Home on Earth: Foundations for a Catholic Ethic of the Environment* (NY: Crossroad, 1989).

[25] See Martin Buber, *I and Thou*, translated by Walter Kaufman (New York: Charles Scribners' Sons, 1970).

[26] See Drew Christiansen, "Ecology, Justice and Development," in *Theological Studies 51*, (1990), 79: "Humanity needs to look more searchingly at itself as it is embedded in nature, not turn away to look at nature alone," cited in Himes and Himes *Fullness of Faith*, 116.

[27] Respectively, see *Mater et Magistra*, 65, *Pacem in Terris*, 11–27; and "Peace with God the Creator," 9, *Centesimus Annus*, 31.37.

[28] John XXIII, *Pacem in Terris*, 132.

[29] John XXIII, *Pacem in Terris*, 135.

[30] The relationship between economic development and a community's overall welfare is treated more fully in c. 9: "Respecting the Limits of Economic Organization."

CHAPTER FIVE

Participating in and for the Common Good

POLITICAL AND ECONOMIC SYSTEMS ALWAYS EMBODY AN understanding of the human, even if they have not expressed it and its underlying assumptions explicitly and critically. Liberalism and capitalism, with their emphasis on self-interest, are founded ultimately upon an anthropology quite different from that which grounds a model of political economy which stresses community. In its traditional sense, liberalism refers to a perspective in political philosophy, especially within the English-speaking world, which abstracts the self-interested person from community, sets individual freedom and rights at odds with the community, and correspondingly stresses contractual theories of society.[1] In contrast, communitarianism and socialism, political and economic philosophies which situate persons in communities, view individual freedom and rights within the context of the community and its common good. Communitarian approaches do not deny self-interest but prefer to focus upon ways to support actions which go beyond self-interest toward the good of others and the community at large.

The different anthropologies guiding liberal and communitarian approaches can also be seen as coming out of theological traditions which have emphasized respectively either the doctrine of Original Sin or of the Trinity. If the emphasis has been primarily from the doctrine of Original Sin, then humanity's capacity to exist in the image and likeness of God has been virtually destroyed. If, however, the emphasis has been primarily from the doctrine of the Trinity, then it is not only possible for humanity to exist in the image and likeness of God, it is humanity's call to do so. This chapter will initially take up the doctrine of Original Sin as understood in Reformation theology, and as subsequently expressed in the anthropologies of Hobbes and Smith. It will then consider a Roman Catholic interpretation of the doctrine of Original Sin as one which incorporates the prior and broader context of the doctrine of the Trinity. For unless both of the doctrines are seen as communicating valuable wisdom about human nature, our understanding of the possible range of individual and communal actions for persons in community will be either hopelessly minimized or unrealistically exaggerated. The chapter will conclude with the suggestions for enhancing an equitable participation in community that are provided by the doctrine of the Communion of Saints.

Reformation and Catholic Views on Original Sin and Society[2]

The Reformation debates on grace and justification focussed on the utter corruption of the human person as a result of the sin of Adam.[3] In its fallen state, humanity's handicapped ability to arrive at knowledge of God, natural things and morality distorted the knowledge and effectively rendered it incapable of being used correctly. Individuals after the fall were radically closed to any possibility of self-giving community, and were locked into selfishness.

Roman Catholicism, like the tradition of the Reformers, also affirmed that Adam's sin had tragic consequences.[4] Unlike the Reformers, however, Roman Catholicism held that human beings were not utterly corrupted, and that humanity still retained the freedom to act in the image of God—that is, with the ability to respond to God's love on behalf of others. Original Sin may have distorted this freedom, but humanity remains human. And it is precisely as human that a longing in the heart for God's self-giving love persists, a longing which is experienced in the call to be self-giving to others. Consequently, the human person, made in the image of God who is self-giving love, remains in that image even after the fall and so is capable, even with great difficulty, of genuine other-directedness.[5]

It is largely Augustine's theological anthropology in the doctrine of Original Sin, as read through the eyes of the Reformers, which found philosophical expression in Thomas Hobbes. In addition to the impact of the Reformers' doctrine of Original Sin upon him, Hobbes' view of human nature was also heavily affected by seventeenth-century physics.[6] Comparing human life with the physical reality of motion, Hobbes proposes that the only factor which contains the motion of one human life is the competing motion of another human life. Ultimately, equality among the competing motions of a variety of human beings, motivated by greed, the desire for security or the hope of glory, is a state of war in which everyone is against everyone else.[7] Since society is merely the controlled war of each against each, no *common* good exists, only a collection of competing individual goods, some of which may from time to time coincide. Entry into civil society is necessary to control the worst excesses of this war of all against each. Membership in civil community allows each person to acquire and enjoy the "gain" of physical goods, and the "glory" of intellectual goods. The basis of such community, however, is not love but self-interest. For individuals would only enter into community to secure their own advantage. "All society, therefore, is either for gain or for glory; that is, not so much for love of our fellows, as for love of ourselves."[8]

Despite the problems with a Hobbesian vision of society as a precariously controlled war, Adam Smith attempted to introduce the idea of the common good into it. Smith suggested that the "problem" of self-interest could become the "solution." He proposed that self-interest could be relied upon to check itself because of the shared human desire for a correspondence of *feeling with* others or what he termed "sympathy."[9] Nothing so effectively advances sympathy, the ability to share others' perceptions of themselves and of oneself, as the drive to "truck, barter, and exchange one thing for another."[10] Thus the free trade for which Smith argued in *The Wealth of Nations* is a prerequisite for the achievement of human community. It was also the expression of a moral stance, which can be interpreted as an outgrowth of Smith's social ethics.

Hobbes' social philosophy, which Smith accepted, can be understood as a secularized version of a Protestant interpretation of the effects of Original Sin. A secularized theological anthropology, based on a Catholic view of Original Sin, results in a very different view of society. The latter acknowledges not only a need to minimize and restrain the evil of self-interest but also a challenge to maximize the good of self-giving. Strategies *for* community must be given priority over concern for limiting or channeling self-interest. Catholic social theory stresses the necessity for persons to express their social nature through the institutions they create to order their lives. Humanity is social by nature and human dignity is "realized in community with others."[11]

Catholicism's criticism of a view of society, reflecting the visions of Hobbes and Smith, challenges the liberal assumption that individuals possess rights prior to society, rights which can be understood and defended outside of the context of the commitments, relationships and involvements that are part of any culture or society.[12] It also challenges the credibility of liberalism's rational economic agent as ahistorical, asocial and disembodied. For Catholics and communitarians, community involves much more than a voluntary contract between atomistic individuals who join together to protect and advance their rights.

Commitment to a communitarian vision of society can sometimes be jeopardized by a sentimental or nostalgic notion of community, rather than be characterized by a politically realistic understanding about what constitutes a contemporary expression of it. Any sort of yearning for pre-industrial experiences of society unaware of the impact of mass communications and huge pluralistic populations cannot serve as a guide for a realistic political approach in our time. Instead, a contemporary political concept of community needs a renewed appreciation of the centrality of public political discourse.[13] Shared political discourse, not an identity of interests or personal intimacy, is needed for political community. In its political expression, shared discourse consists of regular participation in a society's ongoing conversation about its aims, ideals, and practices.[14]

With a realistic and contemporary approach to society, liberalism's view falls short in a number of significant ways. Most seriously, it fosters a political community that speaks of an individual citizen's rights but downplays civic duties and conversation. Secondly, liberalism's concentration on individual rights leads to a progressive loss of interest or participation in the democratic formulation of what constitutes the common good. Lastly, and most fundamentally, liberalism neglects the importance of specific social institutions because it fails to acknowledge that social life is constitutive of the human person.[15]

While the structures of democratic life—civil liberties, a limited constitutional state, pluralistic government—are appealing to the Catholic mind, the commonly held social philosophy underlying these features in the politics of much of the English-speaking world remains problematic. So, Catholicism continues to look within its own tradition for intellectual resources that might provide an alternative foundation for democratic politics. The search, as expressed in this book, involves a Catholic view of persons in community which can support and enrich liberal democracy yet oppose the individualism and myth of self-interest which historically has undergirded liberal institutions.

In developing its view, Catholic teaching hearkens back to the classical period of Western political thought, when society was an order which existed for the mutual exchange of human activities all in service of the common good. The image frequently used by Catholic thinkers to describe this traditional perspective is that of society as an organism. Each part of the organism—that is, each person—contributes to the well-being of the whole. Society, however, can be thought of as an organism only analogically, for human persons cannot simply be subordinated to the whole. Society's proper principle of activity is the common good, and individual persons, through their participation in the common good, form a social unity.[16]

Implied within this description of the Catholic outlook on society are three cardinal principles of Catholic social theory:

personalism, subsidiarity and pluralism.[17] Personalism means that the human person possesses a dignity which cannot be reduced or denied in the name of some collective good. Subsidiarity holds that no organization should be bigger than necessary and that nothing should be done by a larger and higher social unit than can be done effectively by a lower and smaller unit. Pluralism affirms that a healthy society is characterized by a wide variety of intermediate groups freely flourishing between the individual and the state.

A good society fosters such mediating structures so that public life is not equated with the state or governmental life.[18] These principles, along with the tradition's understanding of human nature, reflect Catholicism's optimism regarding the person's ability to act on motives other than self-interest. They also reflect the tradition's conviction that a social order can be shaped in which institutions can embody cooperation and self-giving, and not merely control competition. Unlike Hobbes, the Catholic view does not accept that the state is needed only to apply coercive measures for social order. Recognizing the state's legitimate coercive role, the Catholic view also acknowledges that the state arises naturally from the interaction of persons in order to encourage shared activities and to make available shared goods.

The Common Good: Motivation and Outcome

A Catholic vision of persons in community assumes that the purpose of social life is the attainment of the common good. In the Thomistic tradition the common good was substantially self-evident, objectively knowable, and indivisible.[19] Charles Curran has observed that more recent Catholic Social Teaching about the common good reflects some significant shifts in its anthropological bases.[20] Several new emphases in Catholic social teaching have become important: *freedom, equality* and *participation*. Inasmuch as the understanding of those emphases develops, thinking regarding the common good also develops.

In the "Pastoral Constitution on the Church in the Modern World" of the Second Vatican Council, the Church's emphasis on *personal freedom* is striking: "For its part, authentic freedom is an exceptional sign of the divine image in man."[21] A dramatic change in Catholic teaching on religious freedom provides an example of how its broader understanding of the exercise of freedom vis-a-vis the common good has been recast. Vatican II acknowledged religious freedom as a right grounded on the theory of the limited powers of the state and a recognition that the common good consists of both spiritual and temporal elements.

While the purpose of society is the achievement of the common good, the more narrow purpose of the state is to create and maintain public order. The latter encompasses an order of public peace, public morality and justice. Serving those elements of the common good required for public order, while leaving to others the achievement of dimensions of the common good beyond this task, explains the conciliar approval of the separation of church and state and religious freedom. It also illustrates the council's indirect acknowledgment of a sphere of freedoms which lie beyond the control or jurisdiction of the state. The state, therefore, has a limited role to play in achieving the full breadth of the common good. The temporal element of the common good to be promoted by the state is public order. It is up to other societal bodies to promote additional dimensions of the common good such as spiritual welfare. But this effort on the part of others must be done without resort to the coercive power of the state. This means that considerable personal freedom of belief and activity, an arena of civil liberties, is beyond governmental intrusion even in a society with a communitarian rather than a liberal understanding of the role of the state.[22]

Equality of personhood, like personal freedom, is also very much related to the experience of human dignity and how the common good is formulated. Such equality was opposed in early papal social teaching on the basis that it undermined the organic nature of society. Within the organic model persons performed duties appropriate to their stations in life. Equality made stable role definitions difficult to accept, heightened hopes for social change, and undercut a culture of inherited privilege. While equality in *dignity* was accepted by the papacy as a guiding principle, it was not effectively translated into ideas about political, social or economic equality. So when Leo XIII wrote *Rerum Novarum* in 1891, he did not envision egalitarian justice as the social norm but stressed distributive justice which provided a minimum for all.

As decades passed, however, it became more obvious that equality in dignity needed to be incarnated in social policies and structures. This awareness is a reflection of an increased sensitivity to the immense disparities of wealth and poverty throughout the world with a concomitant interest in narrowing the gaps between rich and poor, workers and management, agricultural and industrial laborers.[23]

The recognition of the need for appropriate economic and political structures, in order to implement corresponding policies, is largely the outcome of the Church's greater sensitivity to equality in the realization of personhood. It has led to a focus in postconciliar teaching on inequality as "the central social problem of our time" which must be attacked through policies and structures that lessen the gaps between groups and nations in our world. At the heart of these assessments is a sense of the divisiveness which inequality creates, as well as the judgment that community is impossible with significant inequality.[24]

The theme of *participation* has also become more important in modern papal social thought in reference to the realization of human dignity and the common good. Papal social teaching now reflects a greater awareness that the participatory nature of communities favors democratic political structures so as to allow for the exercise of self-determination.

Another indication of the importance given to participation in Catholic social teaching can also be seen in the US bishops' pastoral on the economy. In the first draft the bishops asked two questions: "What does the economy do *to* people, and what does it do *for* people?" In later drafts and in the final version a third question was added: "How do people participate in the economy?"[25] Participation becomes a criterion for assessing the moral soundness of an economic system. The more recent calls for active participation within papal and episcopal teaching invite fuller expression for the principles of subsidiarity and pluralism. There is a recognition that healthy social life needs an abundance of human associations and groups so that persons will be able to find a wide array of institutions that give form and structure to participatory community at a grassroots level.

Participation as a moral ideal underscores that the common good requires solidarity, *a devotion to the well-being of others*, an essential disposition of persons in community. For other-directedness to be encouraged, however, people need the access to established institutions in order to participate in the life of the community, to give expression to their social nature, and thereby to contribute to the common good.

Also, as a component in the Catholic understanding of personal dignity, participation presupposes that the formulation of the common good develops through the processes of public conversation and debate. Such a societal project requires structures that encourage participation in the public conversation rather than exclusion. Pluralism in society is best protected if participation in public life is widespread and the common good reflects the consensus of more rather than fewer citizens. David Hollenbach has suggested that we view the common good of civil society as that "measure of the communion of persons that is achievable in society."[26]

A further point in any consideration of the relationship between human dignity and the common good is the issue of human rights. Human rights, whether political, economic or social, are statements about the conditions needed for participatory community to be realised. Human rights in Catholic teaching are moral claims because they are claims to goods which are necessary for the person to participate with dignity in the communal life of a society. Granting rights of empowerment or enablement through social and economic goods like housing, food and health care illustrates the Catholic concern for a person's ability to enter into the life of a community rather than an individualistic concern for self-development apart from social relations.

Radical communitarianism denies the existence of individual rights in the name of the common good while moderate versions of communitarian theory accept the existence of individual rights but challenge the priority which liberalism accords such moral claims.[27] For unless people are able to enter into the life of the group in a meaningful way there are reduced opportunities for self-donation.

The moral imperative of participatory community has a number of implications for economic theory and policies. It points out how such theory has too often presumed that agents acting for self-interest remain independent except when engaged in market transactions. Economic theory ignores that in an interdependent society there are also positive or negative unintended public results of market transactions: "externalities."[28] The net effect of "externalities" reveals a serious and significant flaw of liberal market economics for "the market system underproduces private goods with social benefits and it overproduces private goods with social costs." And, as Charles Wilber notes, when "social costs and benefits diverge from private costs and benefits, what is best for each individual is not what is best for society."[29]

In response to this "serious and significant flaw" of liberal market economics, itself one of the strongest symptoms of an inadequate underlying anthropology, communitarian philosophies and Catholic social theory counter that human life cannot achieve its fullness without lively involvement on the part of all in public life. With a communitarian view, politics and economics are most basically about our common life and the institutions and practices of public life that improve the quality of our life together. In contrast, the myth of self-interest in liberal social and economic theory is most basically about the "rational" realization of individual preferences without an adequately complementary awareness of social responsibility and accountability. That myth is rooted in a vision of human action which arises from a particular theological anthropology. A fundamental but often overlooked reason for the Catholic tradition's uneasiness with and criticism of liberalism is that Catholicism disagrees with that theological anthropology. What is at stake is not only a series of prudential judgments concerning social and economic policy but an understanding of what it is to be human.

A Participatory Communion of Persons[30]

In addition to a Catholic interpretation of the doctrine of Original Sin, another Christian theological symbol that grounds a Catholic understanding of what participation in human community entails is the doctrine of the Communion of Saints. The basis of the doctrine is that Christ's taking on our humanity had two major effects. First, it made it possible for us to share in the life of God. Second, it established our sharing of life with one another as a privileged way in which we experience communion in the life of God.[31] Hence, the doctrine challenges us to work for those political and economic structures which eventually overcome, within the shared life of peoples, the societal "excommunications" based on race, nationality, class, gender, and even space and time. Just as separation from the communion of saints—that is, from Christ and other believers—hinders the sharing in his life-giving spirit, so too separation from a communion of persons hinders a sharing in life which is vital for the development of personhood.

And just as there is a responsibility on the part of all believers to work for that reconciliation which overcomes divisions among believers, so also there is a corresponding responsibility on the part of all persons to work to overcome any of the exclusions or "excommunications" from participating in the full life of community—economic or social or political—by working for a more participatory realization of the common good.

In Vatican II's pastoral constitution "The Church in the Modern World," there is a meditation on humankind's vocation to live in community.[32] On the basis of our creation in the image of the Creator, the plan of God is that humanity should constitute one family and treat one another in a familial spirit. The sacredness of the person is founded upon a cluster of theological claims which assert our inalienable link to the community of the human family: creation, which proclaims our common origin and interrelatedness; redemption, which affirms our shared giftedness and interdependence in Christ; discipleship, which reminds us of our common vocation to proclaim and witness God's love for all peoples and creation; and eschatology, which invites us to assume responsibility for our common destiny.[33]

Social life is not something added onto human life but is essential to our origins, our coming together, our discovery of meaning and our continuing development. The promotion of the common good is a vital concern for all persons. It is through participation in the shared life of a community that the good of all is respected and that each person fulfills his or her worldly responsibilities.

The theological vision of humanity as one family and the Church as a sacramental communion of that unity provides the "deep theory"[34] grounding the importance of all persons participating in the shared responsibilities involved in dedication to the well-being of others; that is, in solidarity. When the Catholic imagination envisions a just society, it depicts a situation in which humans have the capabilities and the opportunities to participate actively in promoting the well-being of others.

The doctrines of the Trinity, Creation, Original Sin, and the Communion of Saints, are all components of the "deep theory" for a communitarian vision of the human person. It is especially from them that notions of justice as participation are derived. It is also from these doctrines that Catholic teaching is committed to a society where the experience of community is made real through the ordering of societal institutions and made available to all through the practice of solidarity. Indeed, it is from these doctrines that Catholic social teaching offers an attractive alternative to "the classical liberal model where society is understood as an artificial contract between autonomous individuals undertaken for self-interest rather than fraternal reasons."[35]

The human vocation to solidarity can be seen as the correlative to the actual interdependence of peoples throughout the world. Wealth and power, however, can provide significant opportunities for people unconsciously to grow progressively more insensitive to the reality of interdependence and the call to solidarity. Indeed, some wealthy people even consciously move on to isolate themselves from much of the experience of their interdependence with the poor and the marginalized. This isolation can be twofold: both from the poor and marginalized within their own countries, as well as throughout the world.[36] The intentional isolation of the wealthy from the poor exacerbates the economic and political "excommunication," of the poor and the marginalized from the wealthy and the politically powerful.

The intentional isolation of the top one-fifth of high earners in First World countries betrays a shocking loss of a sense of solidarity. For solidarity involves a conscious choice for the common good that demands placing limits on specific desires or stated interests. Conversion to solidarity, and the faith vision which undergirds it, also inevitably involves a preferential option for the poor, a strong prejudice in favor of actions which promote a lessening of marginalization. Solidarity as a vision of the universality of our duties to one another means that those already participating in vibrant and sound communal relations need to reach out to those who are left without the means or opportunities to participate in community. Siding with marginalized segments of the community, even when it entails defiance toward other segments, is not a breach of solidarity but an intimation of a truly participatory community.[37]

Solidarity has given new emphasis to the connection between justice and participatory community. Participation is crucial for enabling people to make contributions of themselves and their resources to their communities. If people are left outside the circle, then they are encouraged to act irresponsibly, not altruistically. Indeed, chronic exclusion from significant participation is very often the prelude to irresponsible and hurtful actions. Thus the opportunity to enter into the life of a community, to give oneself away to others in mutually supportive ways, is a marker for assessing whether society is rightly ordered. *"Basic justice demands the establishment of minimum levels of participation in the life of the human community for all persons.* The ultimate injustice is for a person or group to be actively treated or passively abandoned as if they were nonmembers of the human race."[38]

In addition to a faith vision of persons in community, and the importance of participation in community, a growing inequality between as well as within societies presents an even more urgent reason for a commitment in solidarity to the establishment of relative equality. Relative equality is the normative expression of the theological vision of solidarity. The word "relative" means that the equality aimed at is not absolute, a level in which everyone gets the same benefits and shares the same burdens. The idea behind relative equality is that inequalities are held within a defined range set by *moral* limits. A variety of factors such as need, contribution, and the common good may justify differences but there are limits on differences to be permitted. This norm entails "that wealth and resources ought to be regularly redistributed to redress the differences between groups, sectors, and even nations."[39]

Drew Christiansen describes Catholic social teaching as favoring a "strong" form of egalitarianism, one which concentrates on two projects. First of all, it works for the establishment of economic and social institutions which attempt to approximate equal allocation of resources as a norm. In comparison, weak theories permit exceptions in the name of the general welfare or special interests, and require less in the way of institutional support and readjustment. Secondly, a strong egalitarianism requires a redistribution of material goods which would establish guaranteed welfare floors, along with socioeconomic rights.[40] Since a significant aspect of the realization of participation in community is the achievement of greater equity among God's creatures, the growing gap in the possession of the material conditions for human well-being must be both stopped and lessened.[41]

In recent and current Catholic social teaching, inequality has become *the* social question of the age. Unfortunately, the failure of theorists of market economies to look at their theory's assumptions critically about what is good for human persons is one of the main contributing factors to this inequality.[42] So, when the US bishops discuss economic justice they are concerned that there are not sufficient societal safeguards to ensure that one will be included as a participating member in the life of a society. A breakdown of solidarity allows entire classes of people and whole nations to be put on the periphery of our field of vision. Developing a truly inclusive social and global order is the hope held by those who believe that, with a corrective vision of participation in community, economic institutions and practices do not have to aggravate the problem of inequality but can actually begin to contribute to the type of communities which are central to, and generative of, human existence.[43]

The inclusion in public discourse of anthropological insights from the doctrines of the Trinity, Creation, Original Sin, and the Communion of Saints can provide an important contribution toward a critical rethinking of how societies can be organized economically in a more equitable and just fashion. For such insights can add significant weight to any proposed solutions to work for more inclusive and participatory communities. The insights which these doctrines give us about what it means to be human introduce a needed voice in conversations about participation in the economy, the purpose of economies, and how the economy's operation affects persons and societies.

These same insights, however, must be made public more effectively by churches and their theologians that strive to share the possible societal contributions from within the wisdom of the central symbols of the Christian tradition. It is only when that begins to happen that the Christian tradition of wisdom on the human condition, and what it might potentially contribute to a more humane approach to economics, will be able to be heard more readily by those who are not part of the tradition. It is also hoped that with a broader hearing, a more critical dialogue will also be generated from all parties involved. Then, hopefully, a broader consensus of decision and action will also follow. Each chapter in the next section addresses a different aspect of how the Catholic Church, along with other Christian churches, might begin to have a greater impact for the good in the public realm. The first of those chapters begins by offering an evaluation of the strengths and weaknesses of the century-old tradition of Catholic Social Teaching, especially as it has reflected upon and criticized the major ways in which societies have been organized economically.

---

[1] This meaning of liberalism can be found in John Rawls, *A Theory of Justice* (Cambridge: Belknap Press, 1971) and Robert Nozick, *Anarchy, State, and Utopia* (New York: Basic Books, 1974).

[2] For the first two sections of the present chapter I have found Himes and Himes,

Fullness of Faith, c. 2 "Original Sin and the Myth of Self-Interest," 28–54 especially helpful.

[3] See The Formula of Concord, The Synod of Dort, and The Westminster Confession, all cited as examples in Himes and Himes, *Fullness of Faith*, 30.

[4] See Council of Trent, Session 5, canon 1.

[5] See Council of Trent, Session 6, chapter 1, and canon 7.

[6] See Thomas Hobbes, *Leviathan, or the Matter, Forme, and Power of a Common-wealth Ecclesiastical and Civill*, C.B. Macpherson (ed), (New York: Viking Penguin [1651] rpt. 1968), 87.

[7] See Hobbes, *Leviathan*, 185.

[8] Hobbes, *De Cive*, S.P. Lamprecht (ed) (New York: Appleton-Century-Crofts, 1949), 24.

[9] For a more detailed account of Smith's understanding and appraisal of "self-interest" see "Self-Interest: From Unacceptable Vice to Scientific Law," in c.2, 29–32. Also see Hirschman, *The Passions and the Interests: Political Arguments for Capitalism Before Its Triumph*, along with Stephen Holmes' excellent critique of Hirschman in "The Secret History of Self-Interest," in Jane Mansbridge (ed) *Beyond Self-Interest* (University of Chicago Press, 1990), 267–86, esp. 275–81.

[10] Adam Smith, *An Inquiry into the Nature and Causes of the Wealth of Nations*, Edwin Cannan (ed), (New York: Random House, Modern Library, 1937), 13.

[11] National Conference of Catholic Bishops, "Economic Justice for All: Catholic Social Teaching and the US Economy," 28.

[12] See Andrew Greeley, *No Bigger Than Necessary* (NY: Meridian Books, 1977), 92.

[13] See Hannah Arendt, *Men in Dark Times* (NY: Harcourt Brace Jovanovich, 1968), 24.

[14] The importance of shared political discourse is developed further by an appeal to Habermas' theory of communicative action, in c. 7 , 125–35; 131–4.

[15] The three points are gleaned and adapted from Allen Buchanan, "Assessing the Communitarian Critique of Liberalism," *Ethics 99* (1989): 852–82, and Chantal Mouffe, "American Liberalism and Its Critics: Rawls, Taylor, Sandel and Walzer," *Praxis International 8* (1988): 193–206, cited in Himes and Himes, *Fullness of Faith*, 36.

[16] An alternative image sees society as an "organism of social organisms" having a common end. See J. Messner, *Social Ethics; Natural Law in the Modern World*, translated by J. J. Doherty (St.Louis: B. Herder Book Co., 1949), 114–15.

[17] Greeley, *No Bigger Than Necessary*, 10.

[18] For a reflection on the role of the local church congregation as a mediating structure, see Kenneth Himes, "The Local Church as a Mediating Structure," *Social Thought* (1986): 23–30. Also, in the present work, see c. 8 "Contributing to the Emergence of Economic Alternatives."

[19] See Dennis McCann, "The Good to be Pursued in Common," in Oliver Williams and John Houck, (eds) *The Common Good and US Capitalism* (Lanham: University Press, 1987), 158–78 at 164, cited in *Fullness of Faith*, 39.

[20] See Charles Curran, "The Changing Anthropological Bases of Catholic Social Ethics," in C. Curran and R. McCormick (eds), *Readings in Moral Theology, No.5: Official Catholic Social Teaching* (NY: Paulist Press, 1986): 188–218, cited in *Fullness of Faith*, 39.

[21] *The Church in the Modern World*, 17.

[22] For a more detailed argument supporting this conclusion including an explanation of the Augustinian and Thomistic basis for a nontotalitarian view of the state in communitarian thought, see David Hollenbach, "The Common Good Revisited," *Theological Studies 50* (1989): 70–94, cited in *Fullness of Faith*, 43.

[23] Drew Christiansen analyzes this evolution in "On Relative Equality: Catholic Egalitarianism After Vatican II," *Theological Studies 45* (1984): 651–75.

[24] Christiansen, "On Relative Equality," 657–8; 660, cited in *Fullness of Faith*, 43. In c.8 see "The Interdependence Between Equality and Freedom," 150–53.

[25] The various drafts of the pastoral letter are available in *Origins*. The first draft, "Catholic Social Teaching and the US Economy," may be found in v. 14 (1984): 336ff. The two questions are located in the opening paragraph of the letter. By the second draft of the letter, found in volume 15(1985): 258ff, the additional question about participation was added. It remained in all subsequent drafts and the final version of the letter.

[26] Hollenbach, "The Common Good Revisited," 88, cited in *Fullness of Faith*, 45.

[27] Buchanan, "Assessing the Communitarian Critique of Liberalism," 855, cited in *Fullness of Faith*, 46.

[28] They are results which are not considered intrinsic to the action of individuals exchanging goods and services in the market, for example homelessness and pollution. See Charles Wilber, "Economic Theory and the Common Good," in *The Common Good and US Capitalism*, 244–54, cited in *Fullness of Faith*, 48.

[29] Wilber, "Economic Theory and the Common Good," 248, cited in *Fullness of Faith*, 48.

[30] In this final section I am indebted to a number of the key insights in Christiansen's "The Communion of Saints and an Ethic of Solidarity," c. 7 in Himes and Himes, *Fullness of Faith*, 157–83, as well as his "On Relative Equality," *Theological Studies* 45 (1984): 651–75.

[31] See Himes and Himes, *Fullness of Faith*, 163.

[32] See *Gaudium et Spes*, 23–32.

[33] See Himes and Himes, *Fullness of Faith*, 169.

[34] See Ronald Dworkin's *Taking Rights Seriously* (Cambridge, Mass: Harvard University Press, 1977) 177–83. "Deep theory" represents a level of unreflected belief about what counts as fairness or justice between persons, the "tacit intuition or vision that undergirds a conception of justice" (see Anderson, "On Relative Equality," 668). In the present context, the term is used analogously to refer to the doctrines from which a faith understanding of the need for persons to participate in community is ultimately drawn.

[35] Michael Schuck, *That They Be One* (Washington, D.C.: Georgetown University Press, 1991), 187, quoting Raymond Plant, "Community: Concept, Conception, and Ideology," *Politics and Society* 8 (1978): 79–107 at 105, cited in *Fullness of Faith*, 170.

[36] For an excellent account of stark inequality within a society, see Phillip Knightly's "Goodbye To Great Britain," in *The Australian* magazine, April 2–3, 1994, 8–16, esp. p.13: "Britain has always been a class-ridden society . . . . But what has happened now goes further than class. This is very much a two-nation State—the rich and the poor. The wealth gap widens and will continue to do so . . . ."

[37] See John Paul II, *Laborem Exercens*, 8.

[38] USCC, *Economic Justice for All*, 77.

[39] Christiansen, "On Relative Equality," p.652. Christiansen points out that although he first used "relative equality" independently, the term is also referred to by Amy Gutman in *Liberal Equality* (NY: Cambridge University Press, 1980), as well as in Douglas Rae et al, *Equalities* (Cambridge, Mass.: Harvard University Press, 1981), 104–9.

[40] Christiansen, "On Relative Equality," 653.

[41] An illuminating essay explaining the growing emphasis upon equity within Catholic social teaching is "Global Human Rights: An Interpretation of the Contemporary Catholic Understanding," in David Hollenbach, *Justice, Peace, and Human Rights* (New York: Crossroad Publishing, 1988), 87–100.

[42] See "The Interdependence Between Equality and Freedom," in c. 8, 150–53 for an economic analysis of a number of aspects of the problem.

[43] See Robert Bellah et al., *The Good Society* (NY: Alfred Knopf, 1991), 278.

PART TWO

Reconstructing the Context

Appraising Current Church Teaching on Economy

A S PART OF THE CHURCH'S WISDOM AND VISION ABOUT what it means to be a human person in community, the first part of this book affirmed how important it is for people to be able to participate in community on a variety of levels. Such participation is a matter both of justice and freedom. That wisdom, as derived from the doctrinal traditions of Christianity, provides the sources out of which the Church speaks publicly, as well as within her own communities. When the Church's voice is uttered in the public realm, in order to share what the Church has to contribute to the common concerns of the human family, the Church is taking on the role of a public church. As such it shares social responsibility for the common good and envisions its "teaching role" as resting upon "informed participation" in wider social debates.

A public church does not position itself as the source of definitive resolutions to complex sociopolitical questions. Instead, it attempts to move public debate onto questions about moral values, ethical principles and the human and religious meaning of policy choices.[1] There are basically two ways that the Church communicates and shares its values in the public sphere: in a visionary way by communicating larger pictures of human origin, nature and destiny; and in a normative way by a whole range of social, legal and political norms.[2] The tradition of Catholic Social Teaching provides an example of normative communication. This chapter will look at some of the normative expressions of Catholic Social Teaching, along with their strengths and weaknesses, over the last 100 years. Then, in a final section it will ask how effectively that tradition has been communicated in the public realm and in what ways it might begin to reach a broader public with an even greater impact.

A Tradition of Catholic Social Teaching

The century-old tradition of Catholic Social Teaching—that is, of the Church's voice via papal encyclicals on societal problems— addresses a variety of issues of social concern.[3] *Rerum Novarum* (On the Condition of Workers, 1891) by Pope Leo XIII (1878–1903) commenced the tradition. It emphasized the priority of natural law over natural rights in a variety of working-class questions: a just wage, the unassailability of private property, the legitimate scope of state action on economic matters, and the right of workers to form coalitions and associations. The unrestrained free-market system of liberal rationalists, based on the idea of natural rights, was to be endured until corrected, but never approved. Leo XIII, in standing up for human dignity over and above economics and its laws, placed the social question among the top priorities of the Church's concerns, and also made clear the Church's right to be present to the modern world within society. In a remarkable passage, he lays much of the blame for the workers' plight at the feet of the capitalists:

> The present age handed over the workers, each alone and defenceless, to the inhumanity of employers and the unbridled greed of competitors . . . , so that a very few rich and exceedingly rich men have laid a yoke almost of slavery on the unnumbered masses of nonowning workers.[4]

The encyclical, however, also has harsh critical words for socialists, and portrays socialism as a cure worse than the illness:

> To cure this evil, the Socialists, exciting the envy of the poor toward the rich, contend that it is necessary to do away with private possession of goods and in its place to make goods of individuals common to all, ...[5]

According to *Rerum Novarum* the task and duty of the state is to defend the common good and to promote it by means of social legislation.[6] If any one group or class lacked the possibility of getting a fair share of goods, then they were to be helped by the state so that injustice was redressed.[7] Equally significant for this tradition of papal social teaching, however, is the grounding Leo gives to the right of private property. Leo wrote that it is a natural right to possess things privately. Unfortunately, what has gone largely unnoticed has been Leo's accompanying insistence that the right of private property is fundamentally a safeguard for the needy, whose goods must not be expropriated by the state and who deserve from employers the basic material possessions needed to support family life.[8] Although highly critical of the injustices brought on by capitalism, the encyclical did not envision the possibility for advocating either its structural transformation or replacement.[9]

At the height of the world economic collapse during the Great Depression, Pius XI (1922–1939) issued *Quadragesimo Anno* (Reconstructing the Social Order, 1931). For Pius XI the greatest difference in his society from that addressed by Leo XIII is the even greater concentration of wealth in the hands of a few, resulting in an extreme disparity of wealth on the national and international levels.[10] That disparity shows that the market forces of free competition have been displaced by economic dictatorship. Furthermore, those same forces inevitably rob peoples of the moral choices which are part of all aspects of social life.[11]

Despite such strong criticisms Pius makes a distinction between capitalism, understood as economic individualism where profit is an ultimate end in itself, and free enterprise, as a system of exchange of wages and work supported by legitimate ownership of the means of production. In the face of significant reservations about capitalism, however, *Quadragesimo Anno* allows no middle ground of reconciliation between the Catholic Church and socialism. For socialism substitutes the religious doctrine of the nature and destiny of human life with a thoroughgoing materialism. It also substitutes the Christian teaching on human well-being with economic efficiency and productivity.[12] As part of a more acceptable response, the encyclical proposed reconstructing the "juridical and social order" along two lines: the reform of institutions, chiefly of the state, and the renewal of Christian spirit along with the correction of morals.[13] Fundamental to the institutional economic reform was the principle of subsidiarity, illustrated in the collaborative interaction between the state and a variety of corporate, professional and productive orders—all working to promote justice and the common good. The state had a natural right to intervene in economic activity on behalf of the common good.[14]

In the encyclical, no specific form of government is sanctioned, although reference is made to "solidarism," a middle path between capitalist individualism and socialist collectivism. With the solidarist model, local political units and professional corporations, made up of both employers and employed, would direct and limit the possession of capital and the powers of the state.[15] In Pius' view, the heart of *Rerum Novarum* is that labor and capital are interdependent and that solidarism provides a way for that interdependence to be expressed fairly.[16] Also, *Quadragesimo Anno* does not simply "suggest" an alternative to the prevalent forms of economic organization, it insists that Christian charity alone is not a sufficient solution to pressing social and economic problems.[17] For effective remedies, there must be a juridical and social order which can influence the form and shape of all economic life.[18] Reform alone is insufficient; there must be real structural change, if the Church is to cease looking like an extension of the capitalist economic order.[19]

Probably no prior event in the twentieth century had brought about so many changes in the structure and makeup of society than did the Second World War. The pontificate of Pius XII (1939–1958), marked by that war, the start of European reconstruction and the Cold War, contributed to the definition of Catholic Social Teaching through a series of Christmas addresses from 1939 to 1957. Those for 1940, 1941 and 1942 are the most significant.[20] Pius XII introduced some significant shifts in orientation. First, he assigns responsibility to the economically powerful states for working for a new economic order free of the disequilibrium that marked prewar conditions. His message is fundamentally one of hope for a major reconstruction of the social order, not only in Europe but throughout the world. Second, there is a much greater awareness of the importance of economics for human self-definition.

While economics is not the principal formative factor of personhood, Pius XII suggests that one cannot comprehend fully the religious dimensions of human existence without appreciating how profoundly economics affects life for good or for ill. Third, the pope speaks, more clearly than his predecessors, of definite links between war and economic injustice. No analysis of war can be complete without understanding its economic causes.

Finally, although Pius XII does not engage in the detailed discussion of subsidiarity found in *Quadragesimo Anno*, his commitment to the principle can be seen on several levels: smaller economic units within a society must be given room to function; richer nations must not excessively impose on poorer ones; and the individual must have the freedom to engage in economic activity without undue interference from the state. Pius XII's mindset is subtly revolutionary as regards official Catholicism's attitudes toward society. Only a worldwide rethinking and reconstitution of the economic order can secure the human dignity to which all people have a claim. Henceforth, Catholic teaching on economic issues will be animated more by a concern for human dignity than by a fear of social upheaval.

In *Mater et Magistra* (On Christianity and Social Progress, 1961) John XXIII (1958–1963) defined the spirit of cooperation needed for the changed circumstances of the modern world in order to face common crises. It was the first encyclical to link aid to underdeveloped nations to the traditional social questions. One of the economic strategies which the encyclical advocated was co-partnerships and co-ownership of productive capital by the workers and their companies, and a direct role for their professional associations in setting the economic policies of their countries.

Summarising Pius XI's teaching, John emphasized that the norm in economic matters could not be special interests, unregulated competition, economic despotism, or nationalism. Rather, the aim must be a national and international order which respects the norms of social justice by conducting economic activity for the common good.[21] In the move toward social reconstruction *Mater et Magistra* advocated positive, organic state intervention for mutual cooperation.[22] State intervention, in the pontiff's opinion, is a permanent necessity, a sign of the times. Proper intervention by the state, guided by the principle of subsidiarity, involved the directing, stimulating, cooperating, supplying and integrating of a variety of socioeconomic activities.[23]

Pope John XXIII also put the reconstruction of the social order and the relations between the states under the demands of truth, justice, active solidarity and liberty.[24] In order to bring these social principles into action, the pope suggested the technique of small community organization to analyze the causes of misery and formulate a social praxis to press community reconstruction.[25] The technique was created by the Belgian priest Joseph Cardijn (1882–1967) to provide communities of the most poor and vulnerable with a strategy for empowerment. It was, however, *Pacem in Terris* (On Establishing Universal Peace in Truth, Justice, Charity and Liberty, 1963) that showed John's determination to have the Church engage the world especially on behalf of the most needy. On the national and international levels, special attention must be paid to the "weaker members of society."[26]

The powerless have an "option" on the Church's help. In addition, the encyclical entertains the then controversial prospect of some form of accommodation with communism or mutual cooperation for the purposes of ensuring international harmony. The encyclical endorses cooperative endeavors with secular groups by distinguishing between false philosophies "of the nature, origin and purpose of men and the world" and economic, social, cultural and political undertakings in which one may morally discern good and commendable elements that conform to right reason and are lawful aspirations of the human spirit.[27]

Also controversial was John's endorsement of the UN Declaration of Human Rights (December 10, 1948), an endorsement reiterated in 1971 by the Synod of Bishops in *Justice in the World* and in 1979 in John Paul II's *Redemptor Hominis*.[28] The declaration lists not only political rights and freedoms, but also in Article 25, the right to food, clothing, health care, and other forms of social security. The endorsement associated the UN Declaration with the Church's natural law teaching on rights and set it as the basis for dialogue and action with common agencies in modern society. In all situations human beings were the foundation, cause and end of all social institutions, including the economic system.[29]

In Vatican II's *Gaudium et Spes* (Pastoral Constitution on the Church in the Modern World, 1965), the Council continued in the direction of John's proposals for social reconstruction by committing the Church to cooperate in efforts to resolve social inequalities in the face of mounting disparities:

> Extravagance and wretchedness exist side by side. While a few enjoy very great power of choice, the majority are deprived of almost all possibility of acting on their own initiative and responsibility, and often subsist in living and working conditions unworthy of the human person.[30]

This is said against the backdrop of what the Council calls the "revolution of rising expectations" in the economic sphere, as well as the political explosion of newly independent countries; the fear expressed is that social upheaval will result if the dream for a better life is deferred.

It is this unease that Paul VI (1963–1978) echoed in *Populorum Progressio* (On Promoting the Development of Peoples, 1967) when he said, "Human society is sorely ill." He also observed that "development," the new name for peace, has become less and less of a possibility for larger and larger numbers of people. Unfortunately, industrialization's emphasis on the absolute right of private ownership of the means of production, with no limits, has led to a deplorable loss of a sense of social obligations.[31] Where John XXIII had urged that the principles of truth, justice, active solidarity and liberty be implemented by small communities of the most disadvantaged, Paul VI went further and urged the broader body politic to more direct, urgent and concrete engagement in the worldwide social question.[32]

From his extensive travels, Paul VI had become personally aware of the pressing needs of developing nations and the resulting duties of the rich nations. He was also aware that the principle of free trade does not in fact work to regulate international agreements fairly.

Basic economic inequalities in most cases put poorer nations at a disadvantage, so that the market prices "freely" agreed upon are in essence unfair, with the richer nations practicing "economic dictatorship."[33] The encyclical calls for the development of a sense of human solidarity in guaranteeing authentic development in each person.[34] It even opens up the possibility that certain extreme circumstances may make revolutionary strategies morally acceptable.[35]

It is in Paul's apostolic letter, *Octogesima Adveniens* (On the Occasion of the Eightieth Anniversary of the Encyclical *Rerum Novarum*, 1971), that the question of revolutionary strategies, with a number of specific reservations, is developed further.[36] Taken together, both *Populorum Progressio* and *Octogesima Adveniens* have noted that freedom can sometimes mask an ideology of radical autonomy "opposing the freedom of others," and that in the social and political spheres, a more just sharing in decisions and goods is a better basis for the exercise of human freedom and authentic development. *Octogesima Adveniens*, from the perspective of evolution in the Church's social doctrine, moved away from recommending a universalized application of Catholic Social Teaching to a variety of different situations, for example a specific "third way" as a strategy to avoid the extremes of either economic liberalism or socialism.[37] Instead, it calls for a type of local social analysis as preparatory to an appropriate Christian response.[38]

John Paul II (1978–) continues a number of themes of his papal predecessors, while adding his own particular emphases and interpretations. His writings are characterized by a personalist emphasis on the dignity of the person, and an insistence that human relations are not to be taken as given but as the changeable products of human history. He strikes a decisively communitarian note against egoism, possessiveness and class antagonism. In addition, his stance against monopoly capitalism and collectivist socialism reflects a preference for decentralizing political and economic power. Furthermore, his approach for attaining justice is gradualist.[39]

In *Laborem Exercens* (On Human Work, 1981), John Paul II constructs his most detailed analysis of the material and spiritual dimensions of work, based on critiques of communism, liberalism and a defense of "modified socialism." The critique of communism begins by attacking its stress on the priority of material production of goods over the individual and the resulting loss of a sense of the moral value of work. Labor, whether physical, intellectual or artistic, in itself is not a curse, but a liberating necessity in the full realization of one's humanity.[40] The critique of liberalism begins with the question of what it means to be a truly human individual.

Liberalism, in placing capital before labor, robs humans of the resources for creativity and self-development. The subject in liberal thought has been made subordinate to the inviolable market; freedom is reduced to the freedom to acquire property and wealth. This "error of economism" is brought about when labor and capital are separated and set in opposition.[41] In contrast to the critiques of communism and liberalism, the encyclical defends a modified socialism. The right of private property is maintained, but not "the exclusive right to private ownership of the means of production." Under "suitable conditions," socialization of the latter is justified. This distinction is based on a dual notion of property: intrinsically private property such as one's home and car, and capital such as factories, technology and natural resources.[42]

The encyclical thus articulates John Paul's own vision of a just social order, a modified form of socialism built on a new view of human rights, political and economic democracy, and a demand for moral self-consciousness to defend distributory and participatory justice. The Church, in contrast to the pope's personal vision, however, does not sanction any particular system, since none can be a full or adequate embodiment of the Kingdom of God. Even in the recent collapse of the Eastern Bloc, the pope has warned against a superficial sense of satisfaction for liberal capitalism, which has produced such negative effects in the Third World.[43]

Lastly, *Laborem Exercens* entails a critique of liberty as defined in the natural rights tradition: namely, as "freedom from" the external coercion of the state. This restricted view of liberty has no sense of ultimate social goals: the general will, the good society, the Kingdom of God on earth. It has no *positive* sense of ultimate social goals. It does not see that private property, the control of wealth by a few, the existence of extreme poverty and material deprivation, the control of capital over the manner in which work is socially organized, and other such factors, seriously limit the possibilities of each member of society to realize their full human potential. It is in reference to all of these factors that the pope is preaching redemption from the "hidden structures" of economic bondage. Such structures are sinful inasmuch as they contribute to widespread poverty and misery. These "structures of sin" find their origins in specific and personal acts, and cannot be exonerated on the basis of impersonal forces or some material or psychological determinism. Indeed, behind certain economic and political decisions are also motives guided more by a desire for personal monetary gain and ideological influence.[44]

In order to mark the 100th anniversary of *Rerum Novarum*, John Paul II issued *Centesimus Annus* (On the Hundredth Anniversary of *Rerum Novarum*, 1991).[45] It calls for a reform of the free-market system on a global scale in the wake of the collapse of communism and of the associated rapid changes in eastern Europe. After posing the question of whether or not that collapse suggests that capitalism should be the goal of countries rebuilding their economies, the pontiff says that the positive values of the market and of enterprise must, in all situations, be oriented to the common good.[46] John Paul's particular focus is on the humanizing role which the state and its legislation has to take in relation to "business economies." In one of the most telling lines in the encyclical the pope says: "There are collective and qualitative needs which cannot be satisfied by market mechanisms. There are important needs which escape its logic."[47] In addition, the encyclical also argues for basic human needs of the poor in the Third World and their struggle for training, technology and a share of today's high-tech market.

John Paul II's contribution to Catholic Social Teaching develops earlier statements on the common good, and the creative and transcendent nature of human life by recognizing the value of the liberal agenda of civil liberties and political emancipation. He has also insisted, however, that economic, social and cultural rights are also equally normative. Lastly, in his definition of labor, the physical and intellectual activity that creates capital and, more importantly, the moral and ethical substance of humanity, he has contributed some of his most original thinking and embraced intellectually the humanist side of Marx, while rejecting crude communism. His synthesis of classical and critical traditions is bold and challenging.

Probably the most widely agreed upon strength in all of the papal writings is their keeping visible the need for a moral dimension in the operation of the economy. A further strength is the consistent and repeated calls for structural change. They are not satisfied with minor adjustments to address abuses of the system. Reform is but an intermediate measure toward a more fundamental reconstruction.

In terms of the demand for structural change, the encyclicals have often been more progressive than the letters and actions of national conferences of bishops that they either predated or prompted.[48] An additional strength can be discerned in how the encyclicals provide an excellent example of the process by which Roman Catholicism developed a cumulative tradition on social justice. A fourth strength can be observed in the recovery of some largely lost traditions. For example, by rearticulating the natural-law tradition, especially from Augustine to Aquinas, the papal writers renewed an important intellectual school of thought and provided a basis for discussions of political economy apart from, and also alongside, the natural-rights school. Lastly, a fifth strength in the social justice encyclicals can be seen in the way the understanding and role of encyclicals in the life of the Church has come to be interpreted.

Meant originally as a way for the consensus of the faithful to confirm the orthodoxy of the incumbent Bishop of Rome, encyclicals now function as an authoritative guide for the formation of consciences for the faithful and as the basis for dialogue with the wider community. As such, they provide an invaluable tool with which the Church can exercise an extremely widespread influence, not only on its own members, but on world public opinion in general.[49]

The Effectiveness and Impact of Catholic Social Teaching in the Public Realm

In *Theology and Critical Theory*, Paul Lakeland suggests that one of the main reasons for Catholic Social Teaching not being proclaimed more effectively is the lack of, and failure to incorporate, an adequate critical theory within the tradition.[50] In general, critical theory in theology can be understood as a recognition of the distinction between reality and the language used to interpret reality religiously. Without such a distinction religious interpretations of reality are interpreted naively as the reality itself. In addition, without such a theory there is also no awareness of the presuppositions, interests and values which guide, direct and influence such interpretations. In order to see how this is the case it will be important first to outline the problematic elements in Catholic Social Teaching: a confusing openness to contradictory interpretations; an apparent lack of consistency between the principles of the Church's social teachings and the principles which appear to guide its internal governance; the absence of a modern theory of society; and a tendency to resort acritically to religious language and theological concepts.

The problem of contradictory interpretations can be seen by a brief reference to the diverse evaluations of capitalism in Catholic Social Teaching. The different responses of Michael Novak,[51] as an apologist for neoclassical economics, and Donald Dorr,[52] who approaches market economics through the sieve of a socialist critique, are especially to the point at issue. While the degree of difference in the interpretations could be analyzed as reflecting the commentators' selective interpretations and manipulation of the original texts, rather than inconsistency in the author's mind, other factors are also likely to be at work. In the first place, Catholic Social Teaching is not monolithic, and reflects discernible layers of development of doctrine and moral teaching. Thus, John Paul II views the respective weaknesses of both capitalism and socialist systems much more evenly than his predecessors. Second, official church documents seem often to bear the marks of different hands, even when they come nominally from one person.[53] Third, the level of abstraction of the documents means that they are often vulnerable to a scope of applications and associations never envisioned by the author.

The further issue of inconsistency between the principles which guide social teaching and those which appear to direct domestic church administration raises the additional question of their respective guiding motivations, presuppositions and interests. Lakeland believes that the radical source of the inconsistency between the principles of social teaching and ecclesial practice is located in the paradigm of teaching prevalent in the Catholic tradition: namely, a belief that there are some who teach and there are some who are taught. Since this paradigm of teaching is predominantly in possession, the credibility of the Church's liberating social message is greatly handicapped when the latter does not appear to be applied in the same manner within the Church as it is to situations and issues in society. Here, the Church assumes that it can teach in the context of the broader society, but, at least on an official level, has nothing to learn from its own members who move and work in that same society.

In addition, the social message is also greatly handicapped when the Church does not acknowledge how and from whom, outside of its own ranks, it has learned of needs to which it had not previously been either adequately attentive or satisfactorily responsive. An example can be made by reference to John Paul II's *On Human Work*. The encyclical makes a long-overdue identification of the Church with the working poor without recognition of the Church's official distance from the poor for many centuries. The lessons of history are not acknowledged and the Church's debts to others go unrecognized, whether they are to Marx's critique of religion or to liberation theology's preferential option for the poor. Almost thirty years ago *Gaudium et Spes* recognized the need for the Church to learn from the world.[54] While such learning may be going on, the Church does not easily acknowledge officially where and how it is taking, or has taken, place.

The third issue, the absence of a developed modern social theory's analysis of society, presents us with yet another problematic area. The theology of the world in Catholic Social Teaching can be quite perceptive about the significance of historical phenomena. Yet, because it is predisposed to see the world as a part of the divine plan from the standpoint of an economy of salvation articulated in narrowly religious terms, many opportunities for a further and deeper understanding of history are lost. Contributions from historical and related sciences are either unacknowledged or ignored, or even condemned. When human sciences have insights to offer that are not part of the privileged vision of Revelation, as happened in the cases of Galileo and Darwin, they cannot easily be incorporated into the religious worldview. So, for example, while John Paul II's analysis of work in *On Human Work* is excellent in many respects, the unsatisfactory nature of the analysis of work results from the absence of social theory and a premature recourse to the categories of revelation.

A fourth and related problem area is an insufficiently critical recourse to religious language, theological concepts and Scripture. Language is taken to be identical with what it intends and not as an interpretation of the world that is susceptible to error and open to criticism.[55] John Paul II's theology of the world in *Sollicitudo Rei Socialis* (The Social Concern of the Church, 1987) illustrates the problem involved in a premature recourse to Scripture.[56]

The most important of John Paul's observations on today's world is his conviction that geopolitical thinking effectively instrumentalizes the needs of the poor nations to the strategic concerns of the world powers and power blocs. The pope asks how capitalist and socialist economic systems are capable of changes which would promote a more integral development of peoples throughout the world.[57] Problems surface in the pope's own response to the question. He singles out the need for conversion, in the sense of moral awakening that would inspire the will to change relations of power.[58]

Authentic development, based on a converted will, is the political imperative of the Gospel. Also, it becomes possible to look at the present socioeconomic and political reality of the world and read it as a failure to follow out God's mandate to humankind, while proclaiming the need for the Church's Gospel vision to be articulated in the structures of society. The scriptural message confronts human historical failure to produce a renewed commitment to an essentially historical struggle for the realization of justice and peace. Development is part of the divine plan. Christian social ethics and a theology of history, however, also have to acknowledge more seriously that progress has apparently given the human race as many opportunities to confound as to advance the realization of the divine plan.

A critical social theory can help overcome each of the weaknesses which have been noted thus far in Catholic Social Teaching. In conjunction with Habermas's theory of communicative action, which aims at shared understanding as a basis for communal action, there lies a possibility for achieving a more broadly based involvement both in the composition and in the reception of Catholic Social Teaching.[59] Also, theology which engages a critical interpretive framework, such as Habermas offers, has a greatly enhanced capacity to communicate, especially in the public realm. It is a theology which will have diagnosed what disguises the centrality of the Christian message, and thereby will have the potential to proclaim a message of emancipation, within the social, economic, political and cultural conditions of our day. Anything less will be either outdated, irrelevant, incoherent or oppressive. In the next chapter the development and operation of such a theory in the Church's teaching and witness function in reference to the operation of the economy will be considered in more detail.

---

[1] See J. Bryan Hehir, "Church-State and Church-World: The Ecclesiological Implications," *CTSA Proceedings 41* (1986): 54–74; especially 64.

[2] See Robert Gascoigne, "Christian Narrative, Ethics and the Public Forum," in *The Australasian Catholic Record* (April, 1994): 208–18.

[3] English translations are available in the following: David M Byers, (ed) *Justice in the Marketplace: Collected Statements of the Vatican and the US Catholic Bishops on Economic Policy, 1891–1984* (Washington, DC: USCC, Inc., 1985); Claudia Carlen, ed., *The Papal Encyclicals, 1740–1981*, 5 vol. (Ann Arbor, MI: The Pierian Press, 1990); Michael Walsh and Brian Davies, eds., *Proclaiming Justice and Peace: Documents from John XXIII–John Paul II* (Mystic, CT: Twenty-Third Publications, 1984).

[4] *Rerum Novarum*, #6, Byers, 14.

[5] *Rerum Novarum*, #7, Byers, 14. See also Francesco Nitti, *Catholic Socialism* (New York: Macmillan, 1985).

[6] For references to the state's role in economic life see *Rerum Novarum* #s 8–10, 20, 23, 33, 48, 51–5, 67 and 75.

[7] See the following references in *Rerum Novarum*: 38, 40, 45; on cooperation between the classes #s 28, 33; on the number of work hours #59; on child and female labor #60; on wages #s 51, 61–3: and on the right of workers to organize #s 72, 76.

[8] *Rerum Novarum*, #10, Byers, 15; also see #37, Byers, 24.

[9] Giorgio Campanini, *Messagio cristiano ed economia* (Bologna: Edizioni Dehoniane, 1974), 189; also Hans Maier, *Revolution and Church: The Early History of Christian Democracy*, translated by E.M. Schossberger (University of Notre Dame Press, 1969), 265.

[10] See *Quadragesimo Anno* #s 58, 109, Byers, 62 and 75.

[11] See *Quadragesimo Anno*, #14, Byers, 47.

[12] See *Quadragesimo Anno*, #s119, and 120 Byers, 79. Pius also attacked atheistic communism in his later encyclical *Divini Redemptoris* (March 19, 1937). His analysis, however, contends that communism finds its ideological roots in "amoral liberalism," the same source of the capitalist excesses it seeks to overcome (*Divini Redemptoris*, #32, William J. Gibbons, *Seven Great Encyclicals*, NY: Paulist Press, 1963, 188).

[13] Respectively, see *Quadragesimo Anno* 55, 79–80, and 98, 127, 136, 143, along with *Divini Redemptoris* 41, 44, 45 and 47.

[14] See *Quadragesimo Anno* 78, 110, and *Divini Redemptoris* 30, 32, 33, 75 and 76; in reference to public ownership see *Quadragesimo Anno* 28, 114–15. Also see John C. Cort, *Christian Socialism* (Maryknoll, NY: Orbis Books, 1989), 289–96.

[15] Edward Cahill, S.J., "The Catholic Social Movement: Historical Aspects," in Curran and McCormick, *Readings in Moral Theology*, no. 5, 7.

[16] See *Rerum Novarum*, #28, Byers, 28.

[17] See *Quadragesimo Anno*, #4, Byers, 45.

[18] See *Quadragesimo Anno*, #88, Byers, 71.

[19] For a closely related development, see the Pastoral Letter to the Bishops of Mexico, 28 March 1937, *Firmissimam Constantiam in Enchiridion Symbolorum* #s 3775–6, 738–9.

[20] See Byers, *Justice in the Marketplace*, 91–109.

[21] See *Mater et Magistra*, #38, 40, Walsh and Davies, *Proclaiming Justice and Peace*, 9.

[22] *Mater et Magistra*, 20: The state cannot ". . . hold aloof from economic matters; . . . it must do all in its power to promote the production of a sufficient supply of material goods . . . to protect the rights of all its people, and particularly of its weaker members, the workers, women and children."

[23] *Mater et Magistra*, 53.

[24] See *Mater et Magistra*, 212–15; see also *Pacem in Terris*, 86–90, 91–3, 98–9, 120.

[25] See *Mater et Magistra*, #236, Walsh and Davies, 39; see also *Pacem in Terris*, 86–90, 91–3, 98–9 and 120.

[26] *Pacem in Terris*, #56, Walsh and Davies, 56.

[27] See *Pacem in Terris*, #159, Walsh and Davies, 73.

[28] *Justice in the World*, #64 (1), Walsh and Davies, 201; *Redemptor Hominis*, #17.3, Walsh and Davies, 259.

[29] *Mater et Magistra*, 219.

[30] *Gaudium et Spes*, #63.2, Walsh and Davies, 148.

[31] See *Populorum Progressio*, #26, Walsh and Davies, 149.

[32] *Populorum Progressio*, 1, 5 and 15.

[33] *Populorum Progressio*, #58, 59, Walsh and Davies, 157.

[34] *Populorum Progressio*, #20, 18, Walsh and Davies, 147.

[35] See *Populorum Progressio*, #31, Walsh and Davies, 150.

[36] *Octogesima Adveniens*, #26, Walsh and Davies, 176.

[37] See *Octogesima Adveniens*, #s 40, 42, 47.

[38] See *Octogesima Adveniens*, #4. Also "Apostolic Letter of His Holiness Pope Paul VI to Cardinal Maurice Roy" (Vaticanus: Typis Polyglottis Vaticanis, [1971]), 7.

[39] See Gregory Baum, *The Priority of Labour: A Commentary on Laborem Exercens* (NY: Paulist Press, 1982); G. Baum and R. Ellsberg (eds), *The Logic of Solidarity: Commentaries on Pope John Paul II's Encyclical "On Social Concern"* (Maryknoll, NY: Orbis Books, 1989); Peter Hebblethwaite, "The Popes and Politics: Shifting Patterns in 'Catholic Social Doctrine,'" *Daedalus* (Winter 1982).

[40] See *Laborem Exercens*, #9.2, Walsh and Davies, 285.

[41] See *Laborem Exercens*, #13.1, 13.2; Walsh and Davies, 290–1.

[42] See *Laborem Exercens*, #14.2, Walsh and Davies, 293. The letter also picks up the theme of ecology, introduced earlier by Paul VI (see *Populorum Progressio*, #22, Walsh and Davies, 148), and is developed from John Paul II's reading of the creation stories in Genesis cc. 1 and 2. The pope's environmental and ecological concerns reflect a doctrine of the human person as a responsible steward.

[43] See John Paul II, "Is Liberal Capitalism the Only Path?" *Origins* 20:2 (May 24, 1990), #3, 19; the speech was delivered in Durango, Mexico, on May 9, 1990.

[44] See *Sollicitudo Rei Socialis*, #37, USCC, 71; on the topic of "Structures of Sin," see Mark O'Keefe, *What Are They Saying About Social Sin?* (New York: Paulist Press, 1990).

[45] (St. Paul Publications, Homebush, NSW, 1991.) Also see Nancy Sherwood Truitt, "Latin Bishops Look for Liberation in a Market Economy," *The Wall Street Journal* (May 10, 1991), A 11; Editorial, "Pope points toward economic third way for common good," *NCR*, Vol. 27:28 (May 10, 1991), 20; Editorial, "Economic debate can now focus on capitalism," *NCR*, Vol. 27:29 (May 17, 1991), 28.

[46] *Centesimus Annus*, 43. See also *Ibid.*, 42 for more on John Paul's qualified acceptance of market economies.

[47] *Centesimus Annus*, 40. Also, on the logic of the market not being able to deal with needs, see "The Reduction of Needs to Wants" in c. 2, 25–8.

[48] This statement is true in reference both to *Economic Justice for All: Pastoral Letter on Catholic Social Teaching and the US Economy* (United States Catholic Conference, Inc., 1986), and *Common Wealth for the Common Good: A Statement on the Distribution of Wealth in Australia* (Australian Catholic Bishops' Conference: Collins Dove, 1992). In reference to the same point about the former see McCarthy/Rhodes, *Eclipse of Justice*, 40. Also, in *God, Goods, and the Common Good: Eleven Perspectives on Economic Justice in Dialog with the Roman Catholic Bishops' Pastoral Letter* Edited by Charles P. Lutz (Minneapolis: Augsburg Publishing House, 1987), see the entries by Lutz himself, and Sibusiso M. Bengu and Larry Rasmussen. The latter on p. 41 notes: "The underlying economic analysis [is eclectic] . . . [and] for the bishops, a radical faith is to pursue a liberal policy agenda by using gradualist means."

[49] For a more developed presentation of this analysis, see George E. McCarthy and Royal W. Rhodes, *Eclipse of Justice: Ethics, Economics, and the Lost Traditions of American Catholicism* (NY: Orbis Books, 1992), 182–7.

[50] See P. Lakeland, *Theology and Critical Theory: The Discourse of the Church* (Nashville: Abingdon Press, 1990). For the remainder of the chapter I am especially indebted to Lakeland's work in c. 3 "The Value of Critical Theory for Catholic Theology," 70–102.

[51] See Michael Novak, *Freedom With Justice* (NY: Harper & Row, 1984).

[52] See Donald Dorr, *Option for the Poor: A Hundred Years of Vatican Social Teaching* (Maryknoll, NY: Orbis Books, 1983).

[53] See Paul Lakeland, "Distinguishing the Scribes: The Composition of Vatican Documents," *The Month* 7 (June 1974): 595–9.

[54] The notion of the church and the world in dialogue from which both can learn is treated in some detail by Juan Luis Segundo in *The Community Called Church* (Maryknoll, NY: Orbis Books, 1973), particularly in chapter 5. Also see Leonardo Boff's *Church, Charism, and Power: Liberation Theology and the Institutional Church* (NY: Crossroad, 1985), 138–43.

[55] See Jurgen Habermas, *The Theory of Communicative Action. Volume One: Reason and the Rationalization of Society* (Boston: Beacon Press, 1984), 50.

[56] See Paul Lakeland, "Development and Catholic Social Teaching: Pope John Paul's New Encyclical," *The Month* 21 (June 1988): 706–10.

[57] See *Origins* 17 (March 3, 1988): 648, par. 21.

[58] See *Ibid.*, 651, par. 30.

[59] On the importance of a more broadly based involvement see Michael J. Himes and Kenneth R. Himes, "The Myth of Self-Interest," *Commonweal* 125 (September 23, 1988): 493–8.

CHAPTER SEVEN

Stimulating the Conversation

HOW CAN CATHOLIC SOCIAL TEACHING BE COMMUNICATED more effectively in the public realm? This chapter will contend that it would be advantageous to bring the critical theory of Jurgen Habermas to the service of the Church's continuing communication of its tradition of social teaching, as well as to the composition of subsequent contributions to that tradition. At first glance it might not seem likely that the Church could engage Habermas's critical theory easily. That theory and Habermas's social analysis do not include a role for the churches and normative religious traditions, even though there is much in his critique of modern society and discourse ethics that can be interpreted as compatible with the Church's moral vision.[1] This chapter, in addition to highlighting potentially helpful components in Habermas's critical theory, will also acknowledge some of the criticisms of that theory. They have to be taken into account if the churches might ever use it more directly in composing and communicating Catholic Social Teaching in the public realm. The chapter will then conclude by proposing how the churches, in the light of official theology and actual practice, might move closer to becoming what Habermas understands as communities of communicative action.

The Critical Theory of Jurgen Habermas

In *Knowledge and Human Interests*[2] Habermas says that an exercise of reason is "critical" precisely when its impact frees us and others from the interests that constrain us and others from arriving at greater degrees of liberation. Habermas identifies three forms of knowing, each motivated by a particular cognitive interest which structures knowing in a given way: that of the empirical-analytic sciences guided by the interest to gain technical control over a variety of scientific processes; that of the historical–hermeneutic sciences guided by the interest to achieve the greatest possible consensus among participants of a particular tradition; and that of critical social science and philosophy guided by the interest to bring about greater emancipation by moving beyond the rationalizations of uncritical thought.[3] Each knowledge-constitutive interest has its appropriate social medium: respectively, labor, social interaction, and power. Thus, the first deals with the relations between human beings and things to be manipulated, the second with relations between human beings and other human beings, and the third with release through reflective critique from the hidden constraints operative in the other two.

In arguing for the presence of the latter emancipatory interest Habermas begins to develop his *theory of communicative action*. He suggests that the achievement of autonomy and responsibility become possible only in and through the structure of language.[4] All language presupposes the communication of agreement on one point or another. It assumes that there are rules and that the conversation partners are playing by them. The assumption is as necessary to the one who decides to break the rules as to those who abide by them. If everyone breaks the rules, communication is impossible. When the rules are followed, however, language reveals a fundamental orientation to communication which enhances freedom.

The communication made possible by the use of language is preliminary to effective social action.[5] With the latter outcome in mind, Habermas distinguishes between action oriented toward success and action oriented toward understanding. *Action oriented toward success*, in which individuals or groups seek to accomplish specific ends, may be either instrumental or strategic. Habermas further subdivides strategic action into open and concealed strategic action.[6] Open strategic action occurs whenever a recognizable group agrees on a mode of common action. Its objective is effectiveness. Appropriate strategic action oriented to success and claiming effectiveness, however, must also respect the character of a community as simultaneously oriented to a particular set of understandings. Strategic action is appropriate, if it is based on the consensus of the whole body about what is needed to safeguard the community's self-understanding. Concealed strategic action, whether conscious or unconscious, refuses to respect the voices of open discourse.

Action oriented to achieving understanding is only possible in intersubjective, open and free communication. There are three types: *conversation*, concerned with the attainment of *truth*—that is, with a group's establishing that its utterances correspond to the external realities to which they claim to refer; *intersubjective relations regulated by agreed-upon norms*, concerned with *rightness*—that is, with the correctness of the norms and assumptions which guide interpersonal interactions; and *expressive action*, concerned with *sincerity*—that is, with a group's determining that the symbolic representations—both verbal and non-verbal—of its vision and inner self are, in fact, expressive of truthfulness.

Communicative action, a type of action oriented toward understanding, involves the continuing conversation of any human community about the direction and value of its actions, and also presupposes some approximation of an "ideal speech situation."[7] Such a situation is approached when communication proceeds by the force of the better argument; that is, when the speaker has chosen a form of language through which understanding can take place, when the proposition contains some "truth" that can be shared, when the form of communication is "right" for the members of the community concerned, and when the speaker intends to communicate with "sincerity."

When a breakdown occurs in the practice of communicative action, when there is a real or apparent rupture in the search for consensus, Habermas proposes dealing with the problem by an appeal to *discourse ethics*. Discourse refers to the argumentation needed to respond to breakdowns in communication. It also aims at clarifying their causes and restoring channels of communication. If what a group claims as its truth, rightness or sincerity is challenged, and if speakers wish to avoid deceit or force to establish their positions, then one of a number of categories of discourse is needed. Recalling the different validity claims of *conversations* aimed at understanding, *theoretical discourse* is directed at the *truth* claims of a group; *practical discourse* examines the *rightness* of those norms which impact upon interpersonal communications; and *therapeutic discourse* tests the *sincerity* of expressions of personal subjectivity of the members of a group.

Habermas develops his discourse ethics by drawing the idea of communicative action into relation with his critique of the narrow instrumentality of late capitalism.[8] Central to Habermas's critique is the *distinction between "lifeworld" and "system,"* respectively, substructure and superstructure. "Lifeworld" refers to the *shared meanings that make ordinary interaction possible.* It includes social institutions, practices and norms, and also consists of the world of meanings into which we are born and in which we grow up. "Lifeworld" communicates the knowledge and norms that provide the background for the formation of the self and for the legitimation of society. Behind communicative action, there is an implicit "lifeworld." It promotes the development of mutual understanding, the fostering of social integration and solidarity, and socialization as the formation of personal identities.

The structural components of these tasks are culture, society and person. In contrast, "system" refers *to those administrative areas of modern society coordinated by money and power.* Money and power coordinate human action in a way that differs considerably from that which takes place through communication. Indeed, large areas of the "lifeworld"—the public sphere, education, citizenship and the like—have been dissolved and then reconstituted as imperatives of the economic subsystem.[9] Power is also inflexibly tied to bureaucratic roles and hierarchies that are less natural but more easily responded to than communicatively shared understanding. Power, like money, however, takes over areas of the "lifeworld" and then reconstitutes them as the objects of state control. Money converts concrete labour into an abstract commodity in a "free" market economy through the process of commodification, while power converts practical actions guided by values into value-neutral social facts which can be used for a variety of different state purposes.

Society is composed both of "lifeworld" and "system." A successful society holds "lifeworld" and "system" in a unity in which the "lifeworld" has priority. For Habermas, modern capitalist societies are examples of pathological distortions of the equilibrium that should exist between "lifeworld" and "system." In capitalist societies, "systems" are always threatening to instrumentalize the "lifeworld." One indication that they are succeeding is the pervasive feeling in developed capitalist societies that much is beyond the control of individuals or of community action, and that the realities of money and power are simply givens for which communicative action has no option but to make space. The sphere of communicative action is progressively diminished, being forced to live in the space left when vast tracts of modern society have been uncoupled from communicatively shared experience. Habermas's long-term goal is to establish "lifeworld" and "system" in society in the right relationship.

Habermas's *critique of modernity* is an important part of his approach to establish a right relationship. A "lifeworld" under pressure needs to find ways to shorten the process of achieving consensus through communicative action. It can do this either by relying on leadership that depends on and respects consensus formation, or by adopting "steering media" that "uncouple" interaction from the "lifeworld." In the first case, consensus is brought about by "responsible actors." In the second, money and power construct complex networks that no one has to comprehend or be responsible for. The norm-free and value-free networks exclude the shared cultural knowledge, valid norms and accountable motivations of the "lifeworld." "System" integration is uncoupled from social integration.[10]

The uncoupling of "system" and "lifeworld" in contemporary capitalist societies results in the "steering mechanisms" of money and power "colonizing" or eroding the "lifeworld", by deforming its normative and symbolic structures. When that happens, money and power create problems in a number of key areas: family socialization and ego development, mass media and mass culture, and the possibility of protest movements. The modern world then takes one of two forms: welfare-state mass democracy, which, under the pressure of economic crisis, can sometimes be sustained only with authoritarian or fascist orders; or bureaucratic socialism which controls with a political order of dictatorship by state parties. [11] In both cases, the results of the split are managed by transferring the distorting effects upon the system back into the "lifeworld". Then three "pathologies" result: the reduction of communicative rationality to instrumental rationality; the uncoupling of "system" and "lifeworld"; and the colonization of the "lifeworld."

"Lifeworld" pathologies are responsible for modernity's sharp division between private and public life; for private life being viewed as the realm of affect, ethic, religion, art and philosophy; and for private individuals feeling increasingly helpless before the structural forces of the economy or state. While Habermas believes that the division into "lifeworld" and "system" is one of the necessary stages in the development of society, he is also convinced that the "lifeworld" must be the place where the "system" is ultimately grounded.

Unfortunately, throughout the world the power of established economic interests too many times short-circuits steps otherwise being taken to preserve the quality of life, with the resultant transfer of the economy's problems into the "lifeworld" in the form of claims that basic human freedoms are at stake. Since the scale of crises and pathologies is so immense, protest is no longer focused on demanding responses from the political system. In late-capitalist societies single-issue groups seek to defend the world and the human community from the influences of an unchecked system. They are united in their critique of growth and focus either on the defence of class interests, or on opposition to tax reform, to nuclear energy, pollution and deprivation of privacy.[12] Anxiety stirs up feelings of being overwhelmed by an international economic system which is now largely beyond our control.[13]

Habermas warns that the "system" will not solve the problems of the "system." We can only look to the exercise of human rationality in and through the communication community to fight back against human loss of control over the system. A first step is to begin to resist mightily the forces that privatize art, philosophy, ethics and religion, and to promote a vigorous communication community dedicated to a public ethic that will win back control for the "lifeworld" from the "system". In this struggle the churches may play a crucial role by discovering their potential as communication communities oriented to consensus and understanding. Before such a strategy is developed, however, it will be helpful first to address some criticisms of, and a major deficiency in, Habermas's theory of communicative action, prior to suggesting how the Church's social teaching tradition might be enhanced by recourse to it.

Critical Reflections on Habermas's Critical Theory[14]

There are a number of problematic areas in Habermas's critical theory, as well as a more basic problem with his understanding of the scope of morality for any proposed dialogue with Catholic Social Teaching. Niklas Luhmann has challenged Habermas's assumption that modern late-capitalist societies can be understood, organized or governed either by their citizens or in terms of a rational or normative consensus. For Luhmann, rationality no longer has anything to do with rational discourse or with practical decisions about what we should or should not do. Rationality is a property not of the individual or of interacting subjects but of the system. More precisely, rationality is the measure of that system's adaptation to its environment.

When rationality becomes a property of the system, however, power dissolves truth and the public becomes the object rather than the subject of politics.[15] In response, Habermas insists that Luhmann's description of the situation is more symptomatic of the system taking over the proper functions of the lifeworld than it is an argument against retrieving an extremely important possibility for reason in the lifeworld. Indeed, the only way beyond the problem is by greater participation in planning on the part of the community.[16]

Another objection is based on the assumption that the long-term effects of capitalism upon societies and the way they structure themselves is virtually irreversible. When classical capitalist patterns are inserted and/or adapted into societies organized along other economic lines, they inevitably retain the upper hand. Habermas, however, continues to assert that the capitalist work patterns must inevitably run up against normative societal structures which are themselves necessary in order to maintain social integration. Yet this assumption is also challenged on the basis that contemporary expressions of pluralism, characteristic of late-capitalist societies, will not yield to such integration. Habermas's response to this challenge is that there is still a need for a critical social theory to employ the ideal of a workable consensus critically; that is, as a counterfactual, *a more rational future possible criterion.* The latter can show up the limitations of less legitimate capitalist appeals to the common interest such as calls for sacrifices of real living standards "in the interest of national economic development."17

Another criticism levelled at Habermas is that "communicative action" and "communicative rationality" are all faces of the same objectively given forms of power which they seek to address. Critical reflection is completely impotent. Indeed, its possibility is an illusion because all forms of subjectivity, and of intersubjectivity, are merely the inner face of our subjection to power. In response, Habermas argues that the rational potential of the public sphere, of ideal speech, of rational discourse and of communicative reason is actualized only insofar as the interacting participants face one another in a situation that is free of force. The impact of this last stage of criticism is the assertion that interaction is never free of structural force/power, and that "rational discourse" is merely another means of securing it. At one level, then, these objections force Habermas to concede that the process of emancipation involves a kind of forcible "break-in" to established circles of power.

For Habermas this is theoretically problematic. Since rational discourse is not likely to arise from violence, how then do those who stand for a counterfactual consensus break open the circle of those who oppress them? Habermas's defense is firstly to concede that power is indeed coordinated "behind our backs" and that it comes in upon us "from the outside in" as an impersonal structuring force that is both empirically effective and, for the most part, beyond conscious reckoning. However, Habermas does not concede that power is ever *a priori* beyond the exercise of conscious reason. Power as a thing in itself is, for Habermas, a positivist illusion.

While Habermas can be said to have addressed all of the above criticisms with a reasonable degree of credibility, the more basic and underlying problem that has to be faced is the limited scope he assigns to the possibility for norms guiding interpersonal discourse. The main lines of Habermas's concept of the moral are seen in his theory of communicative action. Every statement uttered by a participant in communicative discourse raises three validity claims: that the utterance is *true*, that it is *right*, and that the participants' intentions are *sincere* in the way they are expressed. As a result of his understanding of modernity, Habermas limits the moral domain to an utterance's *rightness* in its interpersonal context. Only those questions which can be decided by communicative discourse are moral questions. The background norms guiding the relations in the interpersonal context are not properly moral because they are personal.

Habermas constructs two principles which, in his view, determine the validity of moral norms: universality and discourse ethics. The former is a rule of argumentation that establishes that the moral rightness of a proposition must be determined through discourse, and that only those things can be discussed which would bring the agreement of all participants. Purely personal statements of value, therefore, cannot be open to argument in discourse ethics. The second principle, that of discourse ethics, is also a procedure for impartially testing the validity of moral norms. It necessitates a distinction between moral norms and evaluative statements or judgments of the good life. Indeed, Habermas argues for a very sharp distinction between evaluative and normative statements, between the good and the just.[18] The implication of this division in the process of discourse ethics is that subjects must take a hypothetical stance toward the personal moral norms which provide the backdrop for their total life context.

Charles Taylor sees Habermas's procedural understanding of morality in his theory of communicative action as a severe weakness. Participants in discourse locate themselves in a common space. If the participants cease to understand the common space in the same way, then it can only be recovered by a process of reaching consensus. Habermas's theory of communicative action argues for a solution which would repair the ruptured common space through dialogue. At this point, Habermas and Taylor stand together. They part company, however, when Habermas attempts to remove background considerations. According to Habermas's procedure, questions of the good must be surgically removed with razor-sharp cuts.

Habermas's solution, at this point, denies an important aspect of the structure of language—namely, that the only way in which consensus can be repaired is through articulating what is already held as antecedently good, in addition to what also proves itself in intersubjective dialogue.[19] While Habermas emphasizes the intersubjective realm he does so in a way in which the subject has no relation to evaluative concerns—that is, to its more important and broader purposes. Habermas recognizes a dimension of the subject which relates to his/her more important purposes, but he removes this dimension from the interpersonal realm. In Habermas's procedural morality, subjects are denied the background which makes sense of their lives. Taylor's point, however, is precisely to locate the subject against the background of its more important purposes.[20]

Resolving moral questions requires an exploration of background understandings, an articulation of the qualitative distinctions which make sense of our lives. Habermas's procedural ethic has ignored such understandings and, thereby, greatly limited the scope of its application. In spite of that limitation, it is my conviction that if his theory of communicative competence were brought to the service of communicating and composing Catholic Social Teaching, not only would the credibility and strength of the latter be greatly enhanced, but that same teaching could go a long way in overcoming the present deficiencies brought on by the limited understanding of moral norms in Habermas's theory. Ultimately, I am assuming that the theory of communicative competence is capable of being applied in a number of contexts and ways not originally envisioned by Habermas.

The Church as a Community of
Communicative Action

Habermas's analysis of modernity focuses upon two of its basic characteristics: greater sophistication in the understanding of human reason resulting from the uncoupling of the "lifeworld" and the "system"; and the decreasing presence of the lifeworld's values in the system resulting in the lifeworld itself becoming "colonized" through the system's media of money and power.[21] Habermas's interpretation of modernity also raises the question of a viable location for public discourse about issues of justice, right and good. Unfortunately, by severing his discourse ethics from religion and religious foundations and institutions, Habermas has not included the Christian churches in his thinking as one possible institutional locus for discourse ethics.

A few reflections on the Roman Catholic Church's official understanding of itself suggest how the Christian Church can be understood as a community of communicative action oriented to understanding. The vision of the Church found in the documents of the Second Vatican Council provides a starting point.

A case can be made that the leading ecclesiological idea of the Council, namely, the Church as a communion,[22] moves the Church to a more obvious concern with communicative action. In portraying the Church as a "communion of the faithful" the Council intended that the first task of the Church's ministry and service for unity is to restore dialogue and communication. Furthermore, the Council also intended that the guiding notion of Church as communion be introduced as far as possible by means of reasoned argument into the process of communication within the Church. The desired outcome of the Council's intention was to build up a full and undivided communion and communication among the faithful.

Unfortunately, and although thirty years have passed since the close of the Council, the Church as a whole is still only at the beginning of its "reception" of communion as Vatican II's leading ecclesiological insight.[23] Perhaps if the Church were to take on a resource such as Habermas's theory of communicative action, along with his critical theory of society, it could go a long way in giving expression to the leading ecclesiological idea which the Council proclaimed as constitutive of its identity.

The lived theology of the Church in the first millennium was that of communion, in contrast to the second millennium in which the formulated theology was of the Church as a perfect society.[24] This concept of communion was recovered and given a central place at Vatican II. Also, according to the Final Report of the 1985 Extraordinary Synod of Bishops, the ecclesiology of communion is the central and fundamental idea of the Council's documents. As a description of the Church's *nature*, not its structures, communion can be understood on a number of levels. Fellowship with God— that is, *trinitarian communion*—provides the most fundamental level of meaning.[25] According to the Council, the "mystery" of the Church means that the Church enjoys a present and partial communion with God—in the Spirit believers have access through Christ to the Father, and in this way share in the divine nature.[26]

Another level of communion is *Eucharistic communion*, a participation in the life of God through Word and Sacrament. Here, the Church is not merely a reflection of the trinitarian communion but also makes that communion present in the world and in human history through its proclamation of the Word and celebration of its sacraments. Eucharistic communion brings about participation in the good things of salvation conferred by God: the Holy Spirit, new life, love, the Gospel and the Eucharist.[27] A third level of communion is the bond among local churches or *ecclesiological communion*. It refers to the unique relationship which exists between the universal Church and the local churches: the universal Church exists only in and through the local churches; the local churches exist only in the communion of the universal Church.[28] It is ecclesiological communion which provides a basis for suggesting greater coresponsibility and collaboration at all levels of church life.

A fourth and further level, *baptismal communion*, comprises all of the baptised in the Church.[29] The shared baptismal dignity of the People of God implies participation in the life of the Church and its mission. A fifth and final level, *world communion*, encompasses the bonds which the Church develops with the world. It provides the basis for the Council's description of the Church as a "universal sacrament of salvation" for the world.[30] That is, the communion to which the Church gives expression on the previous four levels represents the type, model or pattern for the communion of all peoples and nations, as well as for women and men, and rich and poor alike.[31]

It still remains, however, to ask whether the leading ecclesiological idea of Vatican II is adequately taking shape in the life of the Church so as to be able to make the claim that the Church in the wake of Vatican II sees itself as a community oriented toward communicative action and understanding. Creating a church that operates according to the principles of communicative action, where it does not yet exist, will mean engaging in open strategic action that does not distort the essentially communicative character of the community. It will also entail engaging the already existent church in a discourse oriented to truth, rightness and sincerity. Three current developments illustrate how a church intending to reflect the Council's vision of the Church as communion, as well as to operate from a communicative praxis, might organize and structure itself: base Christian communities; churches oriented more toward mission than maintenance; and churches characterized by post-patriarchal feminist emphases.

The phenomenon of base Christian communities, as an example of an alternative way of structuring ecclesial life, has probably received more attention than any other recent development in the Catholic tradition.[32] Grassroots ecclesial communities emerged in Latin America in the 1950s and '60s in the wake of a number of developments: a growing shortage of priests; the consequent large numbers and huge geographical areas of parishes; the spread of primary groups in Church-sponsored educational developments; and responses to forms of local and national oppression. The majority of the developments reflect primarily the socioeconomic and political interests of the people, resulting in a grassroots activism.

A catalyst that led to a more systematic development was the Latin American Bishops' Conference held at Medellin in 1968.[33] One of its intentions was to relate the teaching of Vatican II to the specific situation of the Latin American Church. The bishops attempted to do this in two ways: first, by engaging as many members of the Church as possible to confront the problem of the poverty of the Latin American people; secondly, by pointing out the need for the poor to have a greater role in shaping their own circumstances. They insisted upon genuine opportunities for involvement through one or another form of "mediating structure,"[34] a way for individuals to act collectively and have a greater impact. Medellin promoted the formation of any and every kind of mediating structure, and promised the support of the Church for all initiatives to raise the poor from being objects to becoming subjects of their history.

Base Christian communities are organized on a dialogical and consensual model quite compatible with Habermas's understanding of a community oriented to understanding and open strategic action. They attempt to understand the message of the Scripture and its relation to their life situation. This process can be compared to establishing the validity claim to truth in discourse ethics. Further, the communities are oriented toward the formulation of practical proposals for action. This process can be compared to establishing the validity claim to rightness in discourse ethics. Then the communities aim at conforming to their vision of a world beyond oppression. This process has many similarities with establishing the validity claim to sincerity or truthfulness in discourse ethics. Finally, the strategic actions emerging from their consensus-oriented deliberations are intended to be expressions of the commitment to social, economic and political emancipation that the liberating power of the Gospel has inspired in them.[35]

Churches oriented more toward involvement in the socio-political contexts in which they operate than primarily toward responding to the pastoral needs of their members provide a second example of an emerging form of church organization which reflects a commitment to communicative praxis. They can also be seen as First World examples of the base communities which are more common in Third World settings.[36] Indeed, according to J.B. Metz, many churches in the First World could learn much from the prophetic examples of the Third World base communities. First of all, churches in the Third World offer a way of being person in community and in solidarity which is not distorted by the dismembering bias of bourgeois individualism.[37] Secondly, the Third World churches can begin to suggest to their First World counterparts how to integrate the preaching of salvation with effective action for change in society. Thirdly, First World churches can begin, in their increased involvement in society, to experience a closer sense of community within the ranks of their own members. Unfortunately, such churches have not for the most part yet recognized how they can become agents for the betterment of society. They have not learned how to respond to and resist the economic and political forces that have brought on the increasing fragmentation of society, and the increasing instrumentalization of the individual to larger and more "scientific" forces.[38]

Inasmuch as First World churches allow themselves to become aware of the plight of Third and Fourth World societies, they will discover that they can no longer, while claiming to have a Christian conscience, engage in a "tactical provincialism" whereby they define their political and social identity independently of the poverty, misery and oppression in the Third World. Unfortunately, it simply is not politically palatable to proclaim, in First World countries, that the First World increases its wealth by keeping the Third and Fourth Worlds dependent upon it. Politicians who voice such a position can expect to be removed from office.

In contrast, the Church and the churches' leaders enjoy a particular advantage. They cannot be removed simply by being voted out of office. In this sense, bishops in First World countries especially can function as important pioneering forces, and can help the rest of the churches to move toward the conversion needed in the First World. Bishops who attempt to operate as catalysts to such conversion, however, must themselves recognize the inter-dependence between stemming the erosion of values in society, and the need for them to criticize present social structures and argue for their transformation. For values are not only threatened by bourgeois individualism, but also by certain expressions of liberal-capitalist economies which have used this bourgeois individualism to control not only the economic sector, but the souls of individuals as well. With such an innovative stance, two forces could productively come together—the critique of society presented by papal and episcopal teaching, and the intentions and plans of basic community churches learning from those teachings and moving to give expression to them in their respective societal contexts.

Metz's proposal argues for a dialogical, consensual form of church community by suggesting a convergence between the institutional universal church and the base community church. Unfortunately, he does not clarify how such a convergence might take place. He does not suggest how conversion and maturity might begin to arise in a time of plenty and a culture of affluence.[39] So, it is to a third example of an alternative structuring of church life, the post-patriarchal feminist church, that we turn in order to find strategies for conversion and maturity. Rosemary Radford Ruether suggests "alternative" feminist ecclesial communities.[40] From the perspective of communicative action based on an inclusive, consensus-directed dialogue, Ruether reflects the concerns of so many women who feel that the Church does not recognize the faith maturity which they have to offer and also does not allow an open and free expression of their developed gifts.

Ruether argues further that feminist critique and social analysis are not sufficient as strategies for a more full inclusion within the Christian community, and that nurture within the community also has to include opportunities for symbolizing experiences of liberation from patriarchal oppression in appropriate forms of worship.[41] Ruether says women have to be brought together in order to articulate their own experience and communicate it with each other. Initially, there will be a need to gather apart from the patriarchal influences of present church structures, at least until such time that a sufficiently strong and critical counter-culture is established. It is only then that "women-church" can become church, and also be a constitutive part of the entire church's growth and development.[42]

Since the ultimate intention of women-church is both inclusion within, and as a catalyst of growth for, the entire Church, Ruether is not an advocate for dismantling the institutional church. Her vision of ecclesial community is one of dialogue, equality, consensus, ministry to one another, and sacramental life. She is insistent, however, that the Church face up to its historical relativity and relinquish the myth that some particular historical form of ecclesial institution is the only legitimate one.[43] The institutional church has to learn to see itself as the backdrop for a spirit-filled community, rather than that spirit-filled community itself.

There is much that is compatible in Ruether's vision of women-church with Habermas's consensus community. Its open dialogical structure, its affirmation of the radical equality of all its participants, the applying of ideology critique and historical methodology to the creation of a theory of modernity that is oriented to emancipation, all conform to the model of communicative action. Ruether's critique of the patriarchy of the institution could be repeated in the language of "systematically distorted communication" and "action oriented toward success." Moreover, Ruether's position can be instructive for Habermas inasmuch as the former acknowledges issues of women's oppression that Habermas is sometimes less than adequate in expressing.[44]

By way of summary, both the communion ecclesiology of Vatican II and the communicative action community in Habermas's vision can be brought together productively in order to focus upon the indispensability of human interrelations marked by open and honest communication. The ecclesiology of communion provides a viable background reference otherwise missing in Habermas's moral proceduralism. It also calls for a shift away from a success-driven society toward a community motivated by truth, truthfulness and sincerity. Unfortunately, the Church as a whole has not yet been able to recognize the full implications of this ecclesiology.

The three alternative ways of structuring church life which we have looked at, have all, in their own ways, acted upon the Council's ecclesiology of communion. These newly developing forms of the Church seek open, understanding-oriented dialogue with all who will accept the conditions for communicative action. Such a claim obviously raises the question of the further time yet involved for the Church to receive and act upon the rich understanding of its nature as a communion on many levels. It also raises the further question of whether or not the Church will see in an approach to church life, such as that suggested by Habermas's theory of communicative action, one possible and compatible way of facilitating a more broadly based reception of Vatican II's leading ecclesiological insight.

---

[1] A recent collection of essays explores the possibility for further collaboration between Habermas and Christian theology. See Don S. Browning and Francis Schussler Fiorenza (eds), *Habermas, Modernity, and Public Theology* (NY: Crossroad, 1992), especially the Introduction and c. 1, 3, and 4.

[2] Jurgen Habermas, *Knowledge and Human Interests* (Boston: Beacon Press, 1971).

[3] See *Knowledge and Human Interests*, 309–10.

[4] See *Knowledge and Human Interests*, 314.

[5] See Habermas's essay "What is Universal Pragmatics?" in *Communication and the Evolution of Society* (Boston: Beacon Press, 1979), 1–68; and *The Theory of Communicative Action Volume One: Reason and the Rationalisation of Society; Volume Two: Lifeworld and System* (Boston: Beacon Press, 1984, 1988).

[6] *Reason and the Rationalisation of Society*, 333.

[7] See Habermas, "Towards a Theory of Communicative Competence," in *Inquiry* 13 (1970): 360–75; John B. Thompson, "Universal Pragmatics," in *Habermas: Critical Debates* John B. Thompson and David Held (eds), (Cambridge, MA: MIT Press, 1978), esp. 307–10.

[8] See his *Lifeworld and System: A Critique of Functionalist Reason* (Boston: Beacon Press, 1988). The critique was originally made in *Legitimation Crisis* first published in 1973. The edition I have worked from is translated by Thomas McCarthy and was published by Polity Press in 1988.

[9] See "Economic Imperialism's Threat to the Non-Economic Sectors of Life," in c. 4, 69–71.

[10] See *Lifeworld and System*, 182–4.

[11] See *Lifeworld and System*, 384.

[12] The only exception to this in Habermas's view is the feminist movement which offers a comprehensive alternative vision of society. See *Lifeworld and System*, 393.

[13] See *Lifeworld and System*, 394–5.

[14] In this section I am especially grateful for the incisive critique of Habermas offered by James McEvoy in c. 4, 66-74 of *Freedom in the World: The Significance of Karl Rahner's Theology of Freedom in the Light of Charles Taylor's View of the*

Modern Identity (an unpublished doctoral thesis) The Flinders University of South Australia, Adelaide, 1994.

[15] See Luhmann's *The Differentiation of Society* translated by S. Holmes and Charles Larmore, (NY: Colombia University Press, 1982).

[16] See *Legitimation Crisis*, 136–8.

[17] See Jurgen Habermas, "A Philosophico-Political Profile," in *New Left Review 151*, 1985, 75–105.

[18] See Jurgen Habermas, *Moral Consciousness and Communicative Action*, translated by Christian Lenhardt and Shierry Weber Nicholsen (Cambridge: Polity Press, 1990), 104.

[19] See Charles Taylor, "Language and Society," in *Communicative Action: Essays on Jurgen Habermas's Theory of Communicative Action*, edited by Axel Honneth and Hans Joas, translated by Jeremy Gaines and Doris L. Jones (Cambridge: Polity Press, 1991), 23–35, at 34.

[20] Seyla Benhabib recognizes this problem in Habermas's view of the subject. See her "Autonomy, Modernity and Community: Communitarian and Social Theory in Dialogue," in *Situating the Self: Gender, Community and Postmodernism in Contemporary Ethics* (Cambridge: Polity Press, 1992), 71, 75.

[21] See Hugh Baxter, "System and Lifeworld in Habermas's Theory of Communicative Action," *Theory and Society* 16 (1987): 39–86.

[22] See Francis A. Sullivan, S.J. "The One Church: A Communion of Churches," in *The Church We Believe In* (NY: Paulist Press, 1988), 34–65; esp. 55–65.

[23] See Walter Kasper, *Theology and Church* (London: SCM, 1989), 163, and especially all of c. VIII "The Church as Communion," 148–65. "Reception" is a technical term which refers to the amount of time which has to pass, along with changes in attitude and practice which have to take place, before it can be said that the teaching of a major church council has taken on expression in the life of the Church, and, therefore, has been "received."

[24] L. Hertling, *Communio und Primat*, Miscellanea Historia Pontificiae VII, Rome, 1943. A "perfect society" is one which possesses all of the means needed to accomplish its proper ends.

[25] See the earlier treatment on the social implications of the doctrine of the Trinity in c. 4, 72–4.

[26] See *Lumen Gentium 4, Unitatis Redintegratio 2*.

[27] See *Sacrosanctum Concilium 59* and *51, Lumen Gentium 11, Ad Gentes 9, Apostolicam actuositatem 6, Presbyterorum Ordinis 4, Unitatis Redintegratio 2*, and *Dei Verbum 21*.

[28] *Lumen Gentium 23*; also see Kasper, *Theology and Church*, 157.

[29] See *Lumen Gentium 10, 13*; *Unitatis Redintegratio 2*; *Sacrosanctum Concilium 14*; and *Apostolicam actuositatem 18*.

[30] See especially *Lumen Gentium 48*, and *Gaudium et Spes, 45*.

[31] See *Ad Gentes 11, 23*; *Gaudium et Spes 39*; *Nostra Aetate 1*.

[32] See Alvaro Barreiro, *Basic Ecclesial Communities: The Evangelisation of the Poor* (Maryknoll, NY: Orbis Books, 1982); Leonardo Boff, *Ecclesiogenesis: The Base Communities Re-Invent the Church* (Maryknoll, NY: Orbis Books, 1986); Thomas G. Bruneau, *The Church in Brazil: The Politics of Religion* (Austin: University of Texas Press, 1982); and Harvey G. Cox, *Religion in the Secular City: Towards a Postmodern Theology* (NY: Simon & Schuster, 1984).

[33] See Gremillion, *Peace and Justice*, 445–76, for the texts of some of the Medellin documents.

[34] See Lakeland, *Theology and Critical Theory*, 126, where he describes mediating structures as organizations larger than the individual and smaller than the state. They include student associations, labor unions, political parties, and professional organizations. Also see Kenneth R. Himes, "The Local Church as a Mediating Structure," in *Social Thought* (1986): 23–30.

[35] See Boff, *Ecclesiogenesis*, 2, and 5–6.

[36] See J.B. Metz, *The Emergent Church: The Future of Christianity in a Post-Bourgeois World* (NY: Crossroad, 1981).

[37] For an explanation of how Metz uses "bourgeois" and "bourgeois individualism" in *The Emergent Church*, see Peter Mann's "Translator's Preface," ix: Mann states that Metz uses the phrase to invite First World peoples to understand their own reality as middle class white collar and blue collar workers, as living in a market economy shaped by the "bourgeois" values of competition and exchange. Also, see Metz's *Christianity and the Bourgeoisie* (Concilium 125; Seabury, 1979).

[38] See Sharon Welch, *Communities of Resistance and Solidarity: A Feminist Theology of Liberation* (Orbis Books, 1985). Also see Metz, *The Emergent Church*, 89.

[39] For a fascinating account of how affluence works against the possibility of change and conversion see John Kenneth Galbraith's *The Culture of Contentment* (Penguin Books, 1992).

[40] See her *Women-Church: Theology and Practice of Feminist Liturgical Communities* (San Francisco: Harper & Row, 1985).

[41] See Ruether, *Women-Church*, 3.

[42] See Ruether, *Women-Church*, 59.

[43] See *Ibid.*, 33.

[44] See Nancy Fraser, "What's Critical About Critical Theory? The Case of Habermas and Gender," in *Feminism as Critique*, Seyla Benhabib and Drucilla Cornell (eds), (Minneapolis: University of Minnesota Press, 1987), 31–56.

Contributing to the Emergence of Economic Alternatives

Local Churches as Agents of Social Analysis

TO THE EXTENT THAT CHURCH COMMUNITIES DEVELOP THE skills of communicative competence they will enhance their potential to witness to a lifestyle and values which reflect greater responsibility for the common good. At the same time, they would also exercise a therapeutic effect upon the operation of the economy in the societies where they exist, and take on more characteristics of public churches.[1] When the Church, either in universal teaching or local action, operates as a public church, one of the most important tools available to it is social analysis. Social analysis, a method for planning to bring about constructive change in society, involves a number of moments.[2]

The connecting link for all of the moments is shared experience which grounds a person in the process. The first moment, *insertion* into the lived reality of individuals and communities, entails coming into contact with people's feelings, thoughts, experiences and responses in a situation. The second moment, the task itself of *social analysis*, helps to make sense of present experiences by clarifying their most pertinent historical origins and drawing connections between them. It also examines possible further consequences, delineates linkages among a number of factors, and identifies the most significant actors in a specific context. The third moment, *theological reflection*, involves an effort to understand better the analyzed experience in the light of living faith and the resources of tradition. As the Word of God is brought to bear on the situation, it raises new questions, suggests new insights, and opens new responses. The "core issues" uncovered in the process of analysis give direction to this reflection.

Theological reflection first *sets forth aspects of the Christian faith tradition* that relate to the "core issues" emerging from social analysis, as well as the *lived faith response* to which Christians are invited. Next, it interfaces the highlighted aspects of the *faith tradition* and the suggested *faith response* with further critical questions. Here it is important to ask how our present action or response may be creative or noncreative of the Reign of God, and what action may be appropriate for the future. The emphasis is on action which makes the Reign of God a reality, along with the recognition that we can only begin to know how we might contribute to its inbreaking when we are actually involved in efforts to shape a present expression of it.[3]

The fourth and final moment in the overall process is *pastoral planning*. It is based upon the decisions and actions which are called for by individuals and communities considering the experiences that have been analyzed and reflected upon. This moment also involves designing the response so that it can be most effective, both in the short and long term. Planning means knowing where we are going, and having goals in view. Since all of the moments in the overall process are cyclical and ongoing, every time a pastoral plan is developed and implemented it gives rise to another set of experiences which subsequently must be reflected upon and analyzed in order to do further pastoral planning.

Social analysis is a tool that one can use to identify the underlying causes of situations. Conclusions depend on a variety of factors, including the relative complexity of the situation being studied, the rigor of the questioning put to it, and the accuracy and adequacy of the data available. Even if all the possible data is not at hand, however, the process can still be valuable because it begins to bring issues to light, and to reveal causes, consequences, linkages and trends. So, for example, the process can focus on an isolated issue, such as unemployment, or the policies that address an issue, such as job training, or on the broad structures of the economic, political, social and cultural institutions that have given rise to specific issues and policies.

Gradually, social analysis moves beyond the issues, policies and structures in order to focus on social systems, including primary groups, local communities, nations, and even global enterprises. Also, an adequate analysis of social systems studies the changes in a system over a period of time, as well as provides a cross section of its complexity at a particular moment in history. In addition, such an analysis distinguishes a system's objective and subjective dimensions—that is, its component institutions and organizational behavior patterns, along with the values and ideologies that are the source of its operative assumptions.

Since no social analysis is value-free and is implicitly linked to some ideological tradition, identifying one's biases with one particular vision of society will inevitably bring about conflict with those who hold very different visions. It is very important, nonetheless, for participants to make explicit the values and biases which they bring to the task for the process to be constructive. Otherwise the process will inevitably be dismissed as a less-than-honest attempt either to advantage one's priorities or to enhance one's own sphere of influence.

From a Christian perspective the values and biases which guide and direct social analysis presuppose a viable vision of human community and an adequate view of human motivation, neither of which are presently presupposed by most of neoclassical economic theory. The latter is avowedly individualist and has an intolerably impoverished view of human motivation.[4] If, however, we move to accept a different account of what it means to be a human person in community, such as has been presented in the first part of this book, then we also have to move toward a significant revision of the predominant economic theory and practice in possession. At the moment most alternatives for economic survival are forced to exist in the face of the market's overwhelming influence, an influence which is especially resistant to change or transformation.[5] Acknowledging the strength of such resistance, the World Commission on Environment and Development believed that a more prosperous, just and secure future depended on changes in human attitude which would require education, debate and public participation. Indeed, Christian churches can help by providing contexts in which these intermediate tasks can take place. Such tasks might be seen as succeeding when the individualism of present economic orthodoxy begins to be supplanted with cooperation. A further and equally important sign of success will involve the emergence of a revised understanding of the relationship between equality and freedom, a relationship which we will now look at in more detail in the next section.

The Interdependence Between Equality and Freedom[6]

In all of its approaches to economic organization the Church has to insist on the indispensable need for both equality and freedom as prerequisites for any recognizable commitment to human dignity. Freedom from want and oppression, along with freedom to create and participate fully in society, cannot be exercised, however, except by people who are equal. Equality does not mean that everyone exists at the same socioeconomic level. Rather, it presupposes the removal of the intolerable material inequalities which are becoming more characteristic of market systems. While the latter have certainly proven to be dynamic and adaptable, their limits are especially evident by their apparent inability to redress ever-increasing economic inequalities.

The dominant economic orthodoxy still dismisses serious reflection on economic inequality on the basis that it is a precondition for effective overall economic performance. Without a serious commitment to some type of practical equality however, social, economic and political inclusion in society becomes impossible. For practical equality implies an allocation of resources and income which makes active participation in society possible.

Market economies, despite rhetoric about the equality of individual freedoms in the marketplace, are inherently inequitable, prone to periodic recession and fundamentally incompatible with the values of community, cooperation and ecological balance.[7] Their modern corporate forms centralize power and wealth and recurrently violate democratic principles which require equity and participation in all aspects of economic, social and political life. Ironically, then, the commonly claimed nexus between capitalism and democracy is seriously challenged by the problems brought on by severe inequalities.

The bias in mainstream economics against addressing issues of inequality and income redistribution has been one of the reasons for the development of contemporary political economy, where the centrality of the issues of power, class and economic inequality are reasserted. Unfortunately, sociology, which might have provided assistance in the analysis of inequality, has not been particularly helpful.[8] For there the key concept of class has generally been replaced with a concern for social stratification. The latter makes it more difficult to focus directly upon the economic sources of social inequality, and is associated with the claims that class is a redundant concept in understanding contemporary society. The myth of classlessness is also associated with particular biases in the treatment of democracy in political science. The liberal democratic ideal, however, moves us to ask whether or not the formal equality of rights before the law and in the electoral processes remains possible with the existence of pervasive economic inequalities.[9]

It is much easier to establish the meaning of inequality in quantitative terms than to arrive at a qualitative understanding of it. The distinction between the emphasis in liberal political philosophy on *equality of opportunity* and the emphasis in socialist thought on *equality of outcome* illustrates the problem. Equality of opportunity is seemingly compatible with large inequalities in structures of rewards and with a strikingly unequal society, as long as all have equal opportunity to compete. The liberal concern with equity thereby dissolves into a concern with social mobility, leaving the basic sources of economic inequality untouched. It is a viewpoint which is unacceptable to those whose conception of social justice is disturbed by the wide differences in material living standards and the coexistence of wealth with poverty.

In addition to the difficulties encountered in analyzing economic inequalities scientifically, further problems are met in a number of popular assumptions which dismiss the significance of inequality. The first affirms that major inequalities do not exist. It finds expression in the myth of classlessness and generates misconceptions about the effectiveness of economic and governmental redistributive processes. A second assumption concedes that major inequalities exist, but insists that they result largely from luck rather than stratification brought on by institutional arrangements. A third acknowledges not only that major inequalities exist and that they are systemic, but also insists that they are justified.

There is an almost blind belief in productivity and effort as the decisive determinants of differences in incomes. In addition, there is an unbending conviction about the general possibility of significant social mobility, and an acceptance that ethnicity and gender, and not the economic system, are the major contributors to inequalities. Finally, a fourth assumption asserts that major inequalities do exist, that they are systemic and unjustified, but that they are not crucially important. Regrettably, the combination of a powerful intellectual heritage with particular social biases in the analysis of economic inequality has developed into a massive form of resistance to look at issues and strategies which might lead to a more fair and just society.[10] These powerful impediments against working toward a society marked by the values of equity and social justice are further consolidated by the structure of vested economic interests and the hesitancy by most governments to implement adequate policies of reform.

The recent past has illustrated that the emergence of a principal alternative system of economic organization will not happen easily. Bureaucratic state versions of communism have proven incapable of providing resources and of maintaining the necessary degree of popular support. The recent shifts toward free-market strategies, however, are fraught with capitalism's recurrent problems of recession, trade and debt imbalances, financial instability and a worldwide polarization of rich and poor.[11] In addition, "new right" ideology, popular beliefs and particular economic theories, along with the institutions through which they are disseminated, provide further legitimacy for an unequal society. These elements, rather than any efficiency-equity trade-off, are the fundamental obstacles to a more equitable, and ultimately more efficient, socioeconomic system. An effective challenge to economic inequality will require both a long-term and a thoroughgoing program of social and structural change.

Elements of a Workable Vision

Faced with the obstacles encountered in working for a more equitable society, structural change requires critique, vision, strategy and organization. It is important, then, to turn from a method and program of critique to vision in order to suggest the type of future worth struggling for. There are a number of issues which any vision or system of economic organization has to address: the distribution of wealth, the stimulation of production, the control of the economic process, employment, trade and capital accumulation, government planning versus the dynamics of the free market, and the problems of inflation and recession. While doing this, however, any system also has to remain aware of the ultimate purpose of economic organization: liberation from domination by scarcity and provision with the conditions necessary to a fully human existence—that is, one in which the higher ends of the human family and creativity are possible.[12]

Before the Church can begin contributing to the emergence of economic alternatives within society, it must first clarify for itself and for others the vision of economic organization out of which it intends to operate. If it seeks the source of such a vision in specific areas of its doctrinal tradition, areas which we have looked at in Part One of this book, then its guiding view of the human person in community, a more adequate anthropological foundation for the economic organization of society, will have distinctive characteristics. For example, it will insist that society needs an economy characterized by attitudes which are empowering of individuals and communities, politically participatory, and respectful of ecological limits.

The Church's anthropological starting point would also require a number of agenda items: making it possible for the vast majority of people to become the subjects of their labor; convincing broader sectors of society that economics needs to be freed from the laws of its positivist and questionable scientific imagination;[13] insisting that, instead of self-interest, rights and obligations will be at the heart of the new economics, along with the central concern of enabling people to meet their *needs* and to develop themselves.

An additional assumption might be that a life-giving vision of the economy must also replace the destructive ideology of necessary growth with a recognition of the need for limits to growth, and with a view that the economic system is an organic part of the natural world and not as a machine external to it.[14] Furthermore, the Church might work toward a decentralization which makes democracy in production possible, stressing that the local and national economies will have to become the central focus of interest, rather than the transnational or multinational economy. The task in an alternatively structured society is to see that bureaucracy does not get in the way of responsibility and accountability, and that, if private ownership of the means of production is abolished, industries owned by the community are answerable both to workers and consumers.[15]

Finally, the Church might also hold that in a new economic order the meaning of *money* and *taxes* will be significantly different. Money will be seen basically as a means for facilitating the exchange of goods and services, as well as for creating material incentives and economic cooperation among people. It will no longer be seen primarily as a source of capital and profit in a price system designed merely to give signals to producers about relative demand and supply. Also, in a new economic order, taxes would not be on personal income but on land, on activities that pollute and damage the global environment, on activities which exploit international resources, on imports between one nation and another, and on international currency exchanges.

One possible approach for realizing such a vision and goals, the one to which the augumentation of the present work intends, is social market capitalism.[16] It is based on the principle that while the free market is potentially a useful servant, it is almost certainly a bad master. Also, while the market is an immensely productive tool, it needs to be harnessed to social objectives determined outside of the marketplace itself. The fruits of its productivity should be largely channeled for social purposes.[17] Also, from the standpoint of social justice, the social market approach proposes that we bring the production questions, such as efficiency and productivity, and the distribution questions, such as equality and the meeting of basic human needs, into a socially sensitive and responsive correlation.

Since the social market depends to a considerable degree upon economic incentives, absolute equality is not presumed. Indeed, social market capitalism makes a case for inequality on the basis of its claim that we cannot have adequate production without incentives which ultimately entail some inequalities. We cannot forget, however, that when the theory of social market capitalism was originally formulated it did not envision either the extent or the severity of the inequalities with which we are confronted at the end of the twentieth century. If we appeal to this approach, then we must also incorporate significantly adjusted responses to the contemporary expressions of economic inequality which threaten the social fabric nationally and globally. Also, a definitive priority *must* be assigned to the distribution questions over the production questions in the critical correlation between them.

A second possible approach is democratic socialism. It assigns a central importance to equality. People may not all be equal in natural endowment, but are to be considered equal in value. They should therefore be equal before the law and in economic distribution. In the ideal socialist commonwealth, equality would find expression in each person making his or her creative contribution to the betterment of the whole, and each person receiving what he or she needs out of the abundance created by cooperation.

The solidarity of the human family would replace the individualism of capitalism, and also begin to address the breakdown in Western capitalist society of fundamental social purposes frequently threatened by competitive self-seeking individuals. In contrast, within a society based upon equality, solidarity, and purposeful social planning, cohesion would be greatly enhanced.[18] Even though a strong case can be made for compatibility between democratic socialism and Christianity's concerns with the possible impact of economic organization upon society, democratic socialism cannot be endorsed without reservation. There is a problem with productivity: a worker-controlled state might not democratically agree to devote enough production to capital goods industries rather than to consumer goods.

A related reservation is whether democratic socialism will allow for adequate economic creativity. If social ownership is heavily centralized, then there are likely to be a number of organizational hurdles which might inhibit free creativity. The question of central governmental control also raises the further question about overconcentrations of power and the untoward influence of special interest groups.

A third possible approach, the "steady-state economy," assumes that unlimited economic growth is not possible in a finite world. Its main focus is upon conserving the limited resources and human values that are threatened by more and more production. It is marked by the conviction that our most pressing problem is to replace the economic goal of constantly increasing production, while simultaneously decreasing our use of resources without undermining the health and safety of existing human beings until we have arrived at a steady-state economic balance. Herman Daly defines this point as one in which the total population and the total stock of physical resources are maintained constant at some desired levels by physical production and consumption rates that are equal at the lowest feasible level.[19]

The main thrust of Daly's conception of a "steady-state economy" is reflected in Robert L. Stivers' vision of a "sustainable society,"[20] one whose pattern of economic, political and social life can be sustained for an indefinite future. In economic terms, the "sustainable society" would meet the basic material needs of all people, without sudden and uncontrollable collapse. In political terms, the sustainable society would require institutions capable of distributing the constant stock of economic goods more equitably. Stivers suggests a combination of globally oriented authority with a balancing decentralization of power and the development of small, integrated communities where personal interaction can occur. In social terms, Stivers' vision invokes a call to basics: to faith, to human needs for food, clothing, shelter and health; to liberating structures that provide opportunities for human cooperation and creativity; to throwing off the enslaving forces of affluence.[21]

Despite the attractive aspects of a "steady-state economy" and a "sustainable society," some hard questions still have to be answered. First, in a steady-state economy is it possible to redistribute the world's goods equitably in any kind of foreseeable future? Secondly, will proponents of a "steady-state economy" have to develop greater political influence in order to align the potential benefits of their goals to the most disadvantaged sectors of society? Finally, and perhaps most seriously, will a "steady-state economy" result in a political organization which falls prey to authoritarianism and imperialism? While an exclusively national approach to natural resources can exacerbate the world problem of shortages, and while a recourse to global intervention may be the only way to persuade some governments to greater ecological responsibility, a premature recourse to global intervention might result in measures which bypass the legitimate sovereignty of countries. These questions and others related to "steady-state" economic organization will be treated more fully in the next chapter.

In the meantime, and from all of the above approaches, it is now possible to distill a number of strategies which might begin to give expression to a vision of the economic organization of society which respects the Christian churches' emphases on the prior importance of human communities and the persons which they nurture.[22]

First, there is the need for *new structures for the ownership of the means of production*. One workable possibility is a three-tiered system of ownership, comprising large-scale enterprises which are publicly owned and accountable, small- to medium-scale enterprises organized as workers' cooperatives, and small localized businesses predominantly privately owned and managed. Second, there is also a need for *a guaranteed minimum income system* for all citizens to provide the basis for the elimination of poverty. Such a system could provide a general social safety net and does not depend on each individual's capacity to demonstrate eligibility for selective assistance. Third, *guidelines for reduced wage inequalities* need to be established. A regulated wages system based on increased equality in wage rates between occupations is an important element in achieving a more equitable society. Fourth, *increased flexibility in work and leisure* needs to be established. Each successive recession leaves a higher residue of long-term unemployment.

The traditional goal of full employment becomes ever more elusive. It is necessary to think of long-term measures to harness an increasingly capital-intensive and technologically sophisticated economy to the needs of people for productive and creative lives. Fifth, *a comprehensive program of public expenditure*, including increased expenditure on the social wage, needs to be financed by more progressive income and inheritance taxation. Progressive income tax with no allowances against tax would minimize possibilities of tax avoidance, and would establish a clear relationship between tax and ability to pay. Likewise, a new inheritance tax levied at a progressive rate would inhibit the intergenerational transfer of accumulations of wealth.

These proposals illustrate how a commitment to greater economic equality might influence alternative ways of organizing the economy. They need to be supplemented by analysis of the associated strategies for transition and by careful consideration of the necessary forms of political organization.[23] Achieving progressive change towards a society marked by greater degrees of equality is a massive task, engaging analytical, political and educational resources. Ultimately, what is at stake is humanity's capacity to live together in an economically prosperous, environmentally sustainable and socially harmonious society.

The Church's Potential Contribution

In this final section on the Church's potential contribution to the emergence of more equitable economic alternatives, the focus will be upon local churches in First World settings. The rationale behind such a selection is quite simply that they are almost inevitably situated in countries which have the greatest responsibility for, and impact upon, the way the global economy affects all peoples. Churches operating as communities of communicative action in such settings can make a number of contributions toward an economic organization of societies and cultures which are more respectful of the values and moral structures of those societies and cultures. In general, the contributions can fall into two main categories: the incorporation of community economic development as part of church mission; and critique and pressure on existing economic systems by acting as mediating structures contributing to the emergence of a new economic order.

Political and economic policies which lead to the disintegration of the social fabric, and to death, cannot be passively supported by the Church's knowing or unknowing collaboration in such policies. Unfortunately, unhealthy economic policies have often been operating within the churches themselves. That justifications have sometimes been offered has prompted Ulrich Duchrow to suggest that the global economy is a confessional issue for the churches.[24] Duchrow challenges the churches *first* to see their own financial practices as a theological problem, and *second* to study the present economic ideologies and their effects both within their own countries and abroad.

The US Catholic Bishops in their pastoral on the economy, along with Duchrow, also insist that the internal life of the Church must not only reflect the message it is proclaiming, but that it must be exemplary in doing so.[25] The Bishops point out a number of areas in which there is a need for renewal in the economic life of the Church: wages and salaries; the rights of employees, especially the right to organize and bargain collectively; investments and properties; works of charity; and working for economic justice.[26] It is also important that the paradigm of "justice as participation" in the Bishops' pastoral on the economy becomes the basis of life in the Church so that it can become a credible voice for such participation on the economic level of society.

Another way in which the Christian churches might take on greater economic accountability of their own organization is by moving in the direction of making community economic development a part of their mission proper. The adoption of such development by the churches, proposed in a paper by the American Lutheran Church in 1987,[27] would simultaneously help poor communities and realign the churches' financial resources and management in a future direction that could point to possible developments in broader sectors of the economy. By "mission" the paper understands the work to which God is calling Christians in the world. By "community economic development" the paper means a process of managing human, financial and technical resources so that improved access to jobs, housing, food, education and health care for the peoples of a given community will result.

In seeking capital to support community development, the Church can look to five kinds of assets: its real estate, its own investment funds, the investments it manages for others, such as employee pensions, its operating capital, and the investment resources of its members. The paper also envisions activity by which low-income communities may create the institutional arrangements needed so that they may take care of themselves and not be chronically dependent on outside help. In addition, the paper acknowledges that churches alone can meet only a very small fraction of the capital needs of poor communities. It is only with a number of other organizations with investment capital, for example hospitals, labor unions, universities and community foundations, that the churches will gradually move closer to meeting the needs of poor communities and to contributing to the emergence of economic alternatives. In so doing, they can offer creative models of institutional investor behavior.

In addition to putting its own economic house in order, precisely by incorporating community economic development into its mission, the Church can also begin to become an agent of transition to more equitable systems in society by acting as a mediating structure which provides a critique of, and places pressure upon, existing forms of economic organization. Mediating structures can be understood as institutions standing between individuals in their private lives and the large institutions of public life.[28] Families, neighborhoods, churches and other voluntary organizations all provide examples. From the standpoint of Catholic social thought, the preservation of participatory community is one of the main reasons to utilize the resources of mediating structures whenever possible. To the extent that mediating structures are fostering participatory community, they can simultaneously begin to address what some have described as the phenomenon of the isolated individual's alienation, powerlessness and purposelessness.[29]

Habermas's analysis of capitalism has already indicated how alienation results when the problems of the economic system are projected onto the lifeworld. People are plagued by a feeling and experience of community having broken down. Alienation also brings on a sense of powerlessness: "What can one person possibly do?" In addition, there is also a loss of a sense of meaning about life, or purposelessness. Alienation, powerlessness and purposelessness all denote different aspects of the condition of the isolated individual. Perhaps more than any other institution, local churches as mediating structures can link the isolated individual with other persons, with social power, and with sources of meaning.

Traditionally, the Church has served people in their search for meaning. It, however, must also form individuals with religious imaginations that move them to church-world engagement.[30] Also, since the Second Vatican Council, as has already been noted, there has been a distinct emphasis on church as communion, an emphasis which includes substantial and tangible concern for mission.[31] The mediating structures paradigm underlines the centrality of social ministry in the Christian life, and indicates that the local church is essential to the effort of energizing the Church in times of social change.

In the past the Church very often dealt with social power by providing many essential services itself or through allied agencies. It can no longer, however, maintain a welfare state that parallels federal governments. Instead, the significance of local church communities will largely depend on their ability to relate to the broader society and the new institutions and circles in which people live their lives. Within the Catholic community, an emphasis on local churches as mediating structures is especially important if they are to pick up the challenges put forth in papal encyclicals, national bishops' conferences, or individual episcopal statements on matters of the economy. Within all Christian churches, however, when their local congregations and regions operate as mediating structures, individual members can begin to speak effectively to some of the great social issues.

When local churches in First World countries decide to act as mediating structures to contribute to the emergence of a new economic order, there are a number of specific strategies that they can take up.[32] The *first major strategy* is that local churches become public churches more visibly and more vocally. That is, they will begin to concentrate more forcefully on structural sin and the need to transform social, political, and economic systems and structures that oppress and destroy individuals and communities nationally and globally. In carrying out such a social justice mission, a public church will experience the need to shift priorities in the way it speaks in the public realm; that is, from enunciating moral positions in the first instance, to enunciating structural analyses of social problems as the prior and preparatory project.[33] A public church recognizes that if issues of morality are spoken prior to the need to address the structural issues of justice, it will be significantly less likely that the moral principles will be heard. A public church will greatly weaken its impact in the public realm if it applies specific Christian norms of personal morality to the formation of public policy.

Unfortunately, the Australian Catholic Bishops in their statement on the distribution of wealth in Australia[34] place more emphasis upon the moral issue of redistribution of wealth than upon the structural issue of redistribution of power. They give much more time to moral prescriptions than to the analysis of needed structural changes. It is only at the end of a chapter dealing with some of the structural causes of imbalances in the distribution of wealth that they acknowledge in passing the significance of restructuring power bases as a strategy for correcting imbalances in the distribution of wealth.[35] The bishops do not appear to recognize that the radical source of economic injustice today lies in the concentration of ownership of productive assets in the hands of a few, and that, as a result, great masses of people are excluded from the decision-making processes that determine the control and direction of the productive processes.[36]

Local churches acting in the public realm as mediating structures will also be able to act as grassroots catalysts for the continuing development of diocesan and national positions and statements on the economy. This possibility will eventuate, however, only to the extent that the composition process of official church statements has previously been broadened to include the same variety of peoples within a given church as that needed to give viable expression to church positions and policies. The value of engaging more people in such processes will not only help to raise their consciousness of justice issues, their presence will provide the official church with a consistent contact with the actual needs of the vast majority of people who are affected adversely by unjust economic policies. The churches' broadened base should also include representatives of the government and industry, in order to develop a forum where the Church could clearly voice its concerns and raise consciousness among those most directly involved in giving shape to the structures of society.

In fact, behind all of the efforts to broaden the base of involvement is a mutual consciousness-raising which not only prepares people to address the necessary issues, but helps to create bonds among them that otherwise might never have developed. For such consciousness-raising to become a lasting part of a church's vision, structures have to be set in place for ongoing education for justice from the primary level of education to the university and on both the parish and diocesan levels. Related · dimensions of consciousness-raising will also include the Church's advocacy for the poor through direct lobbying efforts and various organizations within or connected to the Church, as well as the churches' continuing provision of direct services to those in need.

A *second major strategy* in First World countries is the evangelization of the middle class;[37] that is, those who earn wages or salaries rather than deriving their income primarily from the ownership of productive resources. This includes most professional people and middle managers as well as manual laborers, clerical workers, factory workers, retail clerks, office workers, and those in various service occupations. What the Church would hope for through such evangelization would be the conversion of the middle class to a preferential option for the poor and a sense of solidarity with them. The expectation would be that from such an option the middle class would then seek a transformation of oppressive social, political and economic structures.

There are good reasons for churches in the First World targeting the middle class in their evangelization efforts for the sake of economic justice. In most First World countries, the middle class are usually better situated than the poor to gain access to the political processes. If the churches are to operate effectively as public churches, it is the middle classes that the bishops must convince when they address economic and political issues. A further reason is that the middle class have significant vested interests in the preservation of the economic system in which they have enjoyed more than a reasonable amount of success. They must be shown how they, along with the poor, are being affected by the profound changes taking place in society today, especially on the economic level: the centralization of the economy in fewer and fewer giant corporations, the spread of transnational corporations, and the growth of the information revolution. In this context most of the middle class, along with the poor, are experiencing an increasing economic insecurity and sense of powerlessness with regard to political power and control over significant areas of their work life.[38]

The ultimate purpose of the evangelization of the middle class on economic matters is not to call them to do things *for* the poor but to call them to stand in solidarity *with* them and together to seek the transformation of society. This ultimate purpose brings us to a *third major strategy* for the transformation of social, political and economic systems: namely, the establishment of base communities comprising the middle class and the poor.[39] They can provide a vehicle for the middle class, in company with the poor, to come to terms with their own oppression and powerlessness, as well as to struggle to understand and transform the systems that oppress them.

When the middle class and the poor work together in First World base communities, they gradually learn about the mutual needs they have for liberation from an invasive economic system. In such a process the more advantaged might also begin to understand how, either directly or indirectly, their benefts have been won partly at the cost of others' oppression. In addition, by confronting the specific structures that oppress the poor, the middle class will learn the necessity of respecting the poor as architects of their own future. Such collaboration can also enable churches in First World settings to shift their priorities from responding almost exclusively to the pastoral needs of their members to including the formation and preparation for sociopolitical projects aimed at structural change.[40]

Whenever the Church attempts to enter into solidarity with the poor, to identify itself primarily, significantly and credibly with them in order to provide a saving witness on the economy in society, it is inevitably engaging in prophetic action. Gradually as the Church becomes less entangled in the distorting effects of the economy on its own communities it can step back and take an honest look at the system. Only by identifying with the poor in its midst and becoming poor with them, through some type of major institutional alignment, will the Church come to understand and see even more clearly the system that oppresses. As long as the institutional church holds back from working for structural transformation of the economy, it cannot be unaffected by the "self-interest" of the system. Even more importantly, by identifying with the poor in such a commitment, the Church may also learn from them some "home truths." These include its own need for redemption, for dependence on God and one another, and for openness to wherever there is a call to an ultimately Gospel vision of human persons in community.

---

[1] The Church's growth in understanding itself as a public church can be seen partially as a result of coming to terms with a deeper understanding of its social mission. The 1971 Synod of Bishops emphasized that the Church's social mission involves both working for justice and transformation of the world, and also that such action is a constitutive part of the Church's mission (See *Justice in the World*, 6).

[2] What follows represents a summary from Joe Holland and Peter Henriot, *Social Analysis: Linking Faith and Justice* (Center of Concern, 1980), Chapter 1 "Social Analysis: A Tool of Pastoral Action," 3–12.

[3] For more on the two stages involved in theological reflection see Thomas H. Groome, *Christian Religious Education* (San Francisco: Harper & Row, 1980), esp. cc. 9 and 10.

[4] See Timothy J. Gorringe, *Capital and the Kingdom: Theological Ethics and Economic Order* (Orbis/SPCK, 1994), 34.

[5] See James Robertson, *Future Wealth* (London: Cassell, 1989), 10.

[6] Here I have relied significantly on Frank Stilwell's line of argumentation in, *Economic Inequality: Who Gets What in Australia?* (Pluto Press, 1993), 33–9.

[7] For an acknowledgment of these difficulties which, however, does not similarly recognize how the present organization of markets aggravates them, see Julian LeGrand, Carol Propper and Ray Robinson, *The Economics of Social Problems*, 5th edn (Macmillan, 1992). The basic flaw with this well-intentioned book is that it views all social problems through the prism of efficiency in the first instance. As a result, when it goes on to equity issues, they also are framed from the prior perspective of efficiency. In striking contrast, Paul Ormerod in *The Death of Economics* (London: Faber and Faber 1994) appeals to the problems discussed by LeGrand, Propper, and Robinson as more than a sufficient basis for making equality the prior concern, as well as for adopting a new paradigm of economic analysis.

[8] This statement is relevant even in reference to Robert J. Holton's otherwise constructive work *Economy and Society* (London and New York: Routledge, 1992). Holton's main contribution is to have analyzed the relative merits and weaknesses of the traditions of economic liberalism and political economy in the light of the tradition of economic sociology which provides a "culture-inclusive" theory of economy and society. The topics of equality and inequality, however, are neither listed in his subject index, nor treated significantly as distinct issues in his text.

[9] See Arthur Okun, *Equality and Efficiency: The Big Tradeoff* (Washington, DC: Brookings Institution, 1975). Also see "Economic Imperialism's Threat to the Non-Economic Sectors of Life," in c. 4, 69–71.

[10] See S. Rees, G. Rodley, and F. Stilwell (eds) *Beyond the Market: Alternatives to Economic Rationalism* (Sydney: Pluto Press, 1993).

[11] See "Economics in Crisis," in Ormerod's *The Death of Economics*, 3–21.

[12] See J. Phillip Wogaman, *Christians and the Great Economic Debate* (SCM Press, 1977), 139 and 155.

[13] Two recent excellent works which have exposed the tenuous nature of the claim to scientific credibility of both microeconomics and macroeconomics are Paul Krugman, *Peddling Prosperity* (W.W. Norton, 1994), and Paul Ormerod, *The Death of Economics*.

[14] See James Robertson, *The Sane Alternative*, (Minnesota: River Basin Publishing Co., 1979), 36; and Robertson, *Future Wealth*, 14.

[15] A number of recent works deal with the question of small communities whose economic organization has been both alternative and successful: R.D. Putnam, "The Prosperous Community," in *The American Prospect* (Spring, 1993), 36–42; V.B. Luther and M.N. Wall. *Studying Communities in Transition: A Model for Case Study Research and Analysis* (Lincoln, NE: Heartland Center for Leadership Development, 1991); and V.B. Luther. *Clues to Community Survival: A Curriculum for Leadership Development* (Lincoln, NE: Heartland Center for Leadership Development, 1994).

[16] It is generally recognized that the underpinnings for this approach can be found in John Maynard Keynes, *The General Theory of Employment, Interest, and Money* [1936] (London: Macmillan, rpt. 1973). For a fuller treatment of the three approaches to be discussed herein see Wogaman, *Economic Debate*, cc. 6–9.

[17] Wogaman, *Economic Debate*, 99.

[18] See William Coats, *God in Public* (Grand Rapids, Michigan: Eerdmans, 1974), 178.

[19] Herman E. Daly (ed), *Toward a Steady-State Economy* (San Francisco: W.H. Freeman, 1974), 152.

[20] Robert L. Stivers, *The Sustainable Society: Ethics and Economic Growth* (Philadelphia: Westminster Press, 1976).

[21] *The Sustainable Society*, 187, 197 and 201.

[22] The five strategies, developed more fully in Stilwell's *Economic Inequality*, c. 10 "Towards a more equitable society," 85–8, are well suited, and adaptable, to the priorities of a Christian vision.

[23] See Frank Stilwell, *The Accord and Beyond: The Political Economy of the Labour Government* (Sydney: Pluto Press, 1986), c. 9; Frank Stilwell, "New Life on the Left?" *Current Affairs Bulletin*, October 1992; S. Rees, G. Rodley, & Frank Stilwell (eds), *Beyond the Market: Alternatives to Economic Rationalism* (Sydney: Pluto Press, 1993).

[24] See Ulrich Duchrow, *Global Economy: A Confessional Issue for the Churches?* (Geneva, WCC 1987), 125, as cited by Timothy J. Gorringe, *Capital and the Kingdom: Theological Ethics and Economic Order* (SPCK/Orbis, 1994), 141.

[25] See *Economic Justice for All*, (NCCB, 1986), 347.

[26] See *Economic Justice for All*, 351–8.

[27] See the Office of Church in Society of the American Lutheran Church's "Community Economic Development as Mission" (Minneapolis, MN: Augsburg Publishing House, 1987).

[28] I have adapted the definition of "mediating structure" provided by Peter Berger and Richard Neuhaus in *To Empower People* (Washington DC: American Enterprise Institute, 1977), 2. The role of mediating structures in public policy is especially supported by two perspectives on social life found in Catholic Social Teaching: namely, subsidiarity and pluralism. Subsidiarity is the conviction that larger organizations should not usurp the role of smaller bodies as long as the smaller organization is capable and willing to perform its role. Pluralism implies that between the individual and the state a variety of groups should be allowed to function as mediating structures.

[29] See Kenneth R. Himes, "The Local Church as a Mediating Structure," in *Social Thought* (Winter 1985): 23–30, at 23–5.

[30] See Barbara Hargrove, "Churches as Mediating Structures," in *Theology Today* 39 (1983), 385–94, at 389.

[31] See Roger Haight, "Mission: The Symbol for Understanding the Church Today," *Theological Studies* 37, 620–49. Also see Gregory Baum, "Neo-conservative Critics of the Churches," in Gregory Baum (ed), *Neo-conservatism: Social and Religious Phenomenon* (New York: Seabury, 1981), 43–50, at 50.

[32] John A. Grindel's *Whither the U.S. Church?: Context, Gospel, Planning* (Maryknoll, NY: Orbis, 1991), 189–98 suggests specific strategies for local churches in the US. I have adapted some of them so that they might also be applicable to other First World settings.

[33] According to Vatican II's *Declaration on Religious Freedom* (*Dignitatis Humanae*, Vatican II, 1965), 7, the public order has a threefold content: an order of justice, in which the rights of all citizens are effectively safeguarded; an order of peace, which enables human beings to live together harmoniously in society; and an order of public morality understood to be the minimum expression of morality necessary for people to live together in society.

[34] See Australian Catholic Bishops' Conference, *Common Wealth for the Common Good*, (Collins Dove, 1992), c. 6: "Imbalances in the Distribution of Wealth and Some of Their Structural Causes," 83–123.

[35] See *Common Wealth for the Common Good*, 121–2.

[36] See Paul G. King, Kent Maynard, and David O. Woodyeard, *Risking Liberation: Middle Class Powerlessness and Social Heroism* (Atlanta: John Knox Press, 1988), 88, as cited in Grindel, *Whither the U.S. Church?*, 194.

[37] For a broader perspective on some of the problems that might be encountered in such a task see Robert G. Simons, *Is the Gospel Good News for Homo Economicus?* A paper given at the 1994 Conference of the Australian Catholic Theological Association.

[38] See King, et al., *Risking Liberation*, cc. 2 and 3.

[39] On base ecclesial communities in the Third World see Leonardo Boff, *Ecclesiogenesis: The Base Communities Reinvent the Church*, trans. Robert R. Barr (Maryknoll, NY: Orbis Books, 1986). For one possible adaptation of base communities in First World settings see J.B. Metz, *The Emergent Church: The Future of Christianity in a Post-Bourgeois World* (NY: Crossroad, 1981).

[40] Metz's argument for base community churches in First World settings is developed more fully in "The Church as a Community of Communicative Action," in c. 7, 140–2.

CHAPTER NINE

Respecting the Limits of Economic Organization

The words "economy" and "ecology". . . both deal with the *ecos* or "household." One is the *nomos* or "rule of the household"; the other is the *logos* or "structure of the household." Despite this close affinity in the meaning of their names, . . . for many years each developed without regard for the other. Only recently have ecologists begun to raise questions about an economy that has such serious consequences for the human household.[1]

THOMAS BERRY IN A PROVOCATIVE ESSAY ON THE EFFECTS OF economics on the life systems of the world contends that economics as a religious issue can be dealt with basically in two different ways. One is with a religious quest for justice and the well-being of a society in which the basic life necessities are available to all. Another is with an inquiry into the present economy's capacity to sustain itself, and its consequences for the life systems of the earth upon which a sustainable economy depends.[2] Berry is concerned that enough attention is still not directed toward the "deficit" involved in the closing down of basic life systems of the planet through the industrial abuse of air, soil, water and vegetation. Many governments and businesses have still not learned that the "earth deficit" is the ultimate "deficit." Its consequences are so absolute that it makes economic viability and improvement in life conditions for the poor less and less of a possibility.

This deficit in its extreme expression is . . . not simply the death of *a* living process but of *the* living process. . . . This is what makes our problems definitively different from those of any other generation. . . . For the first time we are determining the destinies of the earth in a comprehensive and irreversible manner.[3]

Economics and economists are only beginning to understand that an exhausted planet will inevitably entail an exhausted economy. The primary objective of economic science must become the integration of human well-being within the context of the well-being of the natural world. Regrettably, it is only more recently that Christian moral theologians have begun to deal with the abuse of the natural world in any systematically serious way.[4] Their reflections are helping us to understand the full extent of the task of structuring a human mode of life within the constraints of the earth's ecosystems. For Berry, since inherited concepts of the human cannot address these issues with the breadth required, there is a serious need to rethink revised concepts thoroughly.[5]

It was over twenty years ago that E.F. Schumacher drew our attention to the need to hold economics and the economic organization of societies more obviously accountable to human persons and communities.[6] He was aware that the conclusions and prescriptions of economics change as the underlying picture of humanity and its purpose on earth change. For him, the view of humanity was so basic and radical that any effective reorientation in an approach to economics would require remembering anew what human life is really about. What Schumacher called the "meta-economical" concerns of humankind and nature have to become more adequately incorporated and reflected in the ways economies use resources and distribute them. Indeed, he was convinced that there was a very serious need to rethink, and to be educated to, a new view of the human in order to make a healthier economic organization of society:

Economics is . . . taught without any awareness of the view of human nature that underlies present-day economic theory. . . . Economists are themselves unaware . . . that such a view is implicitly in their teaching and that nearly all their theories would have to change if that view changed.[7]

Today, as Berry and others have pointed out, it is also more obvious that any view of human nature cannot be conceived outside of the context of humanity's dependence on and emergence out of nature and its resources. Three areas of conventional economics, however, still do not reflect an adequate awareness of this fact: its peculiar understandings of growth, development, and measurements of economic welfare. They also show how most market economies fail to acknowledge and respect the environmental limitations within which human communities operate, as well as the need to begin thinking and doing economics in a way which always factors in the limitations which nature places upon economic organization.

The first major section of this chapter will provide a critique of these three areas. Then, in a second part it will suggest in broad outline an alternative economic approach to growth, development, and measures of whole economic progress/welfare. Next, after proposing understandings of growth, development and welfare, which reflect a more adequate approach to human persons and communities, it will look at the additional issue of the relationship between justice and a sustainable development. In a final section, the chapter will suggest some policies for sustainable economic development that move in the direction of community-based economies.

The Growth, Development, and Measurements of Economic Welfare

Conventional economic thinking assumes that *growth* is good and that more growth is better. Unfortunately, it confuses economic growth, one means to an end, with the end itself of increasing human welfare. Such conventional thinking also fails to respect the limits of a finite planet, and is likely to intensify inflation and unemployment, the very economic problems which it is meant to solve.[8] Its pattern of allocating resources, such as water and fossil fuels for industrial production, is so specific and limited, that those same resources are not adequately available for other areas of life. Ultimately, such specialized allocation makes long-term and broadly based growth unsustainable. Closely related to this problem are failures to distinguish between renewable and nonrenewable resources, to take future scarcity into account, to evaluate the costs of environmental degradation, and to make adjustments to ensure that such degradation does not take place.

All of the problems associated with an economics of growth recommend a serious consideration of a steady-state economy. Put most simply, a steady-state economy is one which has constant, not static, and renewable stocks of artifacts and people. In a steady-state economy, births replace deaths and production replaces depreciation. These "input" and "output" rates are to be equal at low levels, so that the life-expectancy of people and durability of artifacts will be high. Both "input" and "output" may be merged into the concept of "throughput." The economy maintains itself by this "throughput" in the same way that an organism maintains itself by its metabolic flow. In a steady-state economy, "throughput" must be within the regenerative and assimilative limits of the ecosystem. Thus, while a steady-state economy can develop qualitatively, it does not grow in a quantitative scale, just as the planet earth, of which the economy is a subsystem, develops without growing.[9]

In addition to the difficulties associated with a commitment to unlimited industrial growth, the corresponding model of *development*, which is part of such a commitment, has also been fraught with problems. While many citizens in industrialized countries experienced a general rise in living standards for a number of decades, they also experienced a great depletion of resources and environmental pollution. Many of these economies are now also vulnerable to the demands of the international market. Furthermore, both in highly industrialized and developing countries the costs of continuing to follow this model far outweigh the benefits. Industrialized countries have been plagued with the problem of recurring and persistent high levels of unemployment.

In much of the so-called developing world, however, this model has ravaged the resources and environments of many countries. All too often it has substituted colonialism with an economic and technological dependence on the industrialized countries, wiping out in the process many traditional economic activities and disrupting the economies of whole regions. Above all, this model of development has left hundreds of millions of people utterly destitute and with an unprecedented vulnerability to famine, starvation and war. In practice, the industrialized model's assumption of development's "trickle-down" effects for developing countries has not worked.

Acknowledging the hurtful effects brought on by growth economics, and the industrial model of development which prescribes growth criteria, it is not surprising that the *indicators* by which conventional economics measures progress are, at best, limited, and, at worst, misleading. Most important among such indicators is the Gross National Product or GNP.[10] GNP measures all of the goods and services which are provided through the market or through government expenditure. The measure is made by "aggregating" all monetary expenditure from information collated from various sources by the state. While the measure was originally used to approximate the cumulative demand for goods and services within a country, the purpose has been expanded as an indicator of overall economic growth. The expansion of the GNP's purpose is based on a number of assumptions: that any significant economic activity is monetary; that all GNP growth is good; that the environment can sustain indefinite growth; and that growth is the panacea for most, if not all, economic problems.

The first assumption, that any significant economic activity is monetary activity, is simply not true. For example, there are a variety of human contributions to the economy which are ignored by GNP measurements: the voluntary economy, the domestic or household economy, and informal work exchange.[11] Unfortunately, the informal economy, compared to the formal economy, does not receive the attention in economic theory or policy that its size and extensive practice warrant. The theory does not recognize that there is a dynamic relationship between the formal and informal economy, and that it is quite possible for one part to grow at the expense of the other.

Consider, for example, the great increase in the number of married women with jobs who previously did domestic work in the nonmonetary economy. GNP will rise both by the wages of the jobs they now do and by their expenditure on laborsaving devices, fast food, child care, and any other goods and services which they previously provided for themselves and their families free of charge. The implications of the GNP's rise in this instance for overall welfare, however, is more difficult to compute. There may even be loss of welfare, if maternal care and home cooking are replaced by day care and take-aways.

The second assumption, that *all* GNP growth is good, is also untrue. For example, if today's extra consumption undermines the natural resource base on which tomorrow's production depends, or contributes to health problems through environmental degradation, then its contribution to welfare is dubious. Increases in GNP take no account of the *social* costs of industrial production. If such costs are nonmonetary, they are simply ignored; if they are monetary they are actually added in to GNP and accounted as benefits. Thus it is quite possible that growth in GNP, far from representing greater human welfare, is actually an expression of greater social costs. The last two assumptions, that the environment can sustain indefinite growth and that growth is the panacea for most economic problems, are challenged by the acknowledgment of environmental and social costs and the need to subtract, rather than add, them to total GNP.

Indicators which add environmental and social costs to the total GNP are inclined to confuse costs and benefits, leave social and environmental factors out of account, and ignore the informal economy altogether as a source of work and wealth. The inadequate indicators betray an overwhelming misconception which the development of alternatives hopes to move beyond.[12] Such a development, in addition to subtracting environmental and social costs, will also have to include indicators of health and other basic human needs as measures of overall welfare. Whether indicators are adequate or inadequate, clarifying or distorting of a situation, they ultimately reflect a community's innermost core values and goals, its understanding of reality.

Paying attention to more of the factors that take away from, or contribute to, overall welfare would itself be an indication of the restoration of mental health to the process of measuring economic welfare.[13] Without the inclusion of such sane indices, and with an almost exclusive recourse to money-based indicators in the formal economy, economists frequently misread situations and prescribe remedies that actually cause them to deteriorate.

An Alternative Approach to Growth, Development, and Measurement of Economic Progress/Welfare

Any theory of economics which seeks to overcome the shortcomings which have been considered in the previous section must, in the first instance, provide a more satisfactory understanding of economic development. In 1975 the Dag Hammarskjold Foundation first coined the term "Another Development" and questioned the fundamental viability of the then prevailing models of economic development. "Another Development" is characterized by a number of principles.[14] First of all, it is *need-oriented*; that is, it begins with the satisfaction of the basic needs of the world's most dominated and exploited peoples. It also simultaneously aims at the humanization of all persons by the satisfaction of their needs for expression, creativity, equality, conviviality and responsibility for their own destiny. Secondly, "Another Development" is also *endogenous*; that is, it comes from the heart of each society as an expression of its values and vision for the future. There is no universal model for development and only a plurality of development patterns can be respectful of the peculiar traits of each society. Thirdly, "Another Development" stresses the importance of *self-reliance*. It recognizes that the primary and persistent source of economic strength in each society comes from the strength of its own members and the viability of its own resources.

While self-reliance needs to be exercised at national and international levels, it can acquire its full potential only if it is firmly grounded in the economic praxis of each community. Fourthly,

"Another Development" is also *ecologically sound*. Communities characterized by such development utilize the resources of the biosphere rationally and in full awareness of the potential of local ecosystems as well as the global and local outer limits imposed on the present and future generations.[15] Fifthly, "Another Development" is based on *structural transformations*. New economic structures are required for reasonable *inclusion in communal self-determination* and *participation in decision-making* by all those affected by it. Although the policies and technologies used to bring these changes about will differ from country to country, the principles are as valid for industrial countries as for those in the Third and Fourth Worlds.

The first and most basic principle of "Another Development" is that it strives to take the concept of *basic human needs* more seriously than does conventional economics. A pervasive shortcoming in the existing economic literature about basic human needs is that the fundamental difference between needs and wants is either not made explicit or is overlooked altogether.[16] This fundamental problem requires a radical reformulation of economic theory. In such a reformulation all human needs are part of a system where they are interrelated and interact.

If they are separated into the categories of having and of being, nine fundamental human needs emerge: permanence/subsistence, protection, affection, understanding, participation, leisure, creation, identity/meaning, and freedom. From such a classification it follows, for example, that housing, food and income are not needs, but satisfiers of the fundamental need of permanence or subsistence. Similarly, education is a satisfier of the need of understanding. Defense, cure and prevention are satisfiers of the need of protection and so on. Overall, fundamental human needs are finite, few and classifiable, as well as the same in all cultures and historical periods. What changes, both over time and through cultures, is the form of the means by which these needs are satisfied. Economic, social and political systems adopt different styles for the satisfaction of the same fundamental human needs. In every system they are satisfied, or not, through the generation, or nongeneration, of different types of satisfiers. In fact, one of the aspects that defines a specific culture is its choice of satisfiers. Cultural change is, among other things, the consequence of dropping traditional satisfiers and adopting new or different ones.

Any fundamental human need that is not satisfied reveals a specific form of *poverty*: poverty of subsistence is due to insufficient income, food or shelter; poverty of protection is due to violence or the arms trade; that of affection is due to authoritarianism, oppression, and exploitative relations with the natural environment; of understanding, to bad quality of education; of participation, to marginalization and discrimination; of identity, to imposition of alien values upon local and regional cultures. In contrast, the understanding of poverty in conventional economics is usually restricted to people who fall below a certain income threshold. When human needs are understood as a system, however, the focus shifts from an economistic description of poverty to a concern with a variety of poverties. A widened concept of poverty clarifies that "poverties" affect both "poor" and "rich" countries. "Another Development" fights all poverties and not just economic poverty. A dynamic process of change can be brought about at the local level both by designing solutions for the problems of poverty, and by stimulating the elements of wealth corresponding to them.

A second principle which characterizes "Another Development" is that as *endogenous* the growth and development of a community is always guided and directed by *its* values and peculiar vision for the future. As a result of this characteristic there is a strategic assumption that the size of any business system can never grow to the point where people no longer have the opportunity to act and interact as creative subjects, or are reduced to becoming efficient objects for an oversized system. Inasmuch as "Another Development" is oriented toward the satisfaction of human needs, it requires a drastic revision of the concept of efficiency. The efficiency of a system should not be measured only in terms of its economic productivity, but also, and more importantly, in terms of its ability to contribute to the satisfaction of the fundamental human needs of those who are, directly or indirectly, affected by that system.

Self-reliance, a third principle of "Another Development," con-stitutes one of its most powerful distinguishing traits. Self-reliance does *not*, in the first instance, mean autonomy or self-sufficiency. Rather, it suggests that communities regenerate or revitalize themselves through their own efforts, capabilities and resources. Practically it means that what can be produced or solved at local levels should be produced or solved there. The same principle holds for regional and national levels. As opposed to the traditional paradigm, where growth goals are often set by transnational corporations, self-reliant development presupposes and demands a more complete and harmonious coordination, one which involves greater cooperation and mutuality, among the various levels of the economy's operation.

"Another Development" recognizes and promotes greater acknowledgment of the interdependence among local, national and international economic developments.[17] For example, actions intended to improve economic performance on the national and international level can have quite a negative impact on the local level. Ultimately, actions at one level of economic activity have to be taken account of at all levels of economic activity. Furthermore, actions intended to improve economic performance on one level require at least one additional action on another level. So, if there is to be an improvement on the level of the local economy, there will have to be at least one additional adjustment on the national and/or international levels of economic management. The dynamics of each level are determined by different rhythms. If changes for the better are to endure on either level, the overall economic rhythms of each level must be adjusted to work in harmony with each other. The experiences of people and groups at each of the levels is most helpful in determining how such "harmonizing" can be brought about.

The persistent inability of conventional economics to incorporate important aspects of the informal economy is a symptom of the problem of inadequate coordination between the local and national/international levels. Economists have excluded the informal sector from conventional economic analysis because they have not been able to agree on how to assign economic value on a national and international level to work carried on outside the formal market or monetary system. Their lack of agreement betrays having become conditioned by economic theories which, instead of assigning value to important and significant nurturing and domestic activities, address only matters which can be measured according to the rules of market value, and then, almost exclusively, at the national and international levels.

Very closely related to "Another Development's" principle of self-reliance is its concern with the satisfaction of human needs of both present and future generations. This concern leads "Another Development" to foster an *ecologically sound concept of development*, one which can ensure the availability of basic resources in the long run. One strategy for achieving this end is the construction of indicators which discriminate between what is positive and what is negative for a process of truly humanized development. For the image which we will have of development will be the image that is provided by its indicators. A sampling of indicators that are needed in order to measure a more adequate understanding of economic progress and welfare might include: resource indicators and resource accounting; an adapted GNP with the social and environmental costs deducted from it; health indicators; social indicators; and finally, ways of taking the informal economy into economic account, so that its contribution to the national economy can be fully appreciated and valued.

A fifth and final principle of "Another Development" asserts that there is a need for the *transformation of economic structures*. Without such a radical change it is unreasonable to expect a greater degree of inclusion in communal self-determination and participation in decision-making. For the needed changes in economic structures to come about, however, a number of changes will also be necessary both in political culture and in the structures of political decision-making.[18] The political philosophy of self-interest, and the interest-group politics of the industrial democracies, are, at present, obstacles to significant change. Structural transformations, both economic and political, then, are interrelated prerequisites for the satisfactory realization of the previous four principles. Such changes are especially necessary for greater coordination among the local, national and international levels of economic management. Without that coordination the self-reliance which is central to

"Another Development" will continue to be systemically handicapped. In addition, it must be said that *all* five principles of "Another Development" are organically linked. No one of them is capable of bringing about the desired outcome. For development itself has to begin to be seen more consistently as a whole, as an integral, cultural process, as the development of every man and woman and of whole men and women.

A variety of different types of *indicators* is needed to measure a type of development which is more realistically whole. One class, resource indicators, includes all natural and human resources, as well as the capital built up by past labor, on which future economic activity depends. At present, a large proportion of the outcome of the production process expressed each year in GNP does not represent any benefit to the quality of life and of the environment. Indeed, it is an actual cost of production and consumption. Unfortunately, the market-centeredness of economic thinking has resulted in a general blindness to environmental and social costs. An adjusted GNP, which subtracts such costs, is sorely needed. During the initial stages of such an adjustment, however, it is unrealistic to expect qualitative and political indicators to have as high a level of precision as do the quantitative indicators which have been in use for a much longer period of time. In the face of this problem, however, it is important to remember that the shift to an Adjusted National Product (ANP) index is a precondition of long-term economic progress.[19]

However much of an improvement an ANP index would be on the current GNP measure, it still would not say anything about how production is distributed in society. An ANP would not tell us whether or not human needs were being satisfied, or whether social goals were being achieved. Progress in these areas needs to be measured directly by indicators that are concerned with how the GNP is used, and with its social results. One way to look at how human needs are being satisfied is through a variety of health indicators. Indeed, the latter can begin to provide a good preliminary indication of needs-satisfaction.[20]

There are certain key health status indicators that reflect broad social and environmental conditions, and that are therefore suitable as indicators of economic progress. The *infant mortality* rate reflects infant deaths within one year of birth, and represents a composite of a number of factors.[21] *Life expectancy rates*, which reflect the personal, social and environmental influences that ultimately cause death, are similarly composite indicators. While infant mortality and life expectancy are useful indicators, there is also a need to reflect the extent to which a population is disabled, either physically or mentally. One attempt to do so has been the development of the concept of *quality-adjusted life expectancy*.[22] In addition to requiring detailed mortality data, calculation of this indicator requires detailed knowledge of minor and major disability rates for a country as a whole, as well as for geographic and social sub-units.

In view of the importance of the data which health expectancy indicators aim at providing, and also acknowledging the difficulty of collecting such data, it may be preferable to develop a composite indicator such as *coherence*.[23] Coherence has three major components. The first, comprehensibility, represents the extent to which individuals find intellectual sense in their lives. The second, manageability, refers to the extent to which people perceive that they have resources at their disposal in order to cope with the challenges which life presents to them. The third, meaningfulness, signifies the extent to which a person's life makes sense emotionally. There is an awareness that people care, and that at least some of life's problems and demands are worth investing energy in. The concept of coherence is concerned with factors that contribute to health, rather than with those that lead to illness.

Some combination of the four health indicators—infant mortality, life expectancy, quality-adjusted life expectancy, and coherence—is both appropriate and feasible for the vast majority of countries. Their use throws light on aspects of economic and social progress that are quite invisible to GNP and other monetary indicators. Their use could also become a standard part of economic assessment and feedback for policy-making at the local, national and international levels. It must be recognized, however, that health indicators cannot by themselves give a full picture of social trends and conditions; for this purpose, social indicators are also required. The latter attempt to develop measures of individuals' well-being across a broad range of social concerns, such as people's relationships, their sense of security, and the productiveness of their activities. While these are difficult to quantify, they are clearly as important for human well-being as more obviously measurable aspects. Social indicators are also concerned with devising measures of crucial social variables which would be part of a model of social change, similar to, but broader in scope than, the conventional economic models.

Social indicators measure individual well-being from a number of aspects. One aspect, *being*, is concerned with the physical and mental state of an individual. It addresses health and knowledge as dimensions of well-being, rather than as part of the functioning of the health-care and educational systems. *Doing*, another aspect, is concerned with the nature of people's activities in all spheres— leisure, paid employment, and household tasks. A further aspect, *having*, is concerned with access to the material conditions necessary to satisfy basic needs. *Relating*, yet another aspect, is about the nature of people's relationships to each other, both within households and among friends, as well as on the level of functioning within the wider social and political system. Finally, *surviving* is concerned with threats to the security of individuals from other individuals, groups, or the state. Attention to specific aspects of well-being provides a basis upon which to evaluate human activities in relation to a number of criteria: the use of time; the quality of activities; the social aspects of activities; the productiveness of activities; and access to activities. Data gathered from the application of such criteria provide far more useful data than bald statistics of employment and unemployment, as well as time spent in leisure activities.

The consideration of human activity patterns as social indicators brings us to the need for a whole economy perspective which would not allow any significant economic activity to be excluded from observation and measure. One way of developing such a perspective is to classify economic activity into an adequate number of commercial and social sectors, moving from the most commercial to the most social: big business, public sector activity, small businesses, collectives and cooperatives, community enterprises, voluntary activity, barter and skills exchange, mutual aid, and household activity.[24]

Formal economic activity includes all of those sectors which operate predominantly and in almost all instances out of commercial motivations. Informal economic activity includes all of those sectors which operate predominantly and in almost all situations out of a social rationale. *Mixed* economic activities involve some combination of both commercial and social motivations. While current measures do not exclude all informal economic activity, many times the data are gathered and reported in ways that bury it and make it impossible to use for further study. For example, some work has already been done to convert informal activity like housework into dollar values and then add them to the GNP.[25] While this work enhances the visibility of neglected economic activities, it is an inadequate measure for evaluating activity in the informal sectors.

If informal activity is measured only by estimated dollar value of final output, the money value will always underestimate the true output and level of activity in relation to formal economic activity. There is a need, therefore, to look for a better indicator of levels of activity in the informal sectors. One such indicator is "time-activity." It is arrived at by multiplying the number of participants by the hours spent in economic activity. It is effectively an extension of current-employment and hours-of-work indicators into the informal sectors. A "time-activity" measure will not represent a dollar value measure of a nation's output, but will show the distribution of human effort among the different formal and informal sectors.

A Sustainable Development that is also Just

Although health and social indicators are more adequate measures of whole economic welfare than standard GNP measures, they still do not go far enough in addressing whether or not the common good is being fostered and nurtured locally, nationally and internationally. Even though they engage a qualitative perspective which strives to give a reading on overall personal welfare and social goods, they are still more strongly individualist than communal in their orientation. At best, they will be able to provide an indirect, and sometimes too vague, measure of the values and visions upon which community and economic health are ultimately based. Work still needs to be done in consolidating and integrating health and social indicators so that they can also become more ostensibly component measures of the overall common good. Measures of sustainable economic development and whole economic welfare, at some point, have to incorporate a way of evaluating whether or not strategies for sustainability and holistic welfare are also just.[26] A focus on justice as the most basic way in which to determine whether or not the common good is being respected provides an initial way of bringing about the desired enhancement of health and social indicators.

Drew Christiansen proposes that a perspective combining sustainability and justice issues also provides the basis for a global agenda. Such an agenda reflects a growing agreement among world leaders about concerns which address environmental quality, development and international justice: reducing atmospheric pollution as the major burden of already industrialized nations; reshaping international economic policies so that they do not result in deforestation and the depletion of other resources in developing countries; and addressing environmental degradation caused by large numbers of poor people, by assisting them to develop more environmentally sensitive ways of meeting their needs.

The ideal of just and sustainable development received one of its most important formulations in the 1986 Report of the World Commission on Environment and Development, *Our Common Future*.[27] While adjustments to the way economies are structured are needed in domestic political institutions, the Commission also recommended that the chief institutional challenge of the 1990s is improved institutional coordination among nations.[28] Coordination of international policies is necessary because otherwise rich and poor nations are likely to differ about the value of economic growth and environmental conservation. Paradoxically, the Commission also pointed out that further controlled economic growth will be necessary to reduce pressures on the environment.[29] At the same time, there will be a need to preserve and restore stocks of environmental resources, to reduce population growth, to develop resource-conserving technologies through recycling and energy efficiency, and to develop new political decision-making processes adequately informed on pertinent environmental concerns.[30] Eventually, environmental policies will have to become a more integrated component in foreign policy agenda.

Some proponents of change advocate coercive policies while others argue for economic incentives in order to restructure growth.[31] Combining both strategies, the Commission recommended a series of measures from reorienting multilateral and bilateral aid to providing new sources of revenue and automatic financing. These include international taxes on the commons, such as ocean fisheries and seabed mining, and taxes on international trade.[32] It is also becoming clearer that within the present international system, national leaders, hopefully in conversation with ethicists, will have to take the initiative on their national agendas in addressing global needs.[33]

Proponents of a just and sustainable development have also found support in John Paul II's 1988 encyclical *Sollicitudo Rei Socialis* (On Social Concern). It insists that respect for nature, the conservation of nonrenewable resources and restriction of pollution are all prerequisities for any adequate notion of development that incorporates a concern for justice. The encyclical also affirms two strong ecological principles: the independent moral status of nonhuman creatures; and the need to think and act in terms of whole environments and ecological systems.[34] The pope's thinking is concurrent with significant developments among theologians reflecting on the resources for environmental theology in the Christian tradition.[35]

The dialogue between Christian theology and environmentalists continues to develop even more challenging perspectives on the value and ethical status of nature. One such example is Deep Ecology, a philosophy and a social program, which is also a spirituality rooted in a vision of the unity of humans, plants, animals and the earth. It is based on an intuition that everything in the biosphere has an equal right to live and to reach self-realization. The movement affirms the intrinsic value of nonhuman life, preservation of ecological and cultural diversity, an economic standard of "vital needs," and a measure of "life quality" rather than "standard of living" for the evaluation of development.[36] For adherents of Deep Ecology, the mainline environmental movement, with its emphasis on sustainable development and conservation, is mainly for people. In contrast, Deep Ecology values nonhuman life "independently of human life" and holds to a policy of noninterference with continuing evolution for animals and for landscapes with their special organisms. Thus, "the satisfaction of nonhuman needs and the improvement of life quality for any nonhuman kind of being" are central to the Deep Ecology platform.[37]

Deep Ecology's emphasis on the value of nonhuman life and ecological systems can be seen to enhance respect for human as well as nonhuman life-forms in the face of a narrow or shortsighted economic approach to human and natural resources. Also, the vital needs standard of Deep Ecology gives a signal to the affluent that environmental reform in the long run will require cutbacks in consumption on their part. While basic needs are a matter of justice to other human beings, an economy of vital needs reminds people of the need for the preservation of a viable ecosystem. Lastly, the standard of life quality, even more than that of vital needs, suggests that there are humanly very satisfying patterns of life which do not entail intensive consumption or high technology.

By weighing things such as environmental quality, leisure, education, and so on, more heavily than material growth, it may be possible for diverse cultures to develop in a way that is more respectful of their histories and values locally, regionally and nationally.[38] Thus Christiansen concludes that while biocentricity may be unsatisfactory as an *ultimate* standard of value, the ethical principles articulated by the Deep Ecology movement point to plausible standards for sustainable development with which Christian ethical considerations on justice and development could be most sympathetic.[39] In his opinion, however, humanity's need to look more searchingly at itself as it is embedded in nature will be assisted better by the theocentric tradition in Christian theology. The latter's insistence on human responsibility to the God of all being seems better able, to him, to generate a properly ordered sense of moral responsibility than the natural piety of Deep Ecology with its emphasis on the undisturbed evolution of the natural world.[40]

Sustainable and Community-Based Economies[41]

It is quite remarkable that more people do not yet perceive that conventional versions of economic progress destroy traditional communities and then replace them with "modern" ones which better fit into conventional economic organization. Indeed, emerging market societies have made it virtually impossible for the continuing existence and experience of community at a variety of levels. Since the concerns of market economies are overwhelmingly national and transnational, they tend to be primarily concerned with the national and international level of community experience. Local community experiences and the support which they offer are simply not addressed with the seriousness which they deserve.

One of the long-term goals of adjusting the operation of market economies, then, needs to be the provision of a *context* in which such local community experiences can grow strong again. With greater sensitivity to the constraints which limited natural resources place upon economic organization, as well as with a greater commitment to enhancing and strengthening community cohesiveness, a more effective approach for enhancing the strength of economic activity and organization at local levels is possible. Third World community development provides an example of such an approach. The village or tribe is taken as a given unit rather than as an aggregate of individuals. The community is made productive in doing what it wants to do *as a community*, and will not give up its relative self-sufficiency. This form of progress is more difficult to introduce into countries where the individualism of economic theory has already expressed itself extensively in corporate life. Nonetheless, it would be possible gradually to place more emphasis, by critical policy initiatives, on the progress of the whole community, rather than upon the productivity of individuals.

Out of the growing interaction between economics and ecology, pressure continues to mount for economic policies that not only include the ecological and social costs, but also gradually shift the primary and increasingly exclusive emphasis of economic management away from the transnational level to a more proportionate and corresponding expression on the local level. A number of policies could help to ensure a better balance and a heightened experience of harmony among the local, national and transnational levels of economic activity.

One proposal previously mentioned as a way to work for a steady-state economy is a more realistic pricing system which includes all social and environmental costs in the price of goods. The social and environmental costs must also include foreseeable costs to future generations. Interestingly, such a pricing system, by drastically working for lessened social, ecological and future costs, would not only reduce the destruction of the environment, but in fact would also require a much higher degree of active involvement in economic management at local and community levels.

Another proposal, that countries voluntarily place limits on a variety of national production sectors, also incorporates the double objective of sustainability and enhanced local management. Such a policy both addresses the problems created by the depletion of nonrenewable resources, and presupposes that the most honest and realistic accounting of how much of a nonrenewable resource might be used is carried out best by the communities from which those resources are taken. So, for example, nations could decide what portion of discovered reserves of minerals could be mined each year. The right to mine that amount could then be auctioned. In those circumstances where no new reserves were discovered, the amount extracted would decline slightly each year. When new reserves were found, or when technology and a higher price made lower grades profitable to mine, the amount allowed would rise. Such a policy could help to avert future crises caused by abrupt depletion of a major resource.

Another policy proposal, geared more toward redressing some of the social costs of economic organization, but which also works for greater local accountability, might include providing a better set of educational opportunities for the young in which to develop the skills and motivation for more regionalised and participatory economies. One of the most devastating effects of the breakdown of adult community in many market societies is that parents and teachers have been left feeling alone and largely impotent in their educational and formative efforts to equip the younger generations to take on a variety of responsibilities for the life of the community. They have not been able to come together in enhancing each other's efforts with the effectiveness that can often be experienced in more cohesive communities. Thus an economic system geared to the strengthening of community will have as one of its main policies the objective of working for the emergence of a more community-based set of educational offerings in which young people will want to learn. Such opportunities will have the advantage of going beyond the very limited objectives whereby many are simply trained to fit into slots in a broader international economic superstructure.

Between local community support and national community business patterns there are intermediate-level economic and political communities. The decentralization of political power which they illustrate provides a source of alternative political and economic organization in a healthy direction. Yet effective local political power has to be matched by effective local economic management. Thus if the local community is to be strengthened by the decentralization of political power, then the economy must also be decentralized. For example, if city businesses are locally owned and managed, they will have a far greater concern for the city and its future than if they are branches of a national corporation that will move them whenever it is profitable to do so. In general, they will contribute to the stability of the community and encourage a sense of belonging on the part of others. If public policy were to encourage community and economic regionalism as policy goals, the proposals made above could be directed to implementing them. In the final and concluding chapter the thesis of this entire book will be seen to have culminated in an argument in favor of community-sensitive local economic organization as a necessary complement to the global economy.

[1] John B. Cobb Jr., *Sustainability: Economics, Ecology & Justice* (Maryknoll, NY: Orbis, 1992), 56.

[2] See *Thomas Berry and the New Cosmology*, edited by Anne Lonergan and Caroline Richards (Mystic, Connecticut: Twenty-Third Publications, 1987), 5–6.

[3] *New Cosmology*, 7.

[4] See Charles M. Murphy, *At Home on Earth: Foundations for a Catholic Ethic of the Environment* (NY: Crossroad, 1989), esp. c. 2, "Home or Hotel: An Ethic for the Earth."

[5] See *New Cosmology*, 19.

[6] See E.F. Schumacher, *Small is Beautiful: A Study of Economics as if People Mattered* [1973] (London: Vintage, rpt. 1993).

[7] *Small is Beautiful*, 73.

[8] See Edward Barbier, *The potential for reviving economic growth: the political economy of resource misallocation* (a paper delivered at the 1984 conference of The Other Economic Summit (TOES), cited in *The Living Economy: A New Economics in the Making*, edited by Paul Ekins [1986] (London & New York: Routledge, rpt. 1990), 10–12. TOES is an independent, international initiative seeking to develop and promote a New Economics, based on personal development and social justice, the satisfaction of the whole range of human needs, a sustainable use of resources, and conservation of the environment. In 1984 and 1985 TOES organized two conferences focused on the London and Bonn Economic Summits respectively.

[9] See Herman Daly, *The steady-state economy: alternative to growth-mania* (a paper given at the 1984 Conference of TOES) cited in *The Living Economy*, 13–14.

[10] I have adapted John Lintott's analysis of GNP as an indicator, along with his list of questions, as the critical basis of my reflections here. See his *National accounting and beyond*, and *Measuring health and human activities* (with Roy Carr-Hill) in *The Living Economy*, 32–8.

[11] See Paul Sparrow, *Unemployment and unvalued work: true costs and benefits* (a paper given at the 1984 TOES Conference), cited in *The Living Economy*, 34.

[12] Indicators which deduct environmental damage and depletion of the earth's natural capital include the Measure of Economic Welfare proposed by William Nordhaus and James Tobin, 1971; Japan's Net National Welfare (Japan Economic Council, 1973); and the Index of Sustainable Economic Welfare proposed by Herman Daly and John B. Cobb in *For the Common Good*, 1989.

[13] See Hazel Henderson, *The indicators crisis: towards post-economic policy tools for*

post-industrial societies (a paper given at the 1984 TOES Conference), cited in *The Living Economy*, 37.

[14] See Dag Hammarskjold Foundation, *Another Development: Approaches and Strategies* (Dag Hammarskjold Foundation, Uppsala, Sweden, 1977), cited in *The Living Economy*, 44.

[15] For an interesting contrast in the estimate of the limitations of natural resources see D. H. Meadows, D. L. Meadows, Jorgen Randers, and William W. Behrens III, *The Limits to Growth: A Report for the Club of Rome's Project on the Predicament of Mankind* (London: Earth Island Limited, 1972); and D. H. Meadows, D. L. Meadows, and Jorgen Randers, *Beyond the Limits: Confronting Global Collapse, Envisioning a Sustainable Future* (Post Mills, VT: Chelsea Green Pub., 1992). The latter report revised some of the former report's severely dire estimates, and, in general, holds out much more hope for long-term prospects of available resources.

[16] See "The Reduction of Needs to Wants," in c. 2, 25–8.

[17] See Manfred Max Neef, *Human-Scale Economics: The Challenges Ahead* (a paper presented at the 1984 conference of TOES), cited in *The Living Economy*, 45–54.

[18] As an example of the changes in the thought processes needed to ground the structural changes, see Robert Ornstein and Paul Ehrlich, *New World, New Mind: Moving toward Conscious Evolution* (New York: Doubleday, 1989).

[19] See Christian Leipert, *Economic growth and its social costs: on the need for an adjusted indicator of net consumption and for a comprehensive statement of "defensive expenditure"—expenditure undertaken to protect society and the environment against damage and other forms of deterioration induced by economic activities* (a paper presented at the 1984 conference of TOES), cited in *The Living Economy*, 139–40.

[20] See Trevor Hancock, *Health-Based Indicators of Economic Progress* (a paper presented at the 1984 conference of TOES), cited in *The Living Economy*, 140–5.

[21] See K. Newland, *Infant Mortality and the Health of Societies*, Worldwatch Institute, Washington, DC, 1981, cited in *The Living Economy*, 141.

[22] See R. Wilkins, and O. Adams, *Healthfulness of Life*, (Montreal: Institute for Research on Public Policy, 1983).

[23] See A. Antonovsky, "The sense of coherence as a determinant of health" in *Advances*, 1(3), 1984, 36–50, cited in *The Living Economy*, 143–5.

[24] The nine sectors are explained more fully by David Ross in *Making the informal economy visible* (a paper presented at the 1984 TOES conference), cited in *The Living Economy*, 155–65; also see the references to Ross on 154–5.

[25] See Ross, *Making the informal economy visible*, cited in *The Living Economy*, 161.

[26] Drew Christiansen's identification of pertinent issues in "Ecology, Justice, and Development," in *Theological Studies*, March 1990 vol. 51, 64–81 provides a very helpful basis for further consideration.

[27] *Our Common Future* (Oxford: Oxford University Press, 1987).

[28] Respectively, see Lester Brown and Edward C. Wolf, "Charting a Sustainable Course," in *State of the World* 1987 (Washington, DC: Worldwatch Institute, 1987), esp. 209–13; and *Our Common Future*, 317. Also see William C. Clark, "Managing Planet Earth," *Scientific American* 261:3 (September 1989), 54.

[29] See *Our Common Future*, 49–52.

[30] See William D. Ruckleshaus, "Toward a Sustainable World," *Scientific American* 261:3 (September 1989) 166–74, esp. 168–9.

[31] Respectively, see Richard O. Brooks, "Coercion to Environmental Virtue: Can and Should the Law Mandate Environmentally Sensitive Lifestyles?" *American Journal of Jurisprudence* 31 (1986), 21–64; and Ruckleshaus, "Sustainable World," 170–1.

[32] *Our Common Future*, 340–2.

[33] See D. Goulet, "Development Ethics and Ecological Wisdom," in *Ethics of Environment and Development*, Goulet 11, 12, as cited in *Ecology, Justice and Development*, 81.

[34] See *Sollicitudo Rei Socialis*, 34.

[35] For example, H. Paul Santmire, *The Travail of Nature: The Ambiguous Ecological Promise of Christian Theology* (Philadelphia: Fortress, 1985), provides a critical survey of the history of Western theology from the perspective of the status of nature.

[36] See Bill Davis and George Sessions, *Deep Ecology: Living as If Nature Mattered* (Salt Lake City: Gibbs Smith, 1985), 64–7.

[37] See Arne Naess, "Sustained Development and Deep Ecology," in *Ethics of Environment and Development: Global Challenge, International Response* (London: Pinter, 1990), 6, as cited in *Ecology, Justice, and Development*, 77.

[38] See Naess, "Sustained Development," 11, cited in *Ecology, Justice, and Development*, 79.

[39] See *Ecology, Justice, and Development*, 79.

[40] Christiansen appeals to James M. Gustafson, *Ethics from a Theocentric Perspective 1: Theology and Ethics* (Chicago: University of Chicago Press, 1981), c.6, "Man in Relation to God and World," and 2: *Ethics and Theology* (1984) c. 7, "Population and Nutrition," esp. 218–50.

[41] See J. B. Cobb, *Sustainability: Economics, Ecology & Justice*, 72–81. I have reworked some of Cobb's policy suggestions to fit in better with my line of argumentation, which addresses the enhancement of local economic management along with environmental concerns for sustainability.

Toward Living Local Economies: A Struggle to Redress an Imbalance

Greater Opportunities for Local Responsibility in the World Market[1]

THE MOVE TOWARD LIVING ECONOMIES, AMONG A VARIETY of tasks, involves a struggle to regain some of the local control for economies that has been lost as the global economy has grown and become more influential worldwide. While there are many positions in the struggle, two from the last ten years continue to be rather prominent. One, which might be called the ecocapitalist position, advocates a highly centralized access to capital and labor. While ecocapitalists aim to reconstruct and diversify goods and services in order to meet the demands for a cleaner and healthier environment, they always do so within the design, priorities and constraints of the global economy. They also tend to collaborate with proponents of self-help welfare. Together they work to restructure the welfare state by opting both to downscale existing social services and to reorganize possible future ones so that they can be set up and dismantled more easily.

A second position, which is headed by ecodecentralists, works to revitalize the self-reliance of local communities by inverting global economic superstructures. The inversion of market relations has to take place on two levels: first, by reducing the present excessively extended range of international exchange relations; and second, by stimulating unpaid work and a variety of nonmonetary economic activities. The argumentation throughout this book is clearly more compatible, both theologically and economically, with the approach of the ecodecentralists. Ultimately, the contemporary struggle between the ecocapitalists and the ecodecentralists moves us to take another look at the historical conflict about who controls the means of production.

The single most important argument used against the ecodecentralists is that the realization of their vision would result in the economic marginalization of their countries. From the perspective of the ecodecentralists, however, it is very important to scale down export–import relations for two reasons. First, there is a need to decrease the vulnerability of even rich societies to crises and collapses abroad. Second, there is a related need to provide a whole new range of opportunities, not tied in as strongly to the global economy as most present opportunities are, in order to be able to shape domestic development with greater sensitivity and responsiveness to local natural and personnel resources. These needs simply cannot be realized if all of the economic processes, products and services of given countries are absorbed into a transnational market where the factors of production can be freely moved around. Rather, their realization will depend upon local markets with greater degrees of *self-reliance*,[2] along with political guidelines which ensure that economic activity is respectful of both the local and international common good.

The present state of dependence of Third World countries on those in the First World provides not only an illustration in favor of the argumentation presented thus far, but a further reason for gaining freedom from the world market. For countries in the South such freedom will mean the ordering of fewer goods and the borrowing of less money from the North. It will also presuppose the South's pulling back on exporting cheap natural resources to the North, as well as the North's restructuring loan repayments to the advantage of the debtor nations. Interestingly, the hoped-for economic freedom of countries in the South has much in common with the grassroots aspirations of proponents of more self-reliant local economies in the North. Both have known only too well the hurtful effects which the global economy can have on local circumstances. Both, therefore, share a very similar objective to regain a more viable degree of economic self-direction at the local level. If such objectives are ever to be realized, there will have to be a shift from the present centralizing tendencies of the global economy to attitudes and strategies which foster many self-reliant, loosely interlinked economies.

Closely related to the problem of gaining freedom from the international market is the need *not* to become overwhelmed by the steadily increasing power of multinational or transnational corporations (TNCs) in that market.[3] That increase becomes visible especially in two trends. One, is the formation of oligopolies, where whole industrial sectors are dominated worldwide by a handful of firms. A second, is the formation of conglomerates, where a single TNC has interests in a wide variety of unrelated activities. These two trends have enormously enhanced TNC power in relation to national governments, the labor force and consumers.

Attempts to restore the balance between TNCs and the people and countries that are affected by them have taken many forms. Some of the most frequent have included: publicity and education; consumer boycotts and campaigns; shareholder actions; international union organization; and international codes of conduct. While all of these are important in the immediate struggles against the abuses of corporate power, they do not strike at the threefold source of TNC power in general: namely, goods and services that consumers will buy; employment opportunities and investment on which people and nations are dependent; and potentially unlimited returns on investment.

The only way in which continuing progress on the wider issues of democracy, accountability and social responsibility can be made is by tackling these sources of power directly. So, for example, individual consumer campaigns need to be broadened into a generalized awareness of TNC products across the board and a determination to buy local products where possible, in order to contribute to the regeneration of the local economy. Similarly, countries need to reduce their dependency on TNCs by fostering their own self-reliance, reducing their dependency on the international market and therefore on TNC technology and productivity. As far as investment is concerned, investors need to become aware of the human, social and environmental consequences of their investments. People and politicians also need to start questioning whether it is still appropriate that the return on capital investment is potentially unlimited.

Since shareholders incur limited risk when they invest, it is not unreasonable that such limited risk should yield only a limited return. Hence the International Cooperative Alliance made representations to the UN Commission on TNC recommending a limited return on investment.[4] At its deepest level the TNC debate is about who should benefit primarily from these giant enterprises and at what social costs: namely, the enterprises themselves, or their shareholders, or the communities on which they depend for natural and human resources. The possible transformation of TNCs into cooperatives offers important insights into that debate. It is an idea whose realization, however, would require that economic and political power be coordinated at all levels. In addition, the transformation of TNCs will also require changing social attitudes and public pressure that will demand that social considerations be put on a par with financial ones.

Cooperatives: An Opportunity for Economic Activity to Be Socially Accountable[5]

In general, cooperatives do business by pursuing common economic, social and educational aims. They usually emphasize democratic organization and self-help, and are committed to joint action for the benefit of everyone involved. In comparison with other forms of business organization, cooperatives operate self-consciously on the basis of ethical values.[6] Their objectives are encoded in the six fundamental principles ratified by the International Co-operative Alliance in 1966: open membership without discrimination; democratic management; a strictly limited return on share capital; equitable distribution of any surplus earnings; provision for education in cooperative principles and techniques; and cooperation between cooperatives at all levels. The two principles which distinguish cooperatives most from limited liability companies are the equal voting among cooperative members and the limited return on share capital. In fact, this last characteristic is sometimes regarded as the cornerstone of the cooperative financial framework.

In contrast, the traditional business structure of Western industrial economies, the limited liability company, is a productive unit with three more or less distinct groups of people: *shareholders*, who contribute capital to the company and who hire *managers*, headed by the board of directors, who hire *workers*. The workers and managers are paid a wage for their labor. Profits are either reinvested in the company, boosting the value of the shares, or distributed to shareholders as dividends. This shareholder/manager/worker relationship can be seen as the producer side of the business equation. The other side of the business equation includes the consumers of the company's products, the suppliers of the company, the community in which the company operates, and society at large. The accountability lines of the limited liability company include those of workers to managers, and managers to shareholders. The company itself is not seen as having any responsibility to its workers beyond their wages or to its suppliers beyond paying their bills. It has no formal responsibility to the community or to the society at large, and its responsibility to its consumers is simply through the price mechanism.

This simple framework of responsibilities has been significantly modified in most industrial economies: employment legislation has given rights to workers; fair trading legislation has given rights to consumers; pollution legislation has sought to protect a company's community and society at large. Moreover, many companies now perceive that they have responsibilities beyond minimum legal requirements, and, in fact, channel business resources and expertise into select community projects. Some companies have even experienced that a heightened sense of social responsibility enhances their business prospects in the community.[7]

Unfortunately, the structure of the limited-liability company ultimately discriminates against such efforts, and makes the integration of social objectives into the structure extremely difficult. Inasmuch as worker cooperatives tend to break down the traditional division between producers, consumers and society at large, they provide an organizational model which explicitly recognizes the social aims and impact of economic activity. They also seek to prevent conflicts between workers, managers and shareholders by vesting functions proper to each group to some extent in all of the people involved in the enterprise.

Cooperatives recognize explicitly that economic activity has a social as well as a financial dimension. Furthermore, they pledge themselves to pursue social and educational, as well as financial, objectives. Unfortunately, a cooperative functioning in an economic system that does not adequately acknowledge the value of social and educational objectives, and, in fact, leaves such objectives to the public sector, is, other things being equal, almost inevitably at a competitive disadvantage with a private company. It is not surprising then, that producer cooperatives will probably remain economically marginal until the economic system within which they operate takes into account their social and educational achievements and makes them some corresponding financial compensation. Thus one of the most important political challenges of the cooperative movement—to include and incorporate the social and educational dimensions which should be part of any evaluation of economic progress and success—is very closely related to the need to develop more holistic measures and indicators of economic and social well-being.

Self-Reliance and Social Responsibility in Local Economic Management: Examples of an Emerging Economic Orthodoxy "From Below"

A number of ventures in imaginative local economic enterprises— rural, urban, regional and national—which incorporate and build upon the principles inherent in self-reliance and cooperation, provide a useful counterweight to many of the assumptions of conventional economic wisdom. One such venture is the Heartland Center for Leadership Development in Lincoln, Nebraska, in the USA. It has been designed to learn from, and communicate, community strategies which have been part of successful economic organization in small rural communities.[8] Reflections on such experiences over the past ten years have reaffirmed the importance of expanding citizen involvement—in contrast to simply increasing consumer consumption—as well as suggesting other new or emerging issues as part of enterprising economic management locally: multicommunity collaboration; the need to link economic development with quality-of-life concerns; and the creation of social capital.

Since the 1960s, increasing citizen involvement in public decision-making has been a primary value of community development.[9] More recently, however, a number of other issues are emerging as equally valuable. A changing global, and therefore regional and local, economic context is suggesting both the possibility and the need for multicommunity collaboration. The latter assumes that small communities will be more efficient in sustaining themselves by clustering or collaborating with other small communities.[10] Also, research is beginning to surface on multicommunity collaboration that offers case studies in collaboration.[11] Case studies that reveal successful models of multicommunity collaboration, analysis of various types of clustering and dissemination of information about collaboration projects are all avenues that should be explored.

Another new issue in local economic leadership for community survival involves the necessary connection between economic development and quality-of-life concerns such as education, housing, health care and the arts. At the local or regional level, economic development has often been treated as a singular activity unrelated to the larger community context. Studies which have looked at effective economic organization in small communities make clear the need to broaden the perspective on economic development to go far beyond industrial recruitment or business development. Quality-of-life concerns are not only linked to economic development but often offer innovative, entrepreneurial opportunities. Heartland Center case studies include examples of very small communities that focused economic development activities on creating childcare centers or subsidized housing with excellent results. Situating economic development in the context of all types of community needs is ostensibly more holistic and practical on the small-town scale.

An additional new issue is that of creating *social capital*. Social capital can be defined as *a system of norms and networks of information and associations that undergird the workings of a community*. Based on the work of Robert Putnam and colleagues who conducted long-term studies of regional governments in Italy, the concept focuses on social interactions within communities that improve the local and regional government.[12] Putnam found that those Italian communities with long-standing social organizations, such as choral societies, displayed additional characteristics that correlated with quality and resident satisfaction in governance and operations. While the level of activity of social organizations was vital for creating economic development, economic development alone did not necessarily contribute to the increased activity of social organizations.

According to Putnam, a sense of civic behavior and social capital comes first and is a precondition for economic development. Putnam's research supports the notion that high visibility in a community can create norms of behavior that positively impact community sustainability. With such visibility comes a generally perceived and acknowledged reciprocity among members of the community, a reciprocity maintained by personal and institutional networks. The result is trust and confidence in social interactions; that is, greater social capital. Perhaps even the creation of new organizations should be considered in the light of creating social capital and the long-term benefits that can be achieved.

One of the more interesting new proposals that combines ideas of social capital, increased citizen participation and more holistic approaches to economic development is the "Communitarian Agenda" developed by Amitai Etzioni. His work, which describes the need for an increased sense of responsibility among citizens and a renewal of basic community institutions, supports Putnam's research.[13] While Etzioni's writing is on an urban and often national scale, much of what he describes as community renewal is applicable to smaller communities. Indeed, when the experiences of local economic management in rural, urban and national settings, based on the ideas of social capital, increased citizen involvement and holistic economic development, are compared, they combine to make a strong argument in favor of the necessity of regaining the widely lost level of local economic management. The community regeneration which is at the heart of the principle of self-reliance, and the cooperation and mutuality which it presupposes, are both fundamental and indispensable components of socially responsible economic organisation.[14]

An emphasis on the importance of human communities and their sustainability in economic activity leads not only to an affirmation of local economic self-reliance, but also to a serious consideration of the local economy as a driving force behind future economic development *in general*. All over the world, small isolated initiatives are being developed in ways which are suggesting principles for a new economic order.[15] One principle, *local prosperity*, addresses the importance of assisting new enterprise and creating jobs as a response to unemployment. Local prosperity depends heavily upon the local circulation of money and investment capital.

Locally generated money probably needs to circulate three times within the community by the purchasing of goods and services from other local people, and thus stimulating further production, before it leaves the local economy. It can contribute to local prosperity in a number of ways: by increasing self-reliance in critical areas such as energy, by establishing local banks to reinvest people's savings in the local economy, and by deliberate attempts at import substitution.

Another major principle is that *the local economy belongs to the community*. A very important part of any vision for a new economic order is a changed understanding of the role and priorities of business. In a potential new order, business would no longer be a means simply to generate more economic growth and profits for a company. Instead, it would become a vehicle through which the visions of a community and its citizens can be realized, the local community and the planet as a whole can be served, and fulfilling, meaningful work can be created for all who desire it. Mutual support would gradually become more important than individual profit.[16] If this shift were to occur, communities might actually begin to structure business agendas with more emphasis on contributing to the community's overall welfare. With a reconstructed role for businesses, local economies will have a better opportunity to become self-renewing through a vital generation of community-based initiatives. They, hopefully, would also be better able to ride the waves of death, growth and change, without suffering widespread poverty or unemployment.

If local economies, however, are to become expressive of a community's compassion as well of its growth vision, they have to find ways to combat the temptations to economic efficiency at the expense of community and environmental values. This factor brings us to a third principle of the new economic order. *Some degree of legislation and control* will also have to be part of it. There will be a need for some type of "codes of conduct" to which all enterprises in the local economy would have to adhere. The codes would have to cover three specific areas. One would concern the relationship of local enterprise with its workforce and the community as a whole. Another code would concern the relationship of the local enterprise with the natural environment and other living creatures. A third code would address the relationship of local enterprise with other people and communities in the same country and abroad. This code would address issues such as the guarantee of fair trading relations, and socially and ecologically sound investment. If such codes were implemented, they would go a long way in ensuring that the creativity and vigor of local enterprise did not degenerate into exploitation at home or abroad.

Reclaiming Economic Organization for Human Communities in the World

Ultimately, the realization of principles for a new economic order, which simultaneously seek to retrieve ecological, humane and spiritual values and to situate economic and status values in a prior context of diverse human communities and cultures in the world, will involve a fundamental shift of beliefs.[17] In order to effect that shift there will be a need to move away from the influence of positivistic science in the earlier part of this century.

In many instances, that influence affected the organization of intellectual disciplines so that there was a deliberate turning away from humanity's creative and spiritual forces which have been treasured by most societies, and highly valued in various religious traditions. The spiritual meanings of significant religious traditions especially had been relegated to a private realm. Any possible impact which they might have had in the public realm was virtually ignored. Indeed, one of the long-term and hoped-for outcomes of the present project is an effective contribution toward reclaiming a voice *in the public realm* for humanity's creative and spiritual needs to be embraced as an indispensable part of society's economic organization.

Modern industrial society, like every other in history, rests on a set of basic assumptions about who we are, what kind of universe we are in, and what is ultimately important to us. Positivistic science, which so confidently set forth the answers to these questions a couple of generations ago, is now a dying orthodoxy.[18] Its basic premises are being challenged anew by the perspectives of faith visions willing to be in dialogue with the contemporary world. With this change comes a long-term shift in value emphasis and priorities, which hopefully will bring about a transformation of industrial society comparable to the breadth of the transformation from medieval to modern society in Western Europe.[19] This, in turn, will subject to radical change the whole concept of economics.

The shift of beliefs will also have to involve what one policy analyst has described as a move away from present expressions of economic fundamentalism.[20] The latter is a product of a limited view of both human nature and society which sees "economic man" as having the right to wealth and being driven by self-interest pushed to the extreme of greed. Because of the possibility of extreme expressions of self-interest, "economic man" joins other individuals in a social contract to create society. Mainline economic theory *believes* that such a view is, in fact, descriptive of the natural state of humanity and that, by implication, the market mechanism is thoroughly "natural." Unfortunately, economic fundamentalism is also very similar to religious fundamentalism:

> Adherents to both believe implicitly in their dogma and seek to make the World comply with the Word. But the resemblance goes deeper: they both believe *man* is individual,

selfish and sinful, forced into civilisation by law, religion and police; creating wealth as a side product of greed. The churches at least see this as sin, while some economists continue to regard it as virtue.[21]

Some of the basic beliefs coming out of economic fundamentalism, which also drive economic policy in many instances, assume that societal order is motivated by fear and that the production of wealth is fueled by greed. With such a view, it is not surprising that proposals to organize societies and economies along the lines of cooperation, mutual support and altruism might be perceived as not only inefficient, but also as theoretically incredible and socially dysfunctional.

A long-term economic reorganization of society, issuing out of a shift in basic beliefs and assumptions, will involve a number of components.[22] The first might be summarized as a shift from a grossly inadequate understanding of what it means to develop as a human person in community, to a more holistic awareness of humanity's dependence on the health of its communities and the planet from which they all draw life and sustenance. Only then will the diverse levels on which persons experience themselves as human beings begin to be respected and responded to. Unfortunately, and in the meantime, the proper subject matter of economics anthropologically is still the exclusive human behavior of choice in the market.

In the standard economic model, choice is, in all cases, taken as the most useful characteristic of how individuals respond to their economic and social environment.[23] Other examples of significant human behaviors simply are not included. A further weakness within this limitation is that the subject matter, as conceived, is of a person who perceives choices and acts upon them. There is no recognition that individuals might ever feel dominated, oppressed, passive, unsure about their abilities, or unaware of alternatives. *There is no acknowledgment that many people in many situations will not perceive that* any *choices are available to them.*

In Part One of this book, we saw how some of the key Christian doctrines can go a long way in helping us develop an understanding of human existence which is respectful of its many-layered texture. Recall how the doctrine of the Trinity portrays human existence as social, with human relationships as a radical source of individual existence and personal development. That same doctrine also affirmed that existence and self-giving love are identical, and that without the right to exercise the power of self-giving it will inevitably become impossible to participate in and enjoy the life of human community.

Recall how the doctrine of Creation extended the necessity and scope of human relationships to include a respectful companionship with all nonhuman creatures, and indeed with the planet on which we all share a home. Recall how the doctrine of Original Sin proposes an understanding of the operation of human freedom, which does not stop with individual freedoms and rights, but encompasses an exercise of freedom based on the common good as both a motivation and outcome of the exercise of freedom.

Lastly, recall how the doctrine of the Communion of Saints invites all persons to an active participatory communion in the civil and economic spheres, in order to become part of a sharing in life which is vital for the development of personhood.

The vision of humanity suggested by these doctrines, one which strongly accounts for the creative and spiritual needs of human persons, along with others, insists that economic organization respects and fosters growth toward the possibility of mature self-giving, of responsible companionship with others and the created order, of inclusive exercises of freedom to work for the common good, and of the stimulation of active participation in all significant levels of human community.[24]

If all the above layers of what it means to be human begin to be reflected more adequately in the modes of organizing society economically, then a number of implications will follow. The present emphasis upon a technological sense of mastery of the modes of production might actually be significantly tempered by a vision more sensitive to the human spirit and more concerned with ethical systems and values.[25] The almost exclusive preoccupation in market societies with individual freedoms and rights might hopefully begin to be replaced with movements for the exercise of freedom which includes political, economic and psychological-cultural freedom. Such movements could go far in bringing about a genuine and holistic liberation of human communities from the disrespectful constraints and priorities of so much of present economic organization.[26] Finally, the democratic ideals of community organization and participation could reasonably be expected to be reinforced more strongly by the social ideals of free education, the economic ideals of equality of opportunity and distribution, and the political ideals of equal justice under law and full participation in government.

Much of the vitality in Western societies has been largely sustained by a strong and broad tradition of respect for all of the significant dimensions which contribute toward the experience of a full and healthy human life. Yet in the aftermath of the industrial revolution something has gone wrong. The potential richness of human consciousness has, in its institutionalized political and economic forms, been reduced to utilitarian perspectives in the service of technology. Technological mastery, guided largely by narrow economic values and an exploitative ethic, has become vulnerable to the priorities of unrestrained economic growth and an inadequately accountable militarism. Holistic human liberation has been usurped economically by large corporations and world financial institutions which have imposed their agendas upon diverse countries in ways that are invasive and obstructive to a more broadly based economic welfare. A more inclusive and participatory expression of political liberation has been stifled by the coercion of large bureaucracies. Even the institution of democracy itself has been compromised in many countries by a set of budgetary goals which have proven to be insensitive to citizen concerns about the well-being of the planet and of future generations.

The task of discovering and following a development path toward a viable global future and sustainable global society presents what is probably one of humanity's greatest challenges at the end of the twentieth century. It involves a willingness to pass through some of the chaos that will ensue when inherited patterns of economic organization, which are progressively seen to be inimical to human community and the planet, are let go of in order to discover more viable alternatives. Perhaps we could hope that some of the most trenchant criticisms which have been leveled against conventional economic wisdom and organization might eventually come to be seen as some of the most promising starting points for constructing economic alternatives that are both more respectful of the varieties of cultures in the human family, as well as of the planet and its resources upon which the life and welfare of all depend.

---

[1] For this section I have found Wolfgang Sachs' *Delinking from the world market: an argument tried out in five steps*, especially helpful. It was originally a presentation at the 1984 TOES conference, and is cited in *The Living Economy*, on 333–44.

[2] Recall that as a principle of "Another Development" self-reliance does *not* mean autonomy or self-sufficiency, but suggests that *communities* regenerate or revitalize themselves through their own efforts, capabilities and resources. See c. 9, 179–81.

[3] See David Ward, "The Rise and Rise of Transnational Companies," in *Science and Public Policy*, vol. 12, no. 2, cited in *The Living Economy*, 340.

[4] See *Multinational Corporations and the International Co-operative Movement*, International Co-operative Alliance, London, 1972.

[5] Here, I have adapted the major point of Paul Ekins in *Co-operation: Where the Social Meets the Economic*, in *The Living Economy*, 282–8, to the structure of the argument in this last chapter.

[6] See Charles Gide (1847–1932), an eminent French cooperator, quoted in International Co-operative Alliance's *Co-operatives in the Year 2000* (ICA, London 1980), 32, 33 and 68, as cited in *The Living Economy*, 282.

[7] See *Business in Society: a new initiative* (London: New Initiative, 1984), 31, cited in *The Living Economy*, 282, fn. 17.

[8] See Vicki Braglio Luther, *Clues to Community Survival: A Leadership Development Curriculum*, especially 10–16, a paper delivered at a Conference on Issues Affecting Rural Communities at James Cook University, Townsville, Queensland, July 1994. The paper, which will be published in the Proceedings of the Conference, brings together a number of lessons from the Centre's experiences. For a comparable set of experiences with similar lessons, but in an urban setting, see Michael Phillips, *What Small Business Experience Teaches About Economic Theory*, cited in *The Living Economy*, 272–82. Phillips recounts the experiences of the Briarpatch Network, an informal association of people and cooperative businesses that believe in open account books, honesty and information sharing. The market behavior and actual experience of the 800-plus

businesses which make up the network provide an empirical base for the development of a new and different approach to economics.

[9] See S. R. Arnstein, "Eight Rungs on the Ladder of Citizen Participation," in *Journal of the American Institute of Planners* 35, 335–57.

[10] H.R. Baker. *Restructuring Rural Communities* (Saskatchewan: University Extension Press, 1993).

[11] B. A. Ciglar, J. C. Stabler, A. C. Jansen, and V. D. Ryan "In Search of Multicommunity collaborations: Three Case Studies," in P. F. Korshing (ed), *Conference Proceedings: Multicommunity Collaboration: An Evolving Rural Revitalisation Strategy* (Ames, Iowa: University Publications), 13–52.

[12] See R. D. Putnam, "The Prosperous Community," in *The American Prospect*, Spring, 1993, 36–42.

[13] See Amitai Etzioni, *The Spirit of Community* (New York: Crown, 1993).

[14] Again, refer to c. 9, 179–81.

[15] See Guy Dauncey's *The new local economic order*, a presentation given at the 1984 TOES conference and cited in *The Living Economy*, 264–72, at 266–7. He cites examples of local economic management in San Jose, California, Llewellyn County, USA; Newport and Nevern, in Dyfed, South Wales; and Bury St. Edmunds, UK.

[16] See Eva Cox, *The Economics of Mutual Support: A Feminist Approach*, in *Beyond the Market*, 270–5, at 271.

[17] See Willis Harman, *The Role of Corporations*, in *The Living Economy*, 344–50. Also for a detailed and developed treatment of the need for economic organization to be more sensitive and responsive to the contexts in which it is applied see *Current Sociology: The Journal of the International Sociological Association* Vol. 35 Number 1 Spring 1987, "Economic Sociology: Past and Present."

[18] See Paul Ormerod, *The Death of Economics* (London: Faber & Faber, 1994). Ormerod argues that the "science" of economics, based upon just such a positivism, is in an unrecognized state of crisis. Indeed, he contends that its achievements have become as limited as those of pre-Newtonian physics.

[19] In this context it is especially interesting to recall Fred Hirsch's contention that the liberal market economy is but a transitional phase on the way from preindustrial economies to those with a more integrated sense of the common good. See his *Social Limits to Growth*, especially c. 12 "The Liberal Market as a Transition Case," 161–77.

[20] See Cox, *The Economics of Mutual Support*, 270.

[21] Cox, *The Economics of Mutual Support*, 271.

[22] While I am in basic agreement with Harman's listing of such components in *The Role of Corporations*, 346–7, I have developed them with significantly different emphases.

[23] Rebecca M. Blank, in *Beyond Economic Man*, 133–43, at 141. Also refer back to c. 4, 65–8.

[24] On each of these doctrinal perspectives on the human, respectively see c. 5, 71–4; 74–8; and c. 5, 88–93; 93–7.

[25] See Fred Hirsch, "The Moral Re-entry," in *Social Limits to Growth* (London and Henley: Routledge & Kegan Paul, 1977), 137–51.

[26] On the role of language in the move toward greater liberation see *Beyond the Market*, Evan Jones, "Economic Language, Propaganda and Dissent," 253–69; and Stuart Rees, "Practices and Policies for Social Justice," 291–304, at 294–8.

References

Atherton, John. *Christianity and the Market: Christian Social Thought for Our Time.* London: SPCK, 1992.

Australian Catholic Bishops' Conference. *Commonwealth for the Common Good: A Statement on the Distribution of Wealth in Australia.* North Blackburn, Vic.: Collins Dove, 1992.

Axelos, Kostas. *Alienation, Praxis, and Techne in the Thought of Karl Marx.* Austin: University of Texas Press, 1976.

Baum, Gregory. *The Priority of Labor: A Commentary on Laborem Exercens.* New York/Ramsey, NJ: Paulist Press, 1982.

Baum, Gregory and Ellsberg, G. (editors). *The Logic of Solidarity: Commentaries on Pope John Paul II's Encyclical "On Social Concern."* Maryknoll, NY: Orbis, 1989.

Becker, Gary S. *The Economic Approach to Human Behavior.* Chicago and London: University of Chicago Press, 1976.

Bellah, Robert et al. *The Good Society.* NY: Alfred Knopf, 1991.

Bellah, Robert et al. *Habits of the Heart.* New York: Harper & Row, 1986.

Benhabib, Seyla. *Situating the Self: Gender, Community and Postmodernism in Contemporary Ethics.* Cambridge: Polity Press, 1992.

Benhabib, Seyla and Cornell, Drucilla (editors). *Feminism as Critique.* Minneapolis, MN: University of Minnesota Press, 1987.

Benne, Robert. *The Ethic of Democratic Capitalism: A Moral Reassessment*. Philadelphia: Fortress Press, 1981.

Boff, Leonardo. *Church, Charism, and Power: Liberation Theology and the Institutional Church*. NY: Crossroad Publishing Co., 1985.

Boff, Leonardo. *Ecclesiogenesis: The Base Communities Re-Invent the Church*. Maryknoll, NY: Orbis, 1986.

Browning, Don S. and Schüssler Fiorenza, Francis. *Habermas, Modernity, and Public Theology*. NY: Crossroad Publishing, 1992.

Buchanan, Allen. *Ethics, Efficiency and the Market*. Clarendon Press, 1985.

Byers, David M. (editor). *Justice in the Marketplace: Collected Statements of the Vatican and the US Catholic Bishops on Economic Policy, 1891–1984*. Washington, DC: United States Catholic Conference, Inc., 1985.

Carlen, Claudia (editor). *The Papal Encyclicals, 1740–1981*. 5 vol. Ann Arbor, MI: The Pierian Press, 1990.

Carroll, John and Manne, Robert (editors). *Shutdown: The Failure of Economic Rationalism and How to Rescue Australia*. Melbourne: The Text Publishing Co., 1992.

Cobb Jr., John B. *Sustainability: Economics, Ecology & Justice*. Mary Knoll NY: Orbis, 1992.

Coleman, John A. (editor). *One Hundred Years of Catholic Social Thought: Celebration and Challenge*. Maryknoll, NY: Orbis, 1991.

Cort, John C. *Christian Socialism*. Maryknoll, NY: Orbis, 1989.

Curran, Charles and McCormick, R. (editors). *Readings in Moral Theology, No.5: Official Catholic Social Teaching*. New York/Mahwah, NJ: Paulist Press, 1986.

Dag Hammarskjold Foundation. *Another Development: Approaches and Strategies*. Uppsala, Sweden, 1977.

Daly, Herman and Cobb, John B. *For the Common Good: Redirecting the Economy Toward Community, the Environment, and a Sustainable Future*. Boston: Beacon Press, 1989.

Dorr, Donald. *Option for the Poor: A Hundred Years of Vatican Social Teaching*. Maryknoll, NY: Orbis, 1983.

Duchrow, Ulrich. *Global Economy: A Confessional Issue for the Churches?* Geneva: WCC Publications, 1987.

Ekins, Paul (editor). *The Living Economy: A New Economics in the Making.* London and New York: Routledge, 1990.

Etzioni, Amitai. *The Spirit of Community.* NY: Crown, 1993.

Ferber, Marianne A. and Nelson, Julie A. (editors). *Beyond Economic Man: Feminist Theories and Economics.* Chicago and London: University of Chicago Press, 1993.

Fromm, Erich. *Marx's Concept of Man.* NY: Frederick Unger Publishing Co., 1961.

Galbraith, John Kenneth. *The Affluent Society,* 3rd ed. New American Library, 1976.

Galbraith, John Kenneth. *The Culture of Contentment.* London: Penguin Books, 1992.

Galbraith, John Kenneth. *A History of Economics: The Past as Present.* London: Penguin, 1989.

Geuss, Raymond. *The Idea of Critical Theory: Habermas and the Frankfurt School.* NY: Cambridge University Press, 1981.

Gorringe, Timothy J. *Capital and the Kingdom: Theological Ethics and Economic Order.* Maryknoll, NY:Orbis/London: SPCK, 1994.

Gouldner, Alvin. *The Two Marxisms: Contradictions and Anomalies in the Development of Theory.* NY: Seabury Press, 1980.

Greeve Davaney, Sheila (editor) *Theology at the End of Modernity* (Essays in Honour of Gordon D. Kaufman) Trinity Press International, 1991.

Grindel, John A. *Whither the US Church?: Context, Gospel, Planning.* Maryknoll, NY: Orbis, 1991.

Habermas, Jurgen. *Communication and the Evolution of Society.* Boston: Beacon Press, 1979.

Habermas, Jurgen. *Knowledge and Human Interests.* Boston: Beacon Press, 1971.

Habermas, Jurgen. *Legitimation Crisis.* Cambridge: Polity Press/Oxford: Basil Blackwell, 1988.

Habermas, Jurgen. *Moral Consciousness and Communicative Action.* Cambridge: Polity Press, 1990.

Habermas, Jurgen. *The Theory of Communicative Action. Volume One: Reason and the Rationalization of Society; Volume Two: Lifeworld and System.* Boston: Beacon Press, 1984, 1988.

Hay, Donald A. *Economics Today: A Christian Critique.* Leicester, UK: Apollos, 1989.

Heyne, Paul. *The Economic Way of Thinking* 4th ed. Chicago: Science Research Associates, 1983.

Himes, Michael J. and Himes, Kenneth R. *Fullness of Faith: The Public Significance of Theology.* New York/Mahwah, NJ: Paulist Press, 1993.

Hirsch, Fred. *Social Limits to Growth.* London and Henley: Routledge & Kegan Paul, 1977.

Hirschman, Albert O. *The Passions and the Interests: Political Arguments for Capitalism before Its Triumph.* Princeton, NJ: Princeton University Press, 1977.

Holton, Robert J. *Economy and Society.* London and New York: Routledge, 1992.

Honneth, Axel and Joas, Hans (editors). *Communicative Action: Essays on Jurgen Habermas's Theory of Communicative Action.* Cambridge: Polity Press, 1991.

Kamenka, Eugene. *Marxism and Ethics* 2nd ed. London: Macmillan, 1970.

Kasper, Walter. *The God of Jesus Christ.* NY: Crossroad Publishing Co., 1984.

Kasper, Walter. *Theology & Church.* London: SCM, 1989.

Kaufman, Gordon D. *Theology for a Nuclear Age.* Philadelphia: Westminster, and Manchester: Manchester University Press, 1985.

Keynes, John Maynard. *The General Theory of Employment, Interest, and Money.* London: Macmillan [1936] rpt. 1973.

King, Paul G., Maynard, Kent, and Woodyeard, David O. *Risking Liberation: Middle Class Powerlessness and Social Heroism.* Atlanta, GA: John Knox Press, 1988.

Krugman, Paul. *Peddling Prosperity: Economic Sense and Nonsense in the Age of Diminished Expectations*. New York/London: W.W. Norton & Co., 1994.

LaCugna, Catherine Mowry. *God For Us: The Trinity and Christian Life*. NY: Harper Collins, 1991.

Lakeland, Paul. *Theology and Critical Theory: The Discourse of the Church*. Nashville: Abingdon Press, 1990.

Lane, Dermot A. *Foundations for a Social Theology: Praxis, Process, and Salvation*. New York/Ramsey, NJ: Paulist Press, 1984.

LeGrand, J., Propper, C., and Robinson R. *The Economics of Social Problems* 3rd ed. London: Macmillan, 1992.

Lonergan, Anne and Richards, Caroline (editors). *Thomas Berry and the New Cosmology*. Mystic, CT: Twenty-Third Publications, 1987.

Lutz, Charles P. (editor). *God, Goods, and the Common Good: Eleven Perspectives on Economic Justice in Dialog with the Roman Catholic Bishops' Pastoral Letter*. Minneapolis, MN: Augsburg Publishing House, 1987.

Lutz, Mark A. *Social Economics: Retrospect and Prospect*. Boston: Kluwer Academic Publishing, 1990.

Lutz, Mark A. and Lux, Kenneth. *Humanistic Economics: The New Challenge*. NY: The Bootstrap Press, 1988.

McBrien, Richard P. *Caesar's Coin: Religion and Politics in America.* NY: MacMillan Publishing, 1987.

McCarthy, George E. and Rhodes, Royal W. *Eclipse of Justice: Ethics, Economics, and the Lost Traditions of American Catholicism*. Maryknoll, NY: Orbis, 1992.

MacIntyre, Alasdair. *After Virtue*. University of Notre Dame Press, 1981.

Mansbridge, Jane J. (editor). *Beyond Self-Interest*. Chicago and London: University of Chicago Press, 1990.

Marty, Martin. *The Public Church*. NY: Crossroad Publishing, 1981.

Marx, Karl. *Early Texts*, Edited by David McLellan. Oxford: Basil Blackwell, 1971.

Marx, Karl and Engels, Frederick. *The Communist Manifesto*. NY: International Publishers Co., Inc., 1948.

Meadows, Donella H. et al. *Beyond the Limits: Confronting Global Collapse, Envisioning a Sustainable Future*. Post Mills, VT: Chelsea Green Pub., 1992.

Meadows, Donella H. et al. *The Limits to Growth: A Report for the Club of Rome's Project on the Predicament of Mankind*. Earth Island Limited, 1972.

Meeks, M. Douglas. *God the Economist: The Doctrine of God and Political Economy*. Minneapolis: Fortress Press, 1989.

Metz, J. B. *The Emergent Church: The Future of Christianity in a Post-Bourgeois World*. NY: Crossroad Publishing Co., 1981.

Meyers, Milton L. *The Soul of Modern Economic Man: Ideas of Self-Interest—Thomas Hobbes to Adam Smith*. Chicago and London: University of Chicago Press, 1983.

Murphy, Charles M. *At Home on Earth: Foundations for a Catholic Ethic of the Environment*. NY: Crossroad Publishing Co., 1989.

Novak, Michael. *Freedom With Justice*. NY: Harper & Row, 1984.

Nozick, Robert. *Anarchy, State, and Utopia*. New York: Basic Books, 1974.

Ormerod, Paul. *The Death of Economics*. London/Boston: Faber & Faber, 1994.

Ornstein, Robert and Ehrlich, Paul. *New World, New Mind: Moving towards Conscious Evolution*. NY: Doubleday, 1989.

Our Common Future. 1986 Report of the World Commission on Environment and Development. Oxford: Oxford University, 1987.

Pannenberg, Wolfhart (Trans. Duane A. Priebe). *What is Man?* Philadelphia: Fortress Press, 1979.

Persaud, Winston D. *The Theology of the Cross and Marx's Anthropology: A View From the Caribbean*. NY: Peter Lang, 1991.

Plamenatz, John. *Karl Marx's Philosophy of Man*. London: Oxford University Press, 1975.

Polanyi, Karl. *The Great Transformation: The Political and Economic Origins of Our Time*. Boston: Beacon Press, 1957.

Preston, Ronald H. *Church and Society in Late 20th Century: The Economic and Political Task.* London: SCM Press, 1983.

Preston, Ronald H. *Religion and the Ambiguities of Capitalism.* London: SCM Press, 1991.

Preston, Ronald H. *Religion and the Persistence of Capitalism.* London: SCM Press, 1979.

Pusey, Michael. *Economic Rationalism in Canberra: A Nation Building State Changes Its Mind.* NY: Cambridge University Press, 1991.

Pusey, Michael. *Jurgen Habermas.* London and New York: Tavistock, 1987.

Rawls, John. *A Theory of Justice.* Cambridge: Belknap Press, 1971.

Rees, S., Rodley, G., and Stilwell, F. (editors). *Beyond the Market: Alternatives to Economic Rationalism.* Sydney: Pluto Press, 1993.

Reich, Robert. *The Power of Public Ideas.* Cambridge, MA: Ballinger Publishing, 1988.

Routh, Guy. *The Origin of Economic Ideas* [1975]. London: Macmillan, rpt.1989.

Ruether, Rosemary Radford. *Women-Church: Theology and Practice of Feminist Liturgical Communities.* San Francisco: Harper & Row, 1985.

Sandel, Michael J. *Liberalism and the Limits of Justice.* NY: Cambridge University Press, 1982.

Santmire, H. Paul. *The Travail of Nature: The Ambiguous Ecological Promise of Christian Theology.* Fortress, 1985.

Schacht, Richard. *Alienation.* London: George Allen and Unwin Ltd., 1971.

Schumacher, E.F. *Small is Beautiful: A Study of Economics as if People Mattered* [1973]. London: Vintage, rpt. 1993.

Schwartz, Barry. *The Battle for Human Nature: Science, Morality and Modern Life.* New York/London: W. W. Norton & Co., 1986.

Sen, Amartya K. *Collective Choice and Social Welfare.* San Francisco: Holder–Day, 1970.

Slavin, Stephen L. *Economics: A Self-Teaching Guide.* NY: John Wiley & Sons, Inc., 1988.

Smith, Adam. *An Inquiry into the Nature and Causes of the Wealth of Nations* [1776]. The Edwin Cannan Text of the Fifth Edition NY: The Modern Library, rpt. 1985.

Smith, Adam. *The Theory of Moral Sentiments* [1759]. Edited by D.D. Raphael and A.L. Macfie. Indianapolis, IN: Liberty Classics rpt. 1982.

Stackhouse, Max L. *Public Theology and Political Economy: Christian Stewardship in Modern Society*. Grand Rapids, MI: Wm. B. Eerdmans, 1987.

Stilwell, Frank. *Economic Inequality: Who Gets What in Australia?* Sydney: Pluto Press, 1993.

Sullivan, Francis A. *The Church We Believe in*. New York/Mahwah, NJ: Paulist, 1988.

Thiemann, Ronald F. *Constructing a Public Theology: The Church in a Pluralistic Culture*. Louisville, Kentucky: Westminster/John Knox Press, 1991.

United States Catholic Conference. *Justice in the Marketplace: Collected Statements of the Vatican and the US Catholic Bishops on Economic Policy 1891–1984*. Washington, DC, 1986.

Walsh, Michael and Davies, Brian (editors). *Proclaiming Justice and Peace: Documents from John XXIII–John Paul II*. Mystic, CT: Twenty-Third Publications, 1984.

Walzer, Michael. *Spheres of Justice: A Defense of Pluralism and Equality*. New York: Basic Books, 1983.

Welch, Sharon. *Communities of Resistance and Solidarity: A Feminist Theology of Liberation*. Maryknoll, NY: Orbis, 1985.

Wesley, Granberg-Michaelson (editors). *Redeeming the Creation: The Rio Earth Summit: Challenges for the Churches*. Geneva: WCC Publications, 1992.

Williams, Oliver and Houck, John (editors). *The Common Good and US Capitalism*. Lanham, MD: University Press, 1987.

Wogaman, J. Philip. *Christians and the Great Economic Debate*. London: SCM, 1977.

Wogaman, J. Philip. *Economics and Ethics: A Christian Enquiry*.

Name Index

A
Adams, O. 193
Antonovsky, A. 193
Aquinas, T. 81, 115
Arendt, H. 98
Arnstein, S.R. 212
Aron, R. 58
Atherton, J. 19, 20, 22, 23
Augustine 115
Axelos, K. 58, 59, 60

B
Baker, H.R. 212
Barbier, E. 192
Baum, G. 121
Becker, G.S. 79
Bell, D. 58
Bellah, R. 101
Benhabib, S. 143
Benne, R. 19
Bentham, J. 40
Berger, P. 21, 22, 168

Berry, T. 171-3
Boff, L. 144
Browning, D.S. xix
Buber, M. 81
Buchanan, A. 19, 21, 98
Byers, D.M. 119, 120

C
Cardjin, J. 110
Carlen, C. 119
Christiansen, D. 81, 99, 100, 186, 194
Ciglar, B.A. 212
Cobb Jr., J.B. 20, 192, 195
Coleman, J.A. 21
Cox, E. 212
Curran, C. 99

D
Daly, H. 20, 167, 192
Darwin, C. 118

Topic Index